Biog
D

MARQUISE DE LA TOUR DU PIN

1770 – 1853

RECOLLECTIONS
OF THE
REVOLUTION AND
THE EMPIRE

FROM THE FRENCH OF THE
"JOURNAL D'UNE FEMME DE CINQUANTE ANS"

BY
LA MARQUISE DE LA TOUR DU PIN

EDITED AND TRANSLATED BY
WALTER GEER

WITH FIFTEEN PHOTOGRAVURE ILLUSTRATIONS

NEW YORK : BRENTANO'S
1920

FOREWORD

THE author of the "Journal of a Woman of Fifty Years," Henriette-Lucie Dillon, was born at Paris, 25 February 1770, and died at Pisa, Italy, 2 April 1853. The 21 May 1787, she married Frédéric-Séraphin, Comte de Gouvernet, who upon the death of his father on the scaffold, 28 April 1794, took the title of Comte de La Tour du Pin de Gouvernet. Under the Second Restoration he was named a Peer of France and given the title of Marquis. The events of his life from the date of his marriage to the epoch of the Hundred Days are told in the following memoirs of his wife. Other details of his career will be found in the Postscript.

In her "Journal" Madame de La Tour du Pin relates all the notable incidents of the period of her life comprised between her childhood and the end of the month of March, 1815, immediately following the return of Napoleon from Elba. Her history from that time on is closely linked with that of her husband, and will be related in that connection.

Her memoirs were written from time to time, with long interruptions. Commenced on the first day of January, 1820, the last pages of the First Part were not finished, or put in final shape, until about twenty years later. The Second Part was not begun until February, 1843, and at the time of her death ten years later had been completed only to the month of March, 1815.

At her death in 1853, she left the manuscript to her only surviving son, Aymar, who in turn willed it to his nephew, Hadelin, Comte de Liedekerke-Beaufort, who confided it a short time before his death to his son Aymar, by whom the memoirs were published in Paris in 1906. The book met with an immediate and well-deserved success, and in a few years reached the sixteenth edition.

In his Preface the Comte de Liedekerke-Beaufort says that with the Marquise de La Tour du Pin disappeared one of the last vestiges of the high society of the period before the Revolution, of which the traditions have to-day completely vanished. The reader of these memoirs cannot fail to appreciate the high qualities of heart and soul and mind shown by the author. Those who knew her, both esteemed and loved her. They united in saying that rarely was greater stability united to greater charms, more constant fidelity to duty to greater kindliness. Endowed with a retentive memory, which recalled in her conversation the varied recollections of so many different periods, Madame de La Tour du Pin interested to the highest degree the thoughtful and serious-minded, as she attracted to her the young, whose tastes she understood and whose faults she excused.

According to the statement of the Editor of the French edition, the recollections brought together in these memoirs by Madame de La Tour du Pin were, in her mind, intended for her only surviving son, Aymar, and were not written originally with the

FOREWORD

idea of publication. They therefore contain many pages of intimate details of family life, and other matters, which would not be of interest to the general public, and which it has therefore been thought advisable to omit from this edition.

WALTER GEER

NEW YORK
July 1920

[v]

CONTENTS

FIRST PART

CHAPTER ONE

1770–1781

CHILDHOOD OF MLLE. DILLON

PAGE

Her Earliest Years.— Members of Her Family.— Her Sad and Precocious Infancy.— Her Maid Marguerite. — Society Before the Revolution.— An Archbishop's Mode of Life.— Toilettes of Men and Women.— Dinners and Suppers.— Château of Hautefontaine.— Louis XVI Jealous of the Hunting Establishment.— Sojourn at Versailles in 1781.— The Queen's Friendship for Madame Dillon   I

CHAPTER TWO

1782–1783

DEATH OF MME. DILLON

Illness of Mme. Dillon.— She is Ordered to the Waters of Spa.— Indignation of Her Mother.— Intervention of the Queen.— Departure for Brussels.— Lord and Lady Dillon.— Lady Kenmare.— Education of Mlle. Dillon.— Sojourn at Brussels.— Visit to the Archduchess Marie-Christine.— Sojourn at Spa.— Return to Paris.— Death of Mme. Dillon.— Description of Hautefontaine.— Purchase of the Folie Joyeuse at Montfermeil   10

CONTENTS

CHAPTER THREE

1783–1786

VISITS TO LANGUEDOC

PAGE

Annual Trip of Mlle. Dillon to Languedoc.— Method of Travel at That Epoch.— The Route to Languedoc.— Nîmes and Montpellier.— Etiquette at Dinners.— Society at Montpellier.— Return of Monsieur Dillon to France.— He Weds Mme. de La Touche.— He Takes the Government of Tabago.— First Plan for the Marriage of Mlle. Dillon.— Sojourn at Bordeaux.— Another Dillon Family.— The Comte de La Tour du Pin and His Son, the Comte de Gouvernet 19

CHAPTER FOUR

1786

MATRIMONIAL PROJECTS

New Marriage Plans.— The Marquis Adrien de Laval.— Fortune of Mlle. Dillon.— Regiments of the Irish Brigade.— Portrait of Mlle. Dillon.— Maréchal de Biron.— Rupture with Monsieur Adrien de Laval.— The Vicomte de Fleury.— M. Espérance de L'Aigle. — The Comte de Gouvernet.— Decision of Mlle. Dillon. 31

CHAPTER FIVE

1787

THE MARRIAGE PRELIMINARIES

Convocation of the Notables.— Return to Paris.— Death of Mme. de Monconseil.— Monsieur de Gouvernet's Marriage Proposal Accepted.—Visit of Mme. d'Hénin.

CONTENTS

PAGE

— Signature of the Contract.— Toilette the Day of the *Fiançailles*.— Politeness of this Epoch.— The Four Lameth Brothers.— The Marriage Contract.— The Comte and Comtesse de La Tour du Pin.— A Visit to the Queen.— At Montfermeil.— The Trousseau and the *Corbeille*.......................... 38

CHAPTER SIX

1787

MARRIAGE AND PRESENTATION AT COURT

A Marriage in High Society at the End of the 18th Century.— The Nuptial Benediction.— The Marriage Souvenirs.— Toilette of the Bride.— Presentation to the Queen.— Rehearsal with the *Maître à Danser*.— The Presentation Toilette.— The Sunday Court.— Portrait of the King.— The Art of Walking at Versailles.— The Mass.— The Royal Dinner.... 43

CHAPTER SEVEN

1787–1788

FIRST SEASON IN SOCIETY

Civil War in Holland.— Feebleness of the French Government.— Mme. de La Tour du Pin at Hénencourt.— Excursion to Lille.— Return to Montfermeil.— The Loges of the Queen at the Theatres.— Mme. de La Tour du Pin in Society. —Mme. de Montesson and the Duc d'Orléans. — Rupture of Mme. de La Tour du Pin with Her Family 52

CONTENTS

CHAPTER EIGHT

1788–1789

EVE OF THE REVOLUTION

PAGE

Sojourn with Mme. d'Hénin.— Monsieur de La Tour du
Pin, Colonel de Royal-Vaisseaux.— Indiscipline of the
Officers of the Regiment.— Prince Henry of Prussia.
— His Taste for French Literature.— The Hôtel de
Rochechouart.— Comte de Chinon, afterwards Duc
de Richelieu.— A Ball at Lord Dorset's.— Approach
of the Revolution.— Popularity of the Duc d'Orléans.
— Causes of the Antipathy of the Queen to the Duc.
— Popularity of English Fashions.— The Origin of
Monsieur de Lally-Tollendal 61

CHAPTER NINE

1789

FALL OF THE BASTILLE

Mme. de Genlis.— Education of the Young Orléans Princes.
— Paméla.— Horse Races at Vincennes.— First
Popular Meetings.— Residence at Versailles.— Sess-
ion of the Opening of the States-General.— Attitude
of the King and Queen.— Feebleness of the Court.
—Departure of Monsieur Necker.—The 14th of July
1789.— Return of Mme. de La Tour du Pin to Paris.—
The Waters of Forges 73

CHAPTER TEN

1789

VERSAILLES INVADED BY THE MOB

Monsieur de La Tour du Pin Père, Minister of War.— Official Dinners.— Commencement of the Emigration.—
Ruin of the La Tour du Pin Family.— The *Contrôle-*

CONTENTS

Général and Mme. de Staël.— Organization of the
National Guard of Versailles.— Monsieur de La Tour
du Pin, Second in Command.— The National Guard
of Paris and Monsieur de La Fayette.—Banquet of the
Gardes du Corps at the Château.— Day of the 5th of
October.— The King at the Hunt.— Paris Marches
on Versailles.— Arrangements for the Defence.— The
Women of Paris at Versailles.— Revolt of the National
Guard of Versailles.— Plan for the Departure of the
Royal Family for Rambouillet.— Invasion of the
Offices of the Ministry.— Hesitation of the King.—
Monsieur de La Fayette with the King.— Calm Re-
established.— Day of the 6th of October.— An Armed
Band Invades the Château.— Massacre of the Gardes
du Corps.— Attempted Assassination of the Queen.—
Presence of the Duc d'Orléans.— Departure of the
Royal Family for Paris.— The King Confides the
Guard of the Palace to Monsieur de La Tour du
Pin.— Mme. de La Tour du Pin Takes Refuge at
Saint-Germain.................................. 84

CHAPTER ELEVEN

1789–1790

VISIT TO SWITZERLAND

Residence of Mme. de La Tour du Pin at Paris.— The
Minister of War at the Hôtel de Choiseul.— Birth of
Humbert.— Kindness of the Queen for Mme. de La
Tour du Pin.— The Fête of the Federation.— The
Garrison of Paris.— Composition of the National
Guard.— Monsieur de La Fayette.— Talleyrand,
Bishop of Autun.— The Spectacle at the Champ-de-
Mars.— The Royal Family.— Excursion to Switzer-
land.— An Adventure at Dôle.— Four Days of Cap-
tivity.— Departure from Dôle.— The Lake of Geneva.

[xi]

CONTENTS

PAGE

— Revolt of the Garrison of Nancy.— Monsieur de
La Tour du Pin Sent as *Parlementaire.*— Suppression
of the Revolt.— Sojourn at Lausanne.— Return to
Paris via Alsace............................... 108

CHAPTER TWELVE

1791–1792

RESIDENCE IN HOLLAND

Sojourn at Paris.— Monsieur de La Tour du Pin Leaves
the Ministry of War.— His Son Refuses the Post.—
Is Named as Minister to Holland.— Residence at Rue
de Varenne.— The Flight of the Royal Family.— Departure for Holland.— The Lameth Family.— Life of
Pleasure at The Hague.— Recall of Monsieur de La
Tour du Pin.— Decree against the Émigrés.— Flight
of La Fayette.— Mme. de La Tour du Pin Returns
to France..................................... 122

CHAPTER THIRTEEN

1793

FLIGHT TO BORDEAUX

Vexations of Travel in France.— Residence at Passy.—
The 21 January, 1793.— Portrait of Monsieur Arthur
Dillon. — Retirement to Le Bouilh. — Bordeaux
and the Federation.— Arrest of Monsieur de La Tour
du Pin Père.— His Son and Daughter-in-Law Take
Refuge at Canoles with Monsieur de Brouquens.—
The Guillotine at Bordeaux.— Birth of Séraphine.—
Flight of Monsieur de La Tour du Pin.— Arrest of
Monsieur de Brouquens.— Confrontation of the
Queen and the Former Minister of War.— Precipitate
Departure of His Son from Bouilh.—Three Months of
Forced Retirement at Mirambeau................. 137

CONTENTS

CHAPTER FOURTEEN
1793–1794
LIFE AT BORDEAUX

PAGE

The Seals at Le Bouilh.— Refuge at Bordeaux with Bonie.
—The Pain de la Section.— The Queue at the Door of
the Butchers and Bakers.— Arrest of the English and
Americans.— A Belle Grisette.— Unexpected Protection.—Mme. Tallien.—Interview with Tallien.—Monsieur de La Tour du Pin Takes Refuge at Tesson.— New
Flight.— Return to Tesson. — The Cartes de Sûreté.. 151

CHAPTER FIFTEEN
1794
DECISION TO LEAVE FRANCE

Alarming Situation of Mme. de La Tour du Pin at Bor-
deaux and of Her Husband at Tesson.—Certificates of
Residence with Nine Witnesses.— Decision to Leave
for America.— The American Vessel "Diane".— Pre-
parations for Departure.— On the Arm of Tallien.
— Passport of the Citizen Latour.— Anxiety over the
Delay.— Return of Monsieur de La Tour du Pin.—
How He Came Back from Tesson................. 163

CHAPTER SIXTEEN
1794
VOYAGE TO BOSTON

Delivery of the Passport.— The Visé by Ysabeau.— Mon-
sieur de Fontenay and his Wife's Diamonds.— Final
Preparations.—Adieux to Marguerite.—Monsieur de
Chambeau Accompanies Us.—Embarkment on the
"Diane".—The Boat and Its Equipment.— Off the
Azores.— The Pilot.—The Port of Boston.— Joy at
Arriving.. 173

CONTENTS

SECOND PART

CHAPTER ONE
1794
ARRIVAL IN AMERICA

PAGE

Adieux to the "Diane".— Joy of Being in a Friendly Country.— Temporary Residence at Boston.— Mr. Geyer.— General Schuyler.— Sale of Superfluous Articles.— Departure for Albany.— Mme. de La Tour du Pin Learns of the Death of her Father.— The Inn at Lebanon.— Arrival at Albany.— Friendly Reception by General Schuyler and the Van Rensselaer Family.— Mrs. Van Rensselaer.— Talleyrand in America.................................... 183

CHAPTER TWO
1794
THE FARM NEAR ALBANY

En Pension with the Van Burens.— Mme. de La Tour du Pin's Father-in-Law.— Apprenticeship as Farmer.— Purchase of a Farm.— Temporary Residence at Troy. — A Log House.— Unexpected Visit of Monsieur de Talleyrand.— News of the 9 Thermidor.— An Appreciation of Monsieur de Talleyrand.— Mr. Law. — Alexander Hamilton.— Beginning of Winter.— First Encounter with the Indians.— Purchase of the First Negro, Minck.— Repairs of the Farm-house. — Activity of Mme. de La Tour du Pin........... 196

CONTENTS

CHAPTER THREE
1795
COUNTRY LIFE

PAGE

Family Life at the Farm.— The Arrival of Spring.— The
Indians.— Their Passion for Rum.—— The Shakers.
— A Visit to Their Establishment.— A Visit from
Messieurs de Liancourt and Dupetit-Theuars.—
Talleyrand and the Banker Morris.— Plans for a
Trip to Philadelphia and New York 210

CHAPTER FOUR
1795
A VISIT TO NEW YORK

Fulton's Invention.— The Trip to New York.— The
Hudson River.— West Point.— Sojourn at New York.
— Alexander Hamilton.— The Yellow Fever.— Pre-
cipitate Departure.— General Gates.— Return to the
Farm.— Death of Séraphine.— Gathering the Apples
and Making Cider.— The Crop of Corn.— Ice in the
River.— Recovery of a Portrait of the Queen 223

CHAPTER FIVE
1796
DEPARTURE FOR EUROPE

News from France.— Return Decided Upon.— Regrets
of Mme. de La Tour du Pin.— The Slaves Receive
Their Liberty.— Departure for Europe.— The Wait
at New York.— Arrival at Cadiz.— The Quarantine.
— Visit of the Customs Officers.— Mode of Travel in
Spain at this Epoch.— A Bull Fight.— Departure
from Cadiz.— The Inns.— Cathedral of Cordova.—
In the Sierra Morena.— At Madrid 237

CONTENTS

CHAPTER SIX
1796–1797
VISIT TO PARIS

PAGE

Departure from Madrid.— The Escurial.— Arrival at Saint-Sébastien.— Bonie Rejoins Us.— Apprehensions on Returning to France.—Arrival at Bayonne.— Monsieur de Brouquens Again.—Arrival at Le Bouilh. — Devastation of the Château.— The Library Saved. — Return of Marguerite.— Birth of Charlotte.— Absence of Monsieur de La Tour du Pin.— Fortune Compromised.— Dispersion of the Family Souvenirs. — Trip to Paris.— Devastation of the Château of Tesson.— Talleyrand, Minister of Foreign Affairs.— Jealousy of Tallien............................... 256

CHAPTER SEVEN
1797–1798
EXILE IN ENGLAND

The 18 Fructidor.— A Promenade in Paris.— Mme. de Staël and Benjamin Constant.— Expulsion of the Returned Emigrés.— Situation of Monsieur and Mme. de La Tour du Pin.— Conduct of Talleyrand and Tallien.— New Exile.— A Friend from America.— Cordial Reception by Lady Jerningham.— Visit of Mme. Dillon.— Mme. de Rothe and the Archbishop of Narbonne.— Lord Dillon.— His Apostasy and Marriage with an Actress.— Lord Kenmare and His Daughter.— Dominating Character of Mme. d'Hénin. — Society of the Emigrés.— Departure for Cossey.— The Races at Newmarket.— Kindness of Lady Jerningham.— Life at Cossey.— The Family Table.— Residence at Richmond with Mme. d'Hénin.— An Inheritance Difficult to Realize.— Money Troubles of Mme. de La Tour du Pin...................... 273

CONTENTS

CHAPTER EIGHT

1798–1799

LIFE AT RICHMOND

PAGE

The Princesse de Bouillon in England.— Birth and Death
of Edward.— Change of Residence at Richmond.—
Facilities of Life in England.— Narrow Circumstances
of Monsieur and Mme. de La Tour du Pin.— Distress
of Monsieur de Chambeau.— He is Aided by Monsieur de La Tour du Pin.— The One Hundred Pounds
of Edward Jerningham.— A Week at London.— An
Eight Days' Excursion.— Plans for Return to France
Abandoned. — The Circulating Library   293

CHAPTER NINE

1799–1800

RETURN TO PARIS

Again at Cossey.— News of the 18 Brumaire.— Plans for
Return to France.— The Wait at Yarmouth.— The
Crossing.— The Debarkment at Cuxhaven.— In the
North of Germany.— The Ball at Wildeshausen.—
Birth of Cécile.— En Route for Holland.— At
Utrecht.— Unexpected Meeting with Mme. d'Hénin.
— Arrival at Paris.— Residence in the Rue de Mi-
romesnil.— Mme. Bonaparte.— Monsieur de Beau-
harnais the Best Dancer in Paris.—The Morality of
Talleyrand.— A Visit to Mme. Bonaparte.— Certifi-
cates of Residence.— At Malmaison.— The Gallery
of Mme. Bonaparte.— Mme. de Staël and Bonaparte   302

CONTENTS

CHAPTER TEN
1800–1808

LIFE AT LE BOUILH

PAGE

Sale of the Paris House.— Departure for Le Bouilh.— Life There.— Education of Mlle. de Lally.— Establishment of the Empire.— Birth of Aymar.— Marriage of Mlle. de Lally and Henri d'Aux.............. 317

CHAPTER ELEVEN
1808

THE EMPEROR AT BORDEAUX

Humbert Leaves for Antwerp.— Grief over the Separation. — Visit of the Emperor to Bordeaux.— His Passage of the River at Cubzac.— Mme. de La Tour du Pin Summoned to Bordeaux. — The Court Assembly. — Presentation to the Emperor.— The Salon of the Empress.— Her Entourage.— Strict Rules for Her Days Dictated by the Emperor.— Anxiety of Josephine over the Rumors of Her Divorce.— A Note from the Emperor.— Departure of the Empress.— Return to Le Bouilh.— Monsieur de La Tour du Pin Appointed Préfet at Brussels.— Mme. de La Tour du Pin, Dame d'Honneur of the Queen of Spain.— Presentation to the Queen.— The Prince de la Paix.— Departure of the Spanish Sovereigns.............. 327

CHAPTER TWELVE
1808–1810

THE PREFECTURE AT BRUSSELS

Commencement of a New Life.— Judicious Choice of Monsieur de La Tour du Pin for the Prefecture.— Departure from Le Bouilh.— Mlle. Fanny Dillon and

[xviii]

CONTENTS

PAGE

the Prince Pignatelli.— Project of Her Marriage with
General Bertrand.— A Delicate Mission to the
Empress Josephine.— Wives of the Officers at
Brussels.— The Dowager Duchesse d'Arenberg.—
Her Suppers.— Her Reception of Monsieur and Mme.
de La Tour du Pin.— A Study of Brussels Society.—
Organization of the House.— Napoleon Obtains Con-
sent of Mlle. Fanny Dillon to Marry General Bertrand.
— Eight Days for the Marriage.— Meeting with
General Bertrand.— Details of the Marriage Arranged
by the Emperor.— Mme. de La Tour du Pin Received
by the Emperor at Saint-Cloud.— Signature of the
Contract.— Marriage at Saint-Leu.— The Emeralds
of Queen Hortense 339

CHAPTER THIRTEEN

1810–1811

VISIT OF THE EMPEROR

The Winter Season at Brussels.— The Ennui of Queen
Hortense.— Arrival of Marie-Louise at Compiègne.—
High Society at Brussels and the Imperial Govern-
ment.— The Guard of Honor.— Napoleon and Marie-
Louise at Brussels.— Dinner with the Emperor.—
Ball at the Hôtel de Ville.— Departure of the Em-
peror.— The Summer at Brussels.— Examination of
Humbert at the Conseil d'Etat.— Humbert Ap-
pointed Sous-Préfet at Florence.— Birth of the
King of Rome.— The Private Baptism.— The Old
Guard 355

CONTENTS

CHAPTER FOURTEEN

1811–1813

AN AUDIENCE WITH NAPOLEON

PAGE

Marie-Louise at Laeken.— Opening of the Russian Campaign.— Movements of Troops.— Monsieur de Liedekerke Demands the Hand of Charlotte de La Tour du Pin.— Humbert is Appointed Sous-Préfet at Sens. — Dismissal of the Préfet of Brussels.— Mme. de La Tour du Pin Leaves for Paris.— Request for an Audience.— Conversation with the Emperor.— Surprise of Monsieur de Montalivet.— Monsieur de La Tour du Pin Appointed Préfet at Amiens.— The Assembly at the Tuileries.— Amiability of Napoleon.— The Last Days at Brussels.— Regrets of the Population.— Marriage of Charlotte................... 365

CHAPTER FIFTEEN

1813–1814

RETURN OF THE KING

Society at Amiens.— The Prefecture.— General Dupont. — Arrival of the Cossacks.— Conversation with Talleyrand.— His Hatred of Napoleon.— Flight of Humbert from Sens.— In the Ante-chamber of Talleyrand.— "Vive le Roi!"— Distribution of White Cockades.— Preparations for the Reception of the King.— The King Enjoys His Dinner.— Ill-nature of the Duchesse d'Angoulême.— Monsieur de La Tour du Pin Re-enters Diplomacy.—Humbert is Appointed Lieutenant of the Black Musketeers.............. 380

CONTENTS

CHAPTER SIXTEEN

1814–1815

THE FIRST RESTORATION

PAGE

Monsieur de La Tour du Pin Envoy to the Congress of
Vienna.— His Wife Accompanies Him to Brussels.—
Alexandre de Lameth, Préfet of Amiens.— Life at
Paris.— Monsieur de Liedekerke Decorated with the
Legion of Honor.— Mme. de Liedekerke Leaves for
Vienna with her Husband.— The Court of Louis
XVIII.— Two Balls at the Duc de Berry's.— Lord
Wellington.— News of the Debarkment of Napoleon
at Cannes.— Mme. de La Tour du Pin Decides to
Leave for Brussels.— She Visits the Minister of
Finance.— A Night of Anxiety.— At Brussels.— Visit
to the King of Holland.— Separation of the Congress
of Vienna.— Mission of Monsieur de La Tour du Pin
to the Duc d'Angoulême...................... 394

POSTSCRIPT

Life of Monsieur and Madame de La Tour du Pin
after the First Restoration.— The Dillon Family.—
Genealogical Table.— Biographical Notes.— History
of the Dillon Regiment........................ 406

ILLUSTRATIONS

PAGE

Marquise de La Tour du Pin .... *Frontispiece*

Comte de La Tour du Pin de Gouvernet 32

La Reine Marie Antoinette 48

Le Marquis de Lally-Tollendal 64

Anne-Louise Necker; Baronne de Staël.............. 96

Princesse d'Hénin 112

Le Conventionnel Tallien 160

Madame Tallien 176

Le Bateau "La Diane" 192

Comte Arthur Dillon 208

Prince de Talleyrand-Perigord 288

Château du Bouilh 304

L'Impératrice Josephine 320

L'Impératrice Marie-Louise 352

Comte Humbert de La Tour du Pin de Gouvernet..... 368

RECOLLECTIONS OF THE REVOLUTION AND THE EMPIRE

FIRST PART

CHAPTER ONE

1770–1781

CHILDHOOD OF MLLE. DILLON

Her Earliest Years.— Members of Her Family.— Her Sad and Precocious Infancy.— Her Maid Marguerite.— Society Before the Revolution.— An Archbishop's Mode of Life.— Toilettes of Men and Women.— Dinners and Suppers.— Château of Hautefontaine.— Louis XVI Jealous of the Hunting Establishment.— Sojourn at Versailles in 1781.— The Queen's Friendship for Madame Dillon.

WHOEVER writes a book, almost always does so with the idea that it will be read either before or after his death. But I do not intend to write a book — merely the journal of my life. If I were only to relate events, a few sheets of paper would suffice for a record of so little interest, but if I undertake to set forth the history of my opinions and my feelings, the journal of my heart, the enterprise is more difficult, for to depict one's self, self-knowledge is essential, and one does not begin to acquire that at fifty years of age. Perhaps

RECOLLECTIONS OF THE REVOLUTION

I shall speak of the past and tell the story of my early years only in episodes and without continuity. I do not pretend to write my confessions, but although I should dislike to reveal my faults, I wish nevertheless to depict myself as I am and as I have been.

I have never written anything except letters to those I love. I have no order in my ideas, and little method. My memory is already much impaired. Moreover, my imagination carries me sometimes so far from the subject I wish to follow that it is difficult for me to pick up the threads so often broken by these digressions. My heart is still so young that I have to look at myself in the mirror to realize that I am no longer twenty years of age. Let me then take advantage of the ardor which still remains, and which the infirmities of age may sweep away at any moment, to relate some facts of a troubled life, but one not so unhappy from the events known to the public, as from the secret afflictions known only to God.

During my earliest years I was a witness of many incidents which should have debased my mind, perverted and corrupted my heart, and destroyed in me every idea of morality and religion. From the age of ten I was present when the conversation was most free, and heard expressed the most ungodly principles. I was brought up in the house of an archbishop, where all the rules of religion were daily violated. I knew from observation that I was taught dogmas and doctrines exactly as I was instructed in history and geography.

[2]

CHILDHOOD OF MLLE. DILLON

My mother had married her cousin, Arthur Dillon, with whom she had been brought up, and whom she regarded only as a brother. She was very beautiful, and the angelic sweetness of her character caused her to be loved by everybody. Men adored her, and women were not jealous of her. Although free from coquetry, she was not sufficiently reserved in her relations with men who took her fancy and who, the world said, were in love with her.

One of her admirers in particular spent his entire life in the house of my grandmother and of my uncle, the Archbishop, where my mother lived. He also went to the country with us. The Prince de Guémené, nephew of the notorious Cardinal de Rohan, was therefore considered by everybody as my mother's lover. But I do not think this was true, for the Duc de Lauzun, the Duc de Liancourt, and the Comte de Saint-Blancard were equally attentive to her. The Comte de Fersen, who was reputed to be the lover of Queen Marie-Antoinette, also came to our house nearly every day. My mother took the fancy of the Queen, who was always impressed by brilliancy. Madame Dillon was much in vogue, and for this reason only she entered the Royal household and became a Dame du Palais. At that time I was seven or eight years of age.

My grandmother, who was a woman of very haughty character, and of infinite ill-nature, running frequently into a rage, enjoyed nevertheless the affections of her daughter. My mother was absolutely under her contol. Entirely dependent upon her mother in money matters, she had never dared to point out, that as the only daughter of her father General de Rothe, who died when she was fifteen years old, she had the right to control her own fortune. My grandmother had taken possession arbitrarily (*de vive force*) of the domain of Hautefontaine, which had been purchased with the funds of her husband. Daughter of a Peer of England of slender fortune, she had received a very small inheritance. But my mother, married at seventeen years of age to a man of eighteen, who had been brought up with her, and who had no property except his regiment, could never find the courage to talk to my grandmother of money matters. The Queen opened her eyes to her interests and encouraged her to demand an accounting. My grandmother was furious, and in place of maternal tenderness, became possessed of an inconceivable rage, such as you find described only in romances or tragedies.

My earliest recollections are of the frightful scenes between my mother and my grandmother, which I was obliged to appear not to notice. Reserve and discretion on my part were absolutely necessary. I contracted the habit of hiding my feelings. I remember that I was shocked by the way in which my mother complained to her friends of my grandmother. My father naturally took the part of my mother. But I knew that he was under great pecuniary obligations to my uncle, the Archbishop, and his position, to me, seemed false.

These reflections developed ideas and experiences which were too precocious in the head of a child of ten years. I never had any infancy. The only person who saved me from these bad influences, and encouraged the thoughts of virtue in my heart, was a maid who could neither read nor write. She was a young peasant, by the name of Marguerite, from the neighborhood of Compiègne. She was very devoted to me and remained in my service nearly all of her life. I knew that Marguerite was worthy of all confidence and that she would rather die than compromise me by an indiscreet word.

The manners and customs of society have changed so much since the Revolution that I wish to retrace in some detail what I recall of the mode of life of my family.

My great-uncle, the Archbishop of Narbonne, rarely visited his diocese. President, ex officio, of the States of Languedoc, he visited this province solely to preside over the meetings of the States, which were in session six weeks during the months of November and December. As soon as the meeting was over he returned to Paris, under the pretext that the interests of his province imperiously claimed his presence at the Court, but, in reality, in order to live *en grand seigneur* at Paris and as a courtier at Versailles.

Besides the archbishopric of Narbonne, which paid him 250,000 francs a year, he had an abbey which was worth 110,000; still another which was worth 90,000; and he received an allowance of more than 50,000 francs for giving dinners every day during the meetings of the States. It would seem that with such an income he should have been able to live honorably and at his ease, but nevertheless he was always in financial difficulties. His style of life at Paris was noble but simple, and the daily fare, although abundant, was reasonable.

At this epoch grand dinners were never given, because every one dined at an early hour — at two-thirty, or three o'clock at the latest. The ladies were sometimes *coiffées*, but never dressed for dinner. The men, on the contrary, were usually dressed in embroidered or plain costumes, according to their age or taste, but almost never in evening dress or in uniform. Those who were not going out in the evening, and the master of the house, were in formal dress and *en négligé*, for the necessity of putting on a hat deranged the fragile edifice of the curled and powdered toupet. After dinner there was general conversation or, sometimes, a game of backgammon. The ladies then retired to dress, and the men awaited them to go to the theatre, if they were to be in the same loge. Those who remained at home received visitors during the afternoon. At nine-thirty in the evening the guests arrived for supper.

The supper was the real event of the day in society. There were two kinds of suppers — those given by persons who had them every day, which permitted a certain number of persons to drop in when they wished, and the more formal affairs, which were more brilliant and more numerously attended, and to which the guests were invited. I speak of the period of my infancy, from 1778 to 1784. I never attended one of these fine suppers, but I have often seen my mother dressing to go to one at the Hôtel de Choiseul or the Palais-Royal.

CHILDHOOD OF MLLE. DILLON

At this time there were fewer balls than later. The costumes worn by the ladies naturally turned dancing into a kind of torture. Every one wore heels three inches high, which put the foot in an unnatural position; a pannier of heavy and stiff whalebone, extending to the right and the left; a coiffure a foot high, surmounted by a bonnet called *pouf*, upon which feathers, flowers and diamonds were piled up, besides a pound of powder and pomade which the least movement caused to fall upon the shoulders: such a scaffolding rendered it impossible to dance with pleasure. But at the suppers, where everybody talked or enjoyed a little music, this edifice was not disturbed.

But to return to my family. We went to the country early in the spring for the whole summer. At the château of Hautefontaine there were twenty-five apartments for guests, and these were often filled. The principal season, however, was during the month of October. It was then that the colonels came back from their regiments, where they had passed four months, less the number of hours necessary to return to Paris, from which city they scattered to the different châteaux to visit their families and their friends.

At Hautefontaine there was a hunting establishment, the expense of which was divided between my uncle, the Prince de Guémené and the Duc de Lauzun. I have heard it said that the expense did not exceed 30,000 francs, but in this sum was not included the outlay for the saddle-horses of the masters — only the dogs, the wages of the huntsmen, who were English, their horses and the keep of the whole establishment. The hunt was held during the summer and autumn in the forests of Compiègne and Villers-Cotterets. The hunt establishment was kept on such a scale that the poor King Louis XVI was seriously jealous.

At the age of seven I took part in the hunt once or twice a week, and when I was ten years old, the day of Saint-Hubert, I broke my leg. They tell me that I showed great courage and did not make a complaint, although it was necessary to carry me five leagues on a stretcher.

My first visit to Versailles was at the time of the birth of the first Dauphin in October, 1781. How often the recollection of these days of splendor of Marie-Antoinette comes to my mind, when I think of the torments and ignominies of which she was afterwards the unfortunate victim. I went to see the ball given by the Gardes du Corps in the Grande Salle de Spectacle, in the Château of Versailles. The Queen opened the ball with a simple young guard. She was dressed in a blue gown all sprinkled with sapphires and diamonds; beautiful, young, adored by all, having just given a Dauphin to France, not dreaming of the possibility of a backward step in her brilliant career, she was already on the edge of the abyss.

I shall not undertake to describe the intrigues of the Court, which my great youth prevented me from judging or even comprehending. I heard it said at the time that the Queen had commenced to take a fancy to Madame de Polignac, who was very pretty, but had little animation. Her sister-in-law, the Comtesse Diane de Polignac, who was older and very *intrigante*, advised her as to the means of securing the royal favor. I recall that Monsieur de Guémené endeavored to warn my mother of this growing favor of Mme. de Polignac, but my mother accepted the Queen's love without thinking to profit by her favor, either to augment her own fortune or to make that of her friends. She felt that she was already attacked by the malady from which she was to perish less than two years later.

At this time my father was in America, at the head of the first battalion of his regiment. The Dillon Regiment had entered the service of France in 1690, at the time that James II had lost all hope of remounting the throne, after the battle of the Boyne. The regiment was commanded at that time by my great-grandfather, Arthur Dillon.*

* A genealogical table of the Dillon family and a brief history of the Regiment will be found at the end of this volume.

CHAPTER TWO

1782–1783

DEATH OF MME. DILLON

Illness of Mme. Dillon.— She is Ordered to the Waters of Spa.—
Indignation of Her Mother.— Intervention of the Queen.—
Departure for Brussels.— Lord and Lady Dillon.— Lady
Kenmare. — Education of Mlle. Dillon. — Sojourn at
Brussels.— Visit to the Archduchess Marie-Christine.—
Sojourn at Spa.— Return to Paris.— Death of Mme.
Dillon.— Description of Hautefontaine.— Purchase of the
Folie Joyeuse at Montfermeil.

MY mother had always been delicate since
the birth of her son, who died at the age
of two years. She did not take any care of
her health. She rode horseback, hunted the stag,
and sang with the celebrated Piccini, who was a
great admirer of her voice. Finally, about the month
of April, 1782, at the age of thirty-one, she had a
hemorrhage.

My grandmother, who did not wish to believe in
the sickness of her daughter, was at last forced to
admit that she was seriously ill. My mother consulted
a physician who then enjoyed a great deal of ce-
lebrity, and he ordered her to go to Spa. It would be
difficult to describe the inconceivable rage of my
grandmother at the idea that her daughter was going
to the springs. She did not wish to accompany her
there and refused her money for the journey. I think

that the Queen came to my mother's help on this occasion. We set out from Hautefontaine for Brussels, where we passed a month.

My uncle, Charles Dillon, had married Miss Phipps, daughter of Lord Mulgrave. He resided at Brussels, as he was not able to live in England on account of his numerous debts. At this time he was still a Catholic. It was only later that he had the unpardonable feebleness to change his religion and become a Protestant, in order to inherit from his maternal great-uncle, Lord Lichfield, who made this a condition of his heritage of 15,000 pounds sterling. Lady Charles Dillon was very beautiful. The year before, she had visited Paris with Lady Kenmare, my father's sister, who was also a great beauty. She went to the Queen's Ball with my mother, and the three sisters-in-law were generally admired. A year had hardly passed before they were in their tombs. All three died at an interval of one week.

As I have already said, I did not have any infancy. At twelve years of age my education was already far advanced. I had read much, but without discrimination. From the age of seven I had been given an instructor. He was an organist of Béziers, named Combes. He was engaged to give me lessons on the clavecin, for at that time pianos were very rare. My mother had one to accompany her voice, but I was not permitted to touch it.

I had always had a great desire to improve my mind. I wished to know everything, from the cuisine to experiments in chemistry, which I made with a little apothecary who lived at Hautefontaine. The gardener was English, and my maid Marguerite took me every day to see his wife who taught me to read in that language, generally "Robinson Crusoe," of which I was very fond.

At eleven years of age, my mother, finding that I was not speaking English as well as formerly, engaged for me an English maid who was expressly brought over from England. Her arrival caused me great chagrin, as I was separated from my former maid, Marguerite.

Returning to my story. At Brussels we stayed in the house of my aunt. She was in the last stages of consumption, but the disease had not impaired her beauty, which was really heavenly. She had two charming children — a boy of four, who afterwards became Viscount Dillon, and a girl who later became the wife of Sir Thomas Webb. I had a great deal of fun with these children. My greatest pleasure was to care for them and to put them to sleep. I already had the maternal instinct. I felt that these poor children would soon be deprived of their mother. I did not realize that I myself was so near the same misfortune.

My mother took me to see Archduchess Marie-Christine, who governed the Low Countries with her husband, Duke Albert of Saxe-Teschen. While my mother was talking with the Archduchess, they showed me a cabinet in which there were portfolios of prints. I have often thought since that this was the beginning of that superb collection of engravings, the finest in Europe, which Duke Albert left to the Archduke Charles.

DEATH OF MME. DILLON

From Brussels we went to Spa, where Monsieur de Guémené rejoined us. It was at Spa that I enjoyed for the first time the dangerous poison of praise and success. The days that there were dances at the Assembly Room, my mother took me there, and the dancing of the *petite française* soon became one of the curiosities of Spa.

The Comte and Comtesse du Nord had just arrived from the interior of Russia, and they had never seen a girl of twelve years dance the gavotte and the minuet. This same princess later became the second wife of the Emperor Paul the First of Russia, and thirty-seven years later, when she met me again as a grave mother of a family, she had not forgotten the little girl of other days. At that time she said many pleasant things regarding the recollections which she had preserved of my grace and, above all, of my beautiful figure.

However, the waters of Spa shortened the days of my poor mother. Nevertheless, she disliked to return to Hautefontaine, as she was certain that she would be greeted there by my grandmother, as usual, with scenes of ill-nature. But my mother had the thought, common to all those who are attacked by this cruel malady of the chest, that she should have a change of air. She wished to go to Italy, and asked first to return to Paris. My grandmother consented, and then for the first time fully realized the unfortunate state of her daughter.

On our arrival at Paris, my grandmother gave my mother her own apartment, as it was the largest in

[13]

the house. During her last moments my mother was well cared for. The Queen came to see her, and every day a groom or a page was sent from Versailles to inquire regarding her. She grew feebler from day to day. In writing these lines, after forty-five years, I still have a feeling of regret that nobody spoke of the sacraments of the Church, or thought of sending for a priest. In this house of an Archbishop there was not even a chaplain. My mother did not realize that the end was so near. The 7th of September, 1782, she died in the arms of my maid.

A good old friend of my mother's, Mme. Nagle, brought me the sad news. In the morning I awoke to find her beside my bed. She told me that my grandmother had left the house, and that I should get up and follow her, and ask for her protection and care; that now I depended on her for my future. She said that my grandmother was on bad terms with my father, who was then in America, and that she might disinherit me. My young heart, which was nearly broken, revolted at the idea of this dissimulation, and the good lady had much trouble in persuading me to allow her to take me to my grandmother. At last I consented, and, as I expected, my grandmother made a great scene of despair, which produced a most painful impression upon me.

After the death of my mother, my grandmother and my uncle went in the month of October, 1782, to Hautefontaine and took me with them, as well as my instructor Monsieur Combes, who occupied himself exclusively with my education.

DEATH OF MME. DILLON

I was very fond of this château, which I knew would one day belong to me. It was a beautiful estate, all *en domaines*, about twenty-two leagues from Paris, between Villers-Cotterets and Soissons. The château, built towards the beginning of the previous century, was situated upon a very steep hill. It overlooked a fertile little valley, or rather gorge, opening out upon the forest of Compiègne, which formed an amphitheatre at the back of the picture. Prairies, woods, ponds of clear water filled with fish, were situated beyond a fine kitchen garden, which you overlooked from the windows of the château. The château itself, although it had no architectural beauty, was convenient, vast, perfectly furnished and well cared for in every detail.

My uncle, my grandmother and my mother had accompanied my father as far as Brest when he embarked in 1779 for the war in the Antilles. On his return my uncle bought at Lorient the whole cargo of a vessel just arrived from India, consisting of Chinese and Japanese porcelains, and Persian cloth of all colors for the hangings of our apartments. All these riches were unpacked, to my great joy, and arranged in the large *garde-meubles*, where the old concierge let me roam with my maid when the weather did not permit me to go out.

During the life of my mother the residence at Hautefontaine had been very brilliant, but after her death all this was completely changed. My grandmother had taken possession, in the absence of my father, of all of my mother's papers, and of all of the correspondence which she had preserved. The fortune of my grandfather had run through her hands, and all of our investments had changed in nature during the minority of my mother. She was only fifteen years of age when she lost her father, General de Rothe, who died suddenly at Hautefontaine, only a short time after purchasing this property. He had bought the château in the name of his wife, under the pretext that it was paid for exclusively with the funds — 10,000 pounds sterling — given as a *dot* to my grandmother by her father, Lord Falkland.

My grandfather had inherited the fortune of his mother, Lady Catherine de Rothe, and also that of his aunt, the Duchess of Perth, both daughters of Lord Middleton, Minister of James II. Another relative had left him, at Paris, the house in which we lived, Rue du Bac, and 4,000 livres of *rentes* upon the Hôtel de Ville of Paris. These two investments were the only ones which remained at the death of Monsieur de Rothe, when my mother came into possession.

My great-uncle, the Archbishop, had lived in the house in the Rue du Bac for twenty years without paying a sou of rent to his niece and without even paying for the repairs. When he left the house after the death of my mother and leased another, he borrowed 40,000 francs on mortgage and used the money for repairs which were urgently necessary. I did not know anything about this debt, which I was obliged to pay myself when I sold the house in 1797. At the death of my mother, all that I received was this house in the Rue du Bac, which was leased for 10 000 francs to the Baron de Staël, who afterwards married the celebrated Mlle. Necker, and the 4,000 francs of income spoken of above. I had no expectations from my father. He had already spent the portion of 10,000 pounds sterling which he had inherited with the Dillon Regiment, of which he was *propriétaire-né*, as heir of his uncles James and Edward, who were killed within two years of each other.

Towards the end of the autumn of 1782, my uncle set out as usual for Montpellier to preside over the States of Languedoc. As Archbishop of Narbonne, he had this prerogative, which he exercised over the period of twenty-eight years.

My grandmother and I remained at Hautefontaine, where we were very lonely. When my grandmother found herself alone at Hautefontaine, in that grand château formerly so animated and brilliant; when she saw the empty stables; when she no longer heard the baying of the hounds and the horns of the hunters, she became desirous of changing her mode of life and of persuading the Archbishop to do the same.

When the Archbishop returned from Montpellier, where he had remained only the time absolutely necessary for the meeting of the States, we went to meet him at Paris. My father at that time was Governor of the island of Saint-Christophe, which he had captured during the expedition in which his regiment had gloriously contributed to the success of the French forces. In his absence my guardians represented to my great-uncle that he should no longer continue to live in my house without paying any rent or even looking after the repairs. He therefore made up his mind to leave the house, and, as already stated, borrowed on mortgage the funds necessary for the repairs.

About this same time my grandmother, who was tired of Hautefontaine, bought, for 52,000 francs, a house at Montfermeil, near Livry, about five leagues from Paris. The price was very moderate, for the land comprised ninety acres. The house, which was in a charming situation, was named Folie-Joyeuse. It had been built by a Monsieur de Joyeuse, who had begun the construction where one ordinarily leaves off. After having laid out a fine court, enclosed by a railing, he built, at the right and left, two wings terminated by two handsome square pavilions. He had then found himself short of the money necessary to build the body of the house, so that the only communication between the two pavilions was by a corridor at least one hundred feet long. His creditors had then seized the house. The park was beautiful, surrounded by walls, with every path terminating at a gate, and all the outlets opening on the forest of Bondy, which was charming in this locality.

The furniture was brought from Hautefontaine, and in the spring of 1783 we were quite well established at Folie-Joyeuse. The first year no repairs were made, but we passed the summer in laying out plans with architects and decorators, which interested me very much.

CHAPTER THREE

1783–1786

VISITS TO LANGUEDOC

Annual Trips of Mlle. Dillon to Languedoc.— Method of
Travel at That Epoch.— The Route to Languedoc.—
Nîmes and Montpellier.— Etiquette at Dinners.— Society
at Montpellier.—Return of Monsieur Dillon to France.—
He Weds Mme. de La Touche.—He Takes the Government
of Tabago.— First Plans for the Marriage of Mlle. Dillon.—
Sojourn at Bordeaux.—Another Dillon Family.—The Comte
de La Tour du Pin and His Son, the Comte de Gouvernet.

IN the month of November, 1783, I learned that
my grandmother would accompany my uncle,
the Archbishop, to the meeting of the States of
Languedoc. This news caused me great joy. At this
time the annual session of the States was a very
brilliant occasion. Peace had just been concluded, and
the English, deprived for three years of the possibility of travelling on the Continent, came over in
crowds, as they did later in 1814. At that time people
did not travel so much in Italy. The fine roads by
Mt. Cenis and the Simplon, and the magnificent
route by the Corniche, constructed during the reign
of Napoleon, were not then in existence. The climate
of the south of France, especially that of Languedoc
and Montpellier, was very attractive.

The thought of this journey, practically the first
I had ever taken, filled me with joy. I will relate

here once for all how we made the trip to Montpellier, as we went there every year until 1786 when
I made my last visit.

We set out in a large *berline* with six horses. My
uncle and my grandmother were seated in the back,
with myself and the secretary of my uncle facing
them, and two domestics upon the box seat in front.
The second *berline*, also with six horses, carried our
two maids and two valets, with two servants upon
the box seat. A *chaise de poste* brought the *maître
d'hôtel* and the chef. There were also three couriers,
one of whom went a half-hour ahead, while the other
two accompanied the carriages. Monsieur Combes,
my instructor, left several days before us by diligence.

Every year the Ministers kept my great-uncle so
long at Versailles that he had hardly sufficient time
to arrive at Montpellier by the day fixed for the
opening of the States. The session could not commence until the Archbishop of Narbonne, who was
President, ex officio, was present.

The delay caused by the Ministers obliged us to
travel as fast as possible — a very disagreeable necessity at this advanced season of the year. As we
needed eighteen horses, the order of the *Administration des Postes* preceded us by several days, in order
that the horses might be ready. We made very long
daily trips. Setting out at four o'clock in the morning, we stopped only for dinner. The *chaise de poste*
and the first courier had preceded us by an hour.
This arrangement permitted us to find the table
ready, the fires lighted, and several good dishes
prepared by our chef when we arrived. The chef

carried with him from Paris, in his carriage, bottles of soup and sauces all prepared, and everything that was necessary to make palatable the bad meals which we found at the hotels. As soon as we arrived, the *chaise de poste* and the first courier set out, so that when we halted for the night we found everything ready for us the same as at noon.

At that time the route, which followed the course of the Rhone as far as Pont-Saint-Esprit, was in such bad order that you ran the risk of being overturned at every moment.

At La Palud we entered the territory of the Comte Venaissin, which belonged to the Pope. It gave me great pleasure to see the guide-post upon which was painted the tiara and the keys. I felt as though we were entering Italy. We left the highway to Marseille and followed an excellent road, which the Papal Government had permitted the States of Languedoc to construct, and which led directly to Pont-Saint-Esprit.

At La Palud my uncle changed his costume. He put on a wadded costume of violet cloth, lined with silk of the same color; silk stockings, also violet in color; shoes with gold buckles; his cordon bleu, and a three-cornered priest's hat ornamented with gold tassels.

As soon as the carriage had passed the last arch of the bridge at Pont-Saint-Esprit, the cannon of the little citadel at this bridge-head fired twenty-one shots. The drums beat a salute, the garrison came out, the officers in full dress, and all the civil and religious authorities presented themselves at the door of the *berline*. If it was not raining, my uncle descended while they attached the eight horses destined for his carriage.

He listened to the harangues which they addressed to him, and replied with affability and incomparable grace. He was very tall, with a noble face, and a voice and air at the same time gracious and assured. He asked for information regarding everything which might interest the inhabitants; listened to the petitions which were addressed to him; and the following year he still remembered the requests which had been made of him the preceding year. All this lasted about a quarter of an hour, after which we set out like the wind, for not only had the postilions been doubled, but the honor of conducting the carriage of so great a personage was warmly appreciated.

In the eyes of the inhabitants of Languedoc the President of the States was a much greater man than the King. My uncle was extremely popular. Although he was very haughty, his arrogance was never shown except to those who were, or who thought they were, his superiors.

We spent the night at Nîmes, where my uncle always had business. One year we spent several days with the Archbishop, which gave me the time to see the antiquities, although the monuments were not as well cared for as at present. They had just commenced to clear up the *Arènes* and had brought to light several new inscriptions.

Finally we arrived at Montpellier. After having travelled 160 leagues of detestable roads, after having crossed torrents without bridges, where you ran the risk of your life, at last we arrived at a route as fine as that of a well-kept estate. We crossed superb bridges perfectly constructed. We traversed cities flourishing with industry and a country which was well cultivated. The contrast was very striking.

The house in which we lived at Montpellier was large and beautiful but very dismal. It was situated in a narrow and sombre street. My uncle rented it all furnished. The apartment which he occupied on the first floor contained very fine Turkish rugs, which were common in Languedoc at that time. The house surrounded the four sides of a square court, one side of which was taken up by the large dining-room, another by a salon of the same dimensions, with six windows, which was hung and furnished in fine crimson damask, with an immense chimney of very ancient design, which to-day would be much admired.

My grandmother and I occupied the lower floor, which was dark even at three o'clock in the afternoon. We never saw my uncle in the morning. We took breakfast at nine o'clock, after which I went out for a walk with my English maid. At three o'clock precisely, it was necessary to be dressed and ready for dinner. We ascended to the salon where we found fifty guests assembled every day except Friday. Saturday my uncle always dined abroad, either with the Bishop or with some great personage of the States. There were never any ladies present at dinner, except my grandmother and myself. Between us were placed the guests most highly regarded. When there were any strangers, especially English, they were seated at my side. At that time every person who had a presentable domestic was served by him at table. Neither carafes nor glasses were placed upon the table. At the large dinners, there were placed upon the buffet silver buckets containing bottles of wine and a glass-stand with a dozen glasses, and any one who wished a glass of wine of any kind sent his servant to obtain it.

I had a servant attached to my person who was at the same time my coiffeur. He wore my livery, which we were obliged to have in red, although in England it was blue, because our stripes were exactly the same as those of the House of Bourbon. If our costumes had been blue, our livery would have been exactly the same as the King's, which was not allowed.

After dinner, which never lasted more than one hour, we returned to the salon which was filled with members of the States who had come for coffee. Nobody sat down, and at the end of a half-hour my grandmother and I descended to our apartment. We then frequently went out to make visits in a *chaise à porteurs*, which was the only means of transportation used in the streets of Montpellier. The fine quarter of the city, which has been built since, was not in existence at that epoch.

On our arrival at Paris, at the beginning of 1784, my father had returned from America. He had been Governor of Saint-Christophe until peace had been declared. After having surrendered the island to the English, he had made a visit to Martinique, where he became strongly attached to the Comtesse de La

Touche, who was the widow, at thirty years, of an officer of the Navy who had left her two children — a boy and a girl. She was very agreeable and very rich. Her mother, Mme. de Girardin, was a sister of Mme. de La Pagerie, the mother of Joséphine, later Empress of the French. At this time she had recently married her daughter to Vicomte de Beauharnais, who had taken her with him to France. Mme. de La Touche had made her plans to go to France with her two children, Alexandre and Betsy, who was later Duchesse de Fitz-James. My father followed them to France, and at this time people began to talk of their marriage. On hearing the news, my grandmother flew into a rage, and nobody could calm her. Nevertheless, it was very natural that my father should wish to marry again, in the hope of having a son. He was only thirty-three years of age and was *propriétaire* of one of the finest regiments of the army. Conducted to France by his grandfather, Arthur Dillon, this regiment had never changed its name, like the other regiments of the Irish Brigade. Without doubt, it would have been better if he had chosen for his new wife the daughter of one of the titled Catholic families of England, but he did not like the English, and he did love Mme. de La Touche. Of a very sweet and amiable character, although feeble, she had the careless and easy-going ways of the Creoles.

The marriage took place, in spite of my grandmother, who made a great fuss. My father wished to have me presented to my stepmother, but he gave up the idea on account of the opposition of my grandmother. She declared that if I ever went out of the house, even for an hour, to visit Mme. Dillon, I should never come back. The only visit that I ever made to my stepmother was in 1786, when my father left to take the position of Governor of the island of Tabago.

My father was very much dissatisfied because he had not been named Governor of Martinique or of Saint-Domingue, as he had acquired the right to demand one or the other of these two posts. During the war he had won the greatest distinction. His regiment had carried off the first success of the campaign by taking by assault the island of Grenade of which the Governor, Lord Macartney, was his prisoner. He had also powerfully contributed to the capture of the islands of Saint-Eustache and Saint-Christophe. He was Governor of this last named island for two years. When he turned it over to the English, at the time of the peace of 1783, the inhabitants gave him many evidences of their esteem and appreciation, of which the echoes reached even to England. My father received the most flattering evidences of this feeling at the time of his visit to England on his return to Europe.

My uncle, the Archbishop, dominated and influenced by my grandmother, instead of lending his support to his nephew to aid him to obtain one of these two governorships of Martinique or Saint-Domingue, did not assist him in any way. My father, therefore, accepted the governorship of Tabago, where he resided until he was elected Deputy of Martinique to the States-General. He left France accompanied by his wife and my little sister Fanny, who later became the wife of General Bertrand. He also took with him as recorder of the island, my instructor, Monsieur Combes.

Before his departure, my father talked with my grandmother of a project which he wished strongly to see carried out. He had known at Martinique, during the war, a young man who was aide de camp to the Marquis de Bouillé, whom the latter liked extremely, and whom my father also highly appreciated. My grandmother objected, without giving the matter much consideration, although the young man was of high birth and would be the head of his house, under the pretext that he was a *mauvais sujet*, that he had many debts and that he was small and homely. I was so young that my father did not insist. He sent my uncle, the Archbishop, a procuration which gave him the power to arrange my marriage when he judged that the time had arrived. However, I often thought of the *parti* whom my father had proposed and searched for information regarding the young man. My cousin, Dominique Sheldon, brought up by my grandmother, and who lived with us, knew him and often spoke to me of him. I learned that he had had indeed a very lively youth, and I made up my mind no longer to think of him.

In 1785 our sojourn in Languedoc was much longer than usual. After the session of the States we went to pass nearly a month at Alais, with the amiable Bishop, who was later Cardinal de Bausset of that city. This trip interested me very much. It

was during this sojourn at Alais that I acquired my
first love for the mountains. This little city, situated
in a charming valley, surrounded by a beautiful
prairie sprinkled with very old chestnut trees, is in
the midst of the Cévennes. Every day we made
some excursions which were really charming. The
young people of the country had formed a mounted
guard of honor for my uncle. They had adopted the
English uniform of the Dillons, red with yellow
facings. They all belonged to the best families of the
country.

To my great regret we set out to pass two months
at Narbonne, where I had never been. As I liked to be
informed regarding all matters of interest in the
places which I visited, I began to look up the histories
of Narbonne from the time of Cæsar to that of
Cardinal de Richelieu, who had formerly occupied the
archiepiscopal château, which was similar to a strong-
hold of the middle ages.

From Narbonne, we went to Toulouse, by way of
Saint-Papoul, where we remained several days.
From there we went to Bordeaux, where we made a
visit of seventeen days with the Archbishop.

I cannot say why Bordeaux interested me more
than the other cities which we had visited. Here we
saw Mme. Dillon, mother of all those Dillons who
have always pretended, but wrongly, to be our
relatives. This lady, who was of a good English
family, had married an Irish merchant named Dillon, whose ancestors had probably come from that
part of Ireland named, until the reign of Queen

Elizabeth, "Dillon's country," where a great number
of the inhabitants, the same as in Scotland, took the
name of their lord. However this may be, this Dillon
had no success in business, and, having raised a
certain sum of money, came to establish himself at
Bordeaux, where he entered into commerce. His wife
was a woman of extraordinary beauty, well known
throughout the province. Her husband died leaving
her with twelve children and with very little fortune,
but possessed of great charms and much courage.
Maréchal de Richelieu befriended her and recommended her to my uncle at the time of one of his trips
to Bordeaux. My uncle promised to look after her
children and kept his word. The three eldest, who
were rather beautiful girls, made very favorable
marriages. The nine sons, who were without exception fine fellows, all had most honorable careers.

At Bordeaux, several days before my departure, my
servant when dressing my hair asked my permission
to go that evening to a château situated at a short
distance, to see some old comrades. He rejoined our
carriages at the passage of the Dordogne, at Cubzac,
not far from the château which he had visited. I
asked the name of the place, and he told me it was
called Le Bouilh, and that it belonged to the Comte
de La Tour du Pin. His son was the young man
whom my father had wished me to marry and whom
my grandmother had refused. I asked my servant
regarding the position of the château and learned
with regret that it could not be seen from the highway. I was very much interested in crossing the river
at Cubzac to learn that the land around belonged

to Monsieur de La Tour du Pin, and I said to myself that perhaps I might some day be the lady of all this fine country. I took good care, however, not to communicate these reflections to my grandmother, who would not have received them with pleasure. Nevertheless, they remained in the back of my head.

CHAPTER FOUR

1786

MATRIMONIAL PROJECTS

New Marriage Plans.— The Marquis Adrien de Laval.—
Fortune of Mlle. Dillon.— Regiments of the Irish Brigade.
— Portrait of Mlle. Dillon.— Maréchal de Biron.—
Rupture with Monsieur Adrien de Laval.— The Vicomte
de Fleury.— M. Espérance de L'Aigle.— The Comte de
Gouvernet.— Decision of Mlle. Dillon.

AT the time of our return to Paris I was sixteen years of age, and my grandmother informed me that she was trying to arrange
a marriage for me with the Marquis Adrien de Laval.
He had just become the head of his family by the
death of his brother, who left a widow twenty years
of age, but no children. The Duchesse de Laval, the
mother of Adrien, had been a great friend of my
mother's. She was very desirous of seeing this marriage brought about, and it was equally agreeable to
me. The name of Laval-Montmorency sounded very
agreeably in my aristocratic ears. Young Laval had
left the *Séminaire* to enter the Army at the death
of his brother. Our fathers were also closely associated, but the principal reason which led me to wish
this marriage was that I would be able to leave the
house of my grandmother. I was no longer a child.
My education had commenced at so early an age
that at sixteen I was as old as other girls at twenty-

five. With my grandmother I led a wretched life. I was very miserable and ardently desired to end this unhappy position. Nevertheless, being in the habit of reflecting upon my fate, I had resolved never to accept, out of spite, a marriage which would not be *en rapport* with my situation in the world.

I was considered to be the sole heir of my grandmother, who had the reputation of being rich, and was so in reality. The fine estate of Hautefontaine, situated about twenty-two leagues from Paris, with a revenue of 50,000 francs from the farms, without counting the woods, the lakes and the fields; a pretty house which she had just purchased about five leagues from Paris, and where my uncle was making extensive repairs; with *rentes* upon the Hôtel de Ville of Paris which she should give me at the time of my marriage; an immense amount of personal property — all this was assured to me, since my grandmother was sixty years of age when I was sixteen.

Who would ever have suspected that my uncle, with over 400,000 francs of income, was in financial difficulties and had persuaded my grandmother to borrow, in order to come to his rescue? All the men who wished to marry me were blinded by these fine appearances. It was also known that, at the time of my marriage, I would have the position of Dame du Palais of the Queen. This, at that time, weighed heavily in the balance in the *grand monde*. *Etre à la Cour* sounded very fine. The Dames du Palais were only twelve in number. My mother had been one, because the Queen personally loved her tenderly;

COMTE DE LA TOUR DU PIN DE GOUVERNET

1727 - 1794

because she was the daughter-in-law of a Peer of England and the granddaughter of another, Lord Falkland; finally, because my father, a distinguished officer, was counted among the very few who could become Marshals of France.

Of the three regiments of the Irish Brigade, Dillon and Berwick were the only ones which had preserved their names. I remember that when Monsieur Walsh was named Colonel of the regiment which took his name, Monsieur de Fitz-James and my father showed a great deal of discontent, on the pretext that he did not belong to any great Irish or English family. The Duchesse de Fitz-James — Mlle. de Thiard — was Dame du Palais, like my mother, and a woman of the same age. But her husband, the third Duc de Fitz-James, who was the grandson of Maréchal de Berwick, and the son of the second Duc, who had also been Maréchal de France, enjoyed a very mediocre military reputation, while my father had greatly distinguished himself during the war which had just finished. At the age of twenty-seven he had been named Brigadier, a grade since suppressed, which represented the rank intermediate between the grade of Colonel and that of Lieutenant-General.

To return to myself. I was then what would be called from every point of view a good match, and since I am on the subject of my personal advantages, I think this is the place to trace my portrait. It will not be very attractive on paper, because I owed my reputation for beauty only to my figure, my general appearance, and not at all to my features.

I had a mass of light blond hair; small gray eyes, with very few eyelashes, most of which I had lost through a severe attack of smallpox at the age of four; I had thin blond eyebrows; a high forehead, and a nose which was said to be Greek, but which was long and too large at the end. My finest feature was my mouth, with very fresh lips, chiselled like those of an antique statue, and beautiful teeth which I have preserved intact at the age of seventy-one. It was said that my face was agreeable, that I had a gracious smile, and, notwithstanding all this, I could be considered plain. However, a large and beautiful figure and a clear and transparent complexion, with a great deal of color, gave me a marked superiority in all gatherings, especially by day, and it was certain that I outshone many women apparently endowed with superior advantages.

At the State dinners given frequently by my uncle during the summers that we passed at Paris, I often saw Maréchal de Biron, the last *grand seigneur* of the time of Louis XIV. Although he was eighty-five years of age, while I was only fifteen, he had taken a great fancy to me. He had me seated at table beside him, and had the kindness to talk with me. At Paris he had a large and beautiful mansion, now that of the Sacré-Cœur, with a splendid garden of three or four acres where there were hothouses filled with rare plants. It was considered a particular honor to be received at his house. One day in speaking with my uncle, he said:

"If I should have the misfortune to lose Mme. la Maréchale de Biron, I would pray Mlle. Dillon to take my name and to permit me to put my fortune at her feet."

He never had this misfortune, however, of which he would easily have consoled himself. His wife survived him and perished upon the scaffold with her niece, the Duchesse de Biron.

The Maréchal died in 1787 or 1788 and had a magnificent funeral. It was the last splendor of the Monarchy.

My marriage with Adrien de Laval fell through, because the Maréchal de Laval, his grandfather, chose for his wife Mlle. de Luxembourg. He married her when he was almost a child and when she herself was hardly eighteen years of age. I regretted this on account of the name.

My grandmother then proposed to me the name of the Vicomte de Fleury, with whom I did not wish to have anything to do. His reputation was bad. He had neither *esprit* nor distinction, and he also belonged to the younger branch of a house without any great reputation. I therefore refused him.

The next candidate was Espérance de L'Aigle, of whom I had seen a great deal during our youth. I did not think that his name was sufficiently illustrious. My decision was perhaps unreasonable, as he was really a very good match. We belonged to the same circle in society. The estate of his father was situated only six or seven leagues from Hautefontaine. All these facts were in favor of our union. Nevertheless, I refused him.

Marriages are made in Heaven. I had taken it into my head to marry the Comte de Gouvernet, notwithstanding the fact that I had never seen him and every one spoke badly of him. I knew that he was small and plain; that he gambled and contracted debts. Nevertheless, my resolution was made. I told my cousin Sheldon that I would marry no one else. He attempted, but without success, to reason me out of what he called my folly.

In the month of November, 1789, we were just about to set out for Languedoc when one morning my grandmother said:

"This Monsieur de Gouvernet continues to come back with his proposals of marriage. Mme. de Monconseil, his grandmother, is endeavoring to get the best of us on all sides; his father is Commandant of a province and will be Marshal of France. He is a man who enjoys the highest consideration in the Army. The Queen herself desires it, for the Princesse d'Hénin, the daughter of Mme. de Monconseil, has spoken to her about it. Therefore think and decide about it."

To which I replied without hesitation, "I have made up my mind. I do not ask for anything better."

My grandmother was stupefied. She hoped, I think, that I would refuse him. She could not conceive why I should prefer him to Monsieur de L'Aigle. In reality, I could not have told why myself. It was an instinct, an impulse coming from Heaven. God had destined me for him.

We set out for Montpellier without any further talk on the subject of this marriage. One morning my grandmother informed me that my uncle had received a charming letter from Mme. de Monconseil; that she extremely desired my marriage with her grandson for whom she had the warmest affection; that she would do everything in her power to bring about our union; but that she was not on good terms with her son-in-law, the Comte de La Tour du Pin, who did not get on well with his wife and had not lived with her for many years. This was the first time that I had heard of this family trouble. Although they did not live together, they were not legally separated, as the family had wished to avoid scandal on account of the Princesse d'Hénin, the sister of Mme. de La Tour du Pin, and also on account of her daughter, the Marquise de Lameth.

The Marquise de Monconseil was then eighty-five years of age, but was still considered beautiful. Her husband, who was an officer, like nearly all the gentlemen of that epoch, had married her very young. He had been a page of Louis XIV and had had a very lively and dissipated youth. He had served in all the wars at the end of the reign of Louis XIV and in those of Louis XV.

At the age of forty, Monsieur de Monconseil left the service and retired to his estate of Tesson in Saintonge. Here he spent most of his life until his death at the age of ninety. He had a fine house at Saintes, where he passed three months during the winter. The rest of the year he lived at Tesson where he himself had laid out and planted the park and gardens. Occasionally, he went to Paris to see his wife, who had a very fine mansion. He was very fond of his grandson, who frequently visited him at Tesson.

CHAPTER FIVE

1787

THE MARRIAGE PRELIMINARIES

Convocation of the Notables.— Return to Paris.— Death of
Mme. de Monconseil.— Monsieur de Gourvernet's Marriage
Proposal Accepted.— Visit of Mme. d'Hénin.— Signature
of the Contract.— Toilette the Day of the *Fiançailles*.—
Politeness at this Epoch.— The Four Lameth Brothers.—
The Marriage Contract.— The Comte and Comtesse de
La Tour du Pin.— A Visit to the Queen.— At Montfermeil.
— The Trousseau and the *Corbeille*.

THE last trip which I made to Montpellier,
during the winter of 1786 and 1787, was to
me the most brilliant of all. Nevertheless, I
was very desirous of returning to Paris where my
fate was to be decided. We set out sooner than I
had expected. My uncle had promised this year to
visit Marseille and Toulon before our return to
Paris. I was rejoicing at this arrangement, when a
courier arrived with the news of the convocation of
the first assembly of the Notables, of which my uncle
was a member. It was necessary, therefore, to set out
for Paris the day after the closing of the session of
the States and to give up our visit to Marseille and
Toulon.

My uncle, who was not feeling very well, wished to
spend the night at Fontainebleau, so that he might
not be too fatigued on his arrival at Paris and be

able to go the next morning to Versailles. We always found our house ready for us, as though we had not left it at all.

The evening of our arrival there were several visitors, among whom was a fat German named Comte de Bentheim, whose wife was a friend of my grandmother's. My uncle at once asked him the news of Paris. He replied: "Mme. de Monconseil is dead."

I turned pale, and my uncle, noticing my agitation, said to me in English that this would not in any way change our plans. For several days I heard nothing except conversation regarding the death of this Mme. de Monconseil, of the grief of her daughter, Mme. d'Hénin, and of her grandson, Monsieur de Gouvernet, who had taken care of her in an admirable manner.

Monsieur de Gouvernet, in the absence of his father, took occasion at once to notify my uncle that the loss of his grandmother would in no way change his desire for his union with our family. He demanded permission of my uncle to go to his father and tell him personally that his demand for my hand would be satisfactory to me and my family. Upon the affirmative response of my great-uncle, he immediately set out for Bordeaux. Before the week was over he had returned from Le Bouilh where he had talked with his father and had arranged to have him write a letter to make a formal demand for my hand. It was settled that he should present himself the following morning at my grandmother's house, but that he was not to see me until after the articles were signed, which was the usage at that time.

This memorable morning I hid myself behind a curtain and saw Monsieur de Gouvernet descend from his carriage and enter the house. He remained a quarter of an hour, and it was arranged that the articles should be signed as soon as they could be drawn up by the notary.

The arrangements were not terminated before the end of the week, and in the meantime Mme. d'Hénin paid a visit to my grandmother. She asked to see me, as I had expected. I was so much afraid of this *grande dame*, so elegant and imposing, who was going to examine me from head to foot, that I could hardly control myself on entering the room. She took my hand and kissed me and then exclaimed: "Ah! la belle taille! Elle est charmante. Mon neveu est bien heureux!"

This visit took place, I think, the eve of the day on which the articles were to be signed. It was not customary for the young lady to be present at the reading of the articles, but as soon as this was over, I was sent for. I was placed beside Mme. d'Hénin and my aunt Lady Jerningham, who took pity on my embarrassment.

My toilette was very simple. I had requested my grandmother to let me order it myself. At that time the gowns which were worn were laced behind and plainly indicated the figure. They were therefore called "sheaths" (*fourreaux*). My robe was of white gauze, without any ornaments, with a sash of dark blue ribbon with fringed ends of brilliant English silk.

From this time on, Monsieur de Gouvernet came

every day for dinner or supper, either at Paris or at Versailles, where my uncle was established since the commencement of the meeting of the Notables.

My grandmother and I remained at Paris, but every day at one-thirty we set out for Versailles where we arrived for dinner at three o'clock.

Monsieur de Gouvernet had presented to my uncle his brother-in-law, the Marquis de Lameth, and two brothers of the latter, Charles and Alexandre. The fourth brother, Théodore, whom I knew later, was not there at the time.

Finally the meeting of the Notables ended, and my uncle returned to Paris, where the day of the signature of the contract was arranged for the first of May. I do not now recall the details of my toilette, but I think that it must have been rose or blue, for the white robe was reserved for the day of marriage.

A few days previously I had made the acquaintance of my future father-in-law, the Comte de La Tour du Pin. He was a little man but very erect, very well built and had been handsome in his youth. He had admirable teeth, fine eyes, an air of assurance and a charming smile. He had served during the Seven Years' War as Colonel of the Regiment called *les Grenadiers de France*, which was composed of the élite of all the other regiments.

The Queen, who approved of my marriage, expressed the desire to see me and asked my uncle to bring me to her, together with Mme. d'Hénin. The day of my visit at Versailles I found myself in the presence of the Queen without really knowing how

I got there. She kissed me and I kissed her hand. She made me sit down beside her and asked me a thousand questions regarding my education and so on, but I was too embarrassed to reply. Finally, taking pity upon my diffidence, the Queen talked with my uncle and Mme. d'Hénin. I am afraid that my timidity made an unfavorable impression on the Queen, which was perhaps never effaced.

We went to Montfermeil about the eighth or tenth of the month of May, 1787. As it was not the etiquette of the time for the *futur* to sleep under the same roof with the young lady whom he was to marry, Monsieur de Gouvernet came every day from Paris for dinner and remained until after supper.

In the vast wardrobes had been brought together the fine trousseau which my grandmother had given me, the price of which exceeded 45,000 francs. It was composed of linens, laces, and muslin dresses. There was not a single silk dress. The *corbeille*, which had been given me by Monsieur de Gouvernet, comprised jewels, ribbons, flowers, feathers and so on.

The present of Mme. d'Hénin was a charming tea service of silver gilt, complete in every respect, with Sèvres porcelain. I think that this gave me more pleasure than anything else. My grandfather, Viscount Dillon, sent me a pair of ear-rings which cost 10,000 francs. I had also received from Monsieur de Gouvernet a fine collection of English and Italian books; also of English engravings, for which I was very grateful.

CHAPTER SIX

1787

MARRIAGE AND PRESENTATION AT COURT

A Marriage in High Society at the End of the 18th Century.—
The Nuptial Benediction.— The Marriage Souvenirs.—
Toilette of the Bride.— Presentation to the Queen.—
Rehearsal with the *Maître à Danser*.— The Presentation
Toilette.— The Sunday Court.— Portrait of the King.—
The Art of Walking at Versailles.— The Mass. — The
Royal Dinner.

I WOULD like to have the power of depicting the
manners of the times of my youth, of which
many details have escaped my memory, and the
occasion of this marriage in high society, at which
figured so many personages, men and women.

The day of my marriage everybody was present
in the salon at noon. The company was composed,
on my side, of my grandmother, Mme. de Rothe,
my great-uncle, the Archbishop of Narbonne, my
aunt, Lady Jerningham, her husband, Sir William
Jerningham, their daughter and eldest son, who was
afterwards Lord Stafford; also of the Messieurs
Sheldon, and their elder brother Monsieur Constable,
my first witness, and the Chevalier Jerningham,
brother of Sir William Jerningham, who was a friend
of my mother and of myself, my second witness.
This was all of my family. The guests included all
the Ministers, the Archbishops of Paris and Toulouse,

Monsieur de Lally-Tollendal, of whom I shall speak later, and several other persons whose names escape me.

The Comte de Gouvernet was born in Paris, Rue de Varenne, at the hôtel of his parents, the 6 January 1759. At the age of sixteen years he entered the military service as a Second Lieutenant of Artillery, and two years later was promoted to be Captain of Cavalry. In 1779 he was appointed aide de camp of the Marquis de Bouillé, Governor of the Antilles, and served under his orders during the last three years of the war in America. During his absence he was promoted to be Colonel en Second of the Royal-Comtois-Infanterie, and was still serving with this regiment at the time of our marriage, 21 May 1787.

The family of Monsieur de Gouvernet was composed of his father and mother; of his uncle, l'Abbé de Gouvernet; of his sister, the Marquise de Lameth; of her husband and his three brothers, Charles, Alexandre and Théodore de Lameth; also of Mme. d'Hénin, his aunt, and of a number of other persons — fifty or sixty in all.

In going to the chapel, we passed through the court. I walked first, giving my hand to my cousin, young Jerningham. My grandmother followed with Monsieur de Gouvernet, and the rest in order. At the altar we found my uncle and the Archbishop of Paris. After a low mass which was said by the Curé of Montfermeil, my uncle gave us the nuptial benediction after having pronounced a very fine discourse.

All the ladies then embraced me in the order of relationship and age. After this a valet de chambre brought a large basket containing the wedding souvenirs, consisting of sword-knots for the men, costing from twenty-five to thirty francs each, and of fans for the ladies, of different prices from twenty-five to one hundred francs. This custom was very expensive.

Let us not forget the toilette of the bride, which was very simple. I had a dress of white crêpe, trimmed with Brussels lace. As veils were not then in vogue, I wore pinners, that is to say, a head-dress having long flaps hanging down the sides of my cheeks. I had a sprig of orange blossoms on my head and a bouquet at my side. For the dinner, which was not served until four o'clock, I put on a pretty toque, with white plumes, to which was attached the sprig of orange blossoms. In the evening a fine concert ended the day.

The following day the greater part of the guests left us. I was married on Monday, and the next day Mme. d'Hénin informed me of the desire of the Queen that my presentation should take place the Sunday following. Mme. d'Hénin added that I ought to accompany her to Paris on Thursday morning to take two lessons in courtesies (*révérences*) of my dancing master; also to try on my presentation costume.

I therefore set out the following morning for Paris in company with my aunt, Mme. d'Hénin, and passed the two following mornings with Monsieur Huart, my dancing master. You cannot imagine anything more ridiculous than this rehearsal of the presentation. Monsieur Huart, a fat man, admirably *coiffé* and powdered, wearing a full skirt, represented the Queen and stood at the end of the salon. He dictated to me what I should do, at one moment personifying the lady who presented me, the next, returning to the place of the Queen in order to indicate the moment when, taking off my glove and bending to kiss the bottom of her robe, she would make the gesture of preventing me from so doing. Nothing was forgotten or neglected in this rehearsal, which was prolonged over a period of three or four hours. My hair was dressed simply, and I wore an ordinary morning costume, over which I had put on a court dress with a large pannier. It was a regular comedy.

Sunday morning after the mass my presentation took place. I was in full court dress (*grand corps*), that is to say, with a corsage expressly made, without shoulder straps, laced in the back, but so narrow that the lacings, four fingers wide at the bottom, revealed a chemise of the finest batiste. This chemise had very short sleeves and no straps, so as to leave the shoulders bare. The top of the arm was covered with three or four rows of white lace falling to the elbow. The neck and shoulders were entirely uncovered. Seven or eight strands of large diamonds, which the Queen had wished to lend me, partially concealed my own. The front of the corsage had the appearance of being laced with rows of diamonds. I also had a number on my head in the form of an aigrette.

Thanks to the good lessons of Monsieur Huart, I had no trouble with the three courtesies, and took off and put on my glove without too much awkwardness. After this I received the accolade of the King; of the Princes, his brothers, the Comte de Provence, afterwards Louis XVIII, and the Comte d'Artois, afterwards Charles X; of the Princes of Condé, Bourbon and d'Enghien. By a piece of good luck, for which I have often thanked Heaven, the Duc d'Orléans was not at Versailles the day of my presentation, and I therefore avoided being kissed by this monster.

The following Sunday I returned to Versailles, and from that time on went there nearly every week with my aunt. Although the Queen had decided that I should be appointed Dame du Palais, only at the end of two years, I was already considered as one, and exercised the functions of the position every Sunday.

It will be interesting perhaps to describe the ceremonial of the Sunday Court in which shone at the time the unfortunate Queen, as etiquette has changed and these details have entered into the domain of history.

The suite of rooms occupied by the Queen, known as the *Grands Appartements de la Reine*, immediately adjoined the *Salon de la Paix*, which was situated at the southwest corner of the main front of the Palace looking out on the gardens. This suite consisted of three rooms — the Queen's bed-chamber, the salon and the antechamber, which was also known as the *Salon du Grand Couvert*. Just beyond was the Queen's Guard Room, which was invaded by the populace the night of 6 October 1789. Adjoining this suite were the *Cabinets de Marie-Antoinette*, frequently called the *Petits Appartements de la Reine*, consisting of a boudoir, library and salon. All of these rooms were extremely small but remarkable for the charm of their decoration. They were lighted by small interior courts, on the other side of which were the King's Guard Room and his first ante-chamber.

At a few minutes before noon the ladies entered the salon which preceded the Queen's bed-chamber. No one sat down except a few aged ladies. There were always at least forty present and sometimes more. Ordinarily, the Princesse de Lamballe, the superintendent of the house, arrived and entered immediately into the Queen's room, where she was making her toilette. The Princesse de Chimay, the sister-in-law of my aunt d'Hénin, and the Comtesse d'Ossun, one a lady of honor and the other lady of the bed chamber, also had the *entrées*. At the end of several minutes an usher advanced to the door of the chamber and called in a loud voice: "Le service!" Then the Dames du Palais for the week, four in number, and other young ladies like myself designated later on to form part of the service also entered. As soon as the Queen had said good-morning to all in turn, with much grace and kindness, the door was opened and everybody entered.

This audience was prolonged until twenty minutes before one. Then the door was opened and the usher announced, "The King." The Queen, always dressed in court costume, advanced towards him with a charming and respectful air. The King nodded to right and left, spoke to some ladies whom he knew,

LA REINE MARIE ANTOINETTE

but never to the young ones. He was so shortsighted that he could not recognize any one at three paces. He was a fat man of medium height, with high shoulders and the worst form that you could imagine. He had the air of a peasant, and there was nothing lofty or royal in his mien. He was always embarrassed by his sword and did not know what to do with his hat. His costume, which was very magnificent, was highly embroidered, and ornamented with the star of the Saint-Esprit in diamonds. He never wore the cordon over his costume, except his fête day and the days of gala and great ceremony.

A quarter before one was the time set to go to the mass. The King and Queen walked side by side, slowly enough to say a word in passing to the numerous courtiers who lined the Gallery. The Queen often spoke to strangers who had been presented to her, to artists and to men of letters. Behind came the ladies in the order of their rank.

It was a great art to know how to walk in these vast *appartements* without stepping on the long train of the lady who preceded you. You could not raise your foot at all, but had to glide it along the floor, which was always very slippery, until you had passed through the Salon d'Hercule. After this you threw the bottom of your robe over one side of your pannier, and having caught the eye of your lackey who awaited you with a large hassock of red velvet trimmed with a golden fringe, you rushed down one of the aisles at the right or left of the chapel in the endeavor to obtain a place as near as possible to the tribune occupied by the Royal family. Your lackey put the hassock before you and you took your prayer book, in which you hardly ever read, for, by the time you were in your place and had arranged the train of your dress and had knelt upon this immense hassock, the mass was already half finished.

As soon as the service was over, the Queen made a profound *révérence* to the King, and then the march back began in the same order in which we had come. Every one returned to the Queen's chamber and chatted while awaiting the dinner hour. At this time, during a period of a quarter of an hour, the King and Queen received the ladies who had come from Paris. We impertinent young things used to call these ladies the *traîneuses*, because they had the skirts of their court costumes so long that you could not see their ankles.

Dinner was served in the first salon, where a small rectangular table was set with two covers, and two large green armchairs were placed one beside the other, touching, with backs so high as entirely to conceal the persons occupying them. The Queen sat at the left of the King. They turned their backs to the chimney, and before them, at a distance of ten feet, was arranged in a circle a line of stools upon which were seated the Duchesses, Princesses and ladies of high rank who had the privilege of the *tabouret*. Behind them stood the other ladies, facing the King and Queen. The King ate with good appetite, but the Queen did not take off her gloves or unfold her serviette, which was a great mistake on her part. As soon as the King had drunk, we had the privilege of leaving, after having made a courtesy.

MARRIAGE, PRESENTATION AT COURT

We regained our *appartements* very much fatigued, and remained quietly in our rooms, so as not to disarrange our coiffures, especially when we had had our hair dressed by Léonard, the most famous of coiffeurs. The private dinners were served at three o'clock which, at this time, was the elegant hour.

The Minister of War, Maréchal de Ségur, who had been present at my marriage, had given my husband a month's leave of absence, so instead of leaving for Saint-Omer, where his regiment was in garrison, he remained with me at Montfermeil. At the end of the month of June it was necessary for him to return to his post and I saw him leave with real chagrin. About the middle of August he came to pass a week at Montfermeil. The Maréchal had consented to this *escapade* on condition that he should not go to Paris. The Colonels in garrison in Flanders were then threatened with the necessity of passing the autumn and winter months with their regiments, on account of the troubles in Holland, in which it seemed that we should be obliged to interfere. But the indecision of the King and the feebleness of the Government did not permit us to take part, which was a great mistake, as it might have turned public opinion from the revolutionary ideas which were beginning to germinate in the heads of the French people.

CHAPTER SEVEN

1787–1788

FIRST SEASON IN SOCIETY

Civil War in Holland.— Feebleness of the French Government.
— Mme. de La Tour du Pin at Hénencourt.— Excursion
to Lille.— Return to Montfermeil.— The Loges of the
Queen at the Theatres.— Mme. de La Tour du Pin in
Society.— Mme. de Montesson and the Duc d'Orléans.—
Rupture of Mme. de La Tour du Pin with Her Family.

MY sister-in-law, Mme. de Lameth, for whom
I had conceived the most tender friendship, had been kept at Paris by the illness
of her younger son until the month of October, 1787.
As the Colonels were still with their regiments and
not able to return, my sister-in-law proposed to me
the first of October that I should accompany her to
the country. My husband could then rejoin us, as
his regiment was in garrison at Saint-Omer, a short
distance from Hénencourt, between Amiens and
Arras. The difficulty was to arrange this trip with
my grandmother, who, in the absence of my husband,
had again assumed her authority over me. Neither I
nor my sister-in-law had the courage to make the
proposition to her. We therefore devised the scheme
of having the request made by my husband himself.
On the appointed day the letter arrived, and my
grandmother, without preamble, brusquely demanded,

"When are you going to leave?" To which I replied trembling that my sister-in-law awaited me. Accordingly, we set out together. Our maids were in my carriage, Mme. de Lameth, her two children and myself, in her carriage.

I have preserved the most charming recollections of this trip. We went to Lille to see the Marquis de Lameth, my brother-in-law, who was there with his regiment. I had never had so much pleasure as during this short journey. With my husband I visited all the establishments, military and civil.

When it was finally decided that France should abandon the Holland patriots to their unfortunate fate, permission was given the Colonels to return to Paris. My husband and I therefore set out for Montfermeil, while my sister-in-law remained in the country until the beginning of winter.

Soon after my return my uncle and grandmother left for Montpellier. It had been arranged that during the absence of my relatives we should live with our aunt, Mme. d'Hénin. As she was to introduce me to society, this arrangement was agreeable and convenient. It was not then customary for a young lady to appear alone in public the first year of her marriage. When she went out in the morning to pay visits or shop, she always took a maid with her in her carriage. Certain old dames carried this rigorism so far as to blame those who went out even with their husbands for a promenade in the Champs-Elysées or the Tuileries gardens, and thought in such cases they should be followed by a lackey in livery.

My husband considered this custom insupportable, and we never submitted to this etiquette.

Once established with my aunt, we found ourselves much happier and more tranquil than with my grandmother. Nearly every evening we went to the theatre, where the performances then ended early enough to permit our going to supper afterwards. My aunt and I had permission to occupy the Queen's boxes. This was a favor which was accorded to only six or eight of the youngest ladies of the Palace. She had a loge at the Opéra, at the Comédie-Française and at the theatre then called the Comédie-Italienne where opéra-comique was given in French. We had only to read the daily papers to make our choice between the different theatres.

These stage boxes were furnished like elegant salons. Every box had a large antechamber, well heated and lighted; and a private staircase communicated with the antechamber where the servants remained. At the entrance was a porter in the King's livery. You never had to wait a moment for your carriage. Generally we went to the Comédie-Italienne for the first piece, which was always the best, and to the Opéra for the ballet.

Since I am now established with my aunt, this is the moment to speak of the society in which she moved, which was the most elegant and the most highly considered in Paris, and by which I was adopted the first year that I was out. This clique was composed of four very distinguished ladies, joined together from their youth by a friendship which in their eyes represented a sort of religion, and which was perhaps the only one that they possessed! These four ladies, very highly esteemed on account of their rank in the world, were, besides Mme. d'Hénin, the Princesse de Poix, the Duchesse de Biron and the Princesse de Bouillon.

At the time of my marriage, my aunt, Mme. d'Hénin, was thirty-eight years of age. She had espoused, at the age of fifteen, the Prince d'Hénin, younger brother of the Prince de Chimay, who was only seventeen. They were admired as the handsomest couple who had ever appeared at court. The second year of her marriage Mme. d'Hénin had an attack of smallpox, and this malady, which they did not then know how to treat properly, left upon her face an eruption which was never cured. However, she was still very beautiful when I knew her, with fine hair, charming eyes, teeth like pearls, a superb figure and a very noble air. Until the death of her mother she resided with her. Monsieur d'Hénin had an apartment in the house of Mme. de Monconseil, but although he was not judicially separated from his wife, he nevertheless resided apart with an actress of the Comédie-Française, who was ruining him. The Court justified by its indifference these kinds of liaisons. It was laughed at as the most simple thing in the world.

At that time the ladies of high society were marked by the audacity with which they made a parade of their love affairs. These intrigues were known almost as soon as formed, and when they were durable, they acquired a sort of consideration. In the society of *les princesses combinées*, as they were called, there were exceptions however to these blamable customs. Mme. de Poix, who was deformed, lame, and crippled a great part of the year, had never been accused of any intrigues. When I first knew her, she still had a charming face, although forty years of age. She was the most amiable person in the world.

Mme. de Lauzun, who was later Duchesse de Biron, after the death of my respectful admirer, the Maréchal of that name, was an angel of kindness and goodness. After the death of the Maréchale de Luxembourg, her grandmother, with whom she had lived, and who kept the finest house in Paris, she had bought a hôtel, Rue de Bourbon, looking out on the river. This she had arranged with simple elegance, in harmony with her handsome fortune and the modesty of her character. She lived here alone, for her husband, following the example of Monsieur d'Hénin, passed his time with an actress of the Comédie-Française. Since the death of his mother, whose happy influence had kept him in good company, he had mixed with the habitués of the Duc d'Orléans (*Egalité*), who corrupted all who approached him.

The Duchesse de Lauzun had a very curious library, with many manuscripts of Rousseau, among others that of "La Nouvelle Héloïse," entirely written in his own hand; also a quantity of letters and notes which he had written to Mme. de Luxembourg.

The Princesse de Bouillon had married, when very young, the last Duc de Bouillon, who was an imbecile and a cripple. She lived with him in the Hôtel de Bouillon upon the Quai Malaquais. He was never seen, because he remained always in his apartment with the persons who looked after him. During the summer he went to his place at Navarre, the fine estate which later belonged to the Empress Joséphine. But I think that Mme. de Bouillon never went there.

She was a person of great spirit and charm and, I think, was the most distinguished of my acquaintances. At no time could she have been pretty. She was exceedingly thin, almost a skeleton, with a flat German face, *retroussé* nose, wretched teeth and yellow hair. With all this, she had so much *esprit*, such original ideas, and her conversation was so amusing that she attracted and enchanted everybody. Her kindness to me was very great and I was quite proud of it.

Nevertheless this homely and spirituelle Princesse had had one or several lovers. She was bringing up a little girl who, in a striking manner, resembled her as well as the Prince Emmanuel de Salm-Salm. He passed for being the lover whom she had adopted for life, but certainly at that time he was only a friend. A very tall man, as thin as his mistress, he always appeared to me to be insipid, although he was said to be learned. I would like to believe that, but he hid his treasures, and I cannot recall anything of his conversation.

The Chevalier de Coigny, brother of the Duc, who was first equerry of the King, was supposed, before the time of my marriage, to be the lover of my aunt. At least he had that reputation. Later on he formed a strong attachment for Mme. de Monsauge, wife of the *fermier général* and mother of the charming Comtesse Etienne de Durfort, whom he afterwards married. I was very fond of this fat chevalier who was of so gay and amiable a nature. As he was fifty years of age, I talked with him as often as possible. He recounted to me a thousand anecdotes which I remembered and which perhaps would be amusing if I were to relate them. Destined to live in the *grand monde* and at the Court, I listened with interest to his recitals, for a knowledge of past times was useful to me.

A mansion which we all visited, and where I was received with the most affectionate familiarity, was that of Mme. de Montesson. She loved my husband like a son. After the death of his grandmother, Mme. de Monconseil, he had lived there until the day of his marriage. She received me with extreme kindness. I was also bound by ties of friendship to Mme. de Valence, the daughter of her niece, Mme. de Genlis. Mme. de Valence was three years older than myself and was then considered a model young woman.

It is well known that Mme. de Montesson was the legitimate wife of the Duc d'Orléans, the father of Philippe-Égalité, to whom she had been married by the Archbishop of Toulouse. The King was unwilling to recognize this marriage, and she ceased to visit the Court. The Duc d'Orléans gave up his residence in the Palais-Royal to establish himself in a house, Rue de Provence, adjoining that which Mme. de Montesson had bought in the Chaussée-d'Antin. The separating walls were torn down and the two gardens were united. The Duc always kept his separate entrance, Rue de Provence, with a Swiss in his livery, while Mme. de Montesson also had her private entrance. But the courts remained connected.

FIRST SEASON IN SOCIETY

The house of Mme. de Montesson bore a very good reputation. She saw the best company in Paris and the most distinguished, from the oldest sets to the youngest. She no longer gave large parties, as during the life of the Duc d'Orléans, which I much regretted. She immediately adopted me for a daughter, and from her great experience in the world, her conversation and her counsels were very useful to me. Hardly a day passed without my visiting Mme. de Valence, and often when the hour was advanced, Mme. de Montesson kept me for dinner.

On her return to Paris my grandmother came to see me. She soon learned from my conversation of my success in the world and the fine reception which I had received from a large number of persons whom she disliked. From this moment I think she resolved to seize the first occasion which presented itself to oblige us to leave my uncle's house. Nevertheless, for the moment I returned to the Hôtel Dillon, where they had arranged for me a charming *appartement* in the *mansardes*, which was reached unfortunately by a small turning staircase.

I do not remember the circumstances which finally led to the rupture with my relatives. After several months of repeated quarrels my grandmother requested us to leave her house. In spite of my tears and the intervention of my uncle, the Archbishop, whose affection we had gained, but who feared my grandmother too much to offer any opposition, we were obliged to leave the Hôtel Dillon never to return. This was about the month of June, 1788.

My aunt received us at her house with great kindness. It was nevertheless a great chagrin for me to be separated from my family. This epoch was one of the most painful of my life. It was the first real grief that I had ever known, and the remembrance is still painful, although I cannot in any way reproach myself for having provoked it.

CHAPTER EIGHT

1788–1789

EVE OF THE REVOLUTION

Sojourn with Mme. d'Hénin.— Monsieur de La Tour du Pin, Colonel de Royal-Vaisseaux.— Indiscipline of the Officers of the Regiment.— Prince Henry of Prussia.— His Taste for French Literature.— The Hôtel de Rochechouart.— Comte de Chinon, afterwards Duc de Richelieu.— A Ball at Lord Dorset's.— Approach of the Revolution.— Popularity of the Duc d'Orléans.— Causes of the Antipathy of the Queen for the Duc.— Popularity of English Fashions.— The Origin of Monsieur de Lally-Tollendal.

MY aunt, Mme. d'Hénin, received us at her house in the Rue Verneuil, and gave me quarters on the ground floor looking out on a very dismal little garden. As we did not wish to be an expense to her, our cook prepared our servants' meals, and also our own when my aunt dined out or had company for dinner. My maid, Marguerite, who had never left me, refused all the offers and even prayers of my grandmother in order to accompany me.

The summer of 1788 we passed at Passy in a house which Mme. d'Hénin had leased, together with Mmes. de Poix, de Bouillon and de Biron. My aunt and I lived there all the time, while these ladies came there in turn.

Monsieur de La Tour du Pin had been appointed Colonel of the regiment of Royal-Vaisseaux. This body of troops was in a state of great indiscipline, not by the conduct of the soldiers and the under-officers, which was excellent, but by the attitude of the officers, who had been spoiled by their former Colonel, Monsieur d'Ossun, husband of the Queen's *Dame d'Atours*. When my husband, who was very severe in the matter of discipline, arrived at his regiment, he found that these gentlemen were not attending to their duties. Having ascertained that during the daily drills the regiment was commanded by the under-officers and the Lieutenant-Colonel, Monsieur de Kergaradec, Monsieur de La Tour du Pin declared that, as he expected to be present at the drills every morning at sunrise, he should require that the officers also be present. This order raised a perfect storm of discontent, and punishments, arrests, prison — no measures could determine the officers to fulfil their duties. In this way the summer passed.

In the autumn a camp for manœuvres was to be formed at Saint-Omer under the command of the Prince de Condé. The first manœuvre, which should have been executed in a model manner, was very unsatisfactory, and Monsieur de La Tour du Pin was furious. He reported to the Prince regarding the bad spirit of the regiment, or rather that of the officers. The Prince declared that if, at the next manœuvre, the officers did not do better, he would put them all under arrest for the duration of the camp, and that the companies would be commanded by the under-officers. This order had the desired effect and there was no further insubordination.

While these events were happening at Saint-Omer, I was living very pleasantly at Passy with my aunt and with one or two of her friends. I often visited Paris, and also passed some time at Berny with Mme. de Montesson, who was always full of kindness for me. Here I met very frequently old Prince Henry of Prussia, brother of the Great Frederick. He was a man of much capacity, both military and literary, and a great admirer of all the philosophers whom his brother had attracted to his court, and particularly of Voltaire. He knew our literature better than any Frenchman.

As I am not writing a history of the Revolution, I shall not speak of all the conversations, arguments and disputes that the difference of opinions occasioned in society. For my eighteen years these discourses were very boring, and I endeavored to divert myself by visiting as often as possible a charming house where I was attached by ties of friendship since the period of my youth, and especially from the day that I had been obliged to leave my relatives. The Hôtel de Rochechouart was one of those patriarchal mansions which will never be seen again and where several generations mingled, *sans gêne, sans ennui, sans exigence*.

Mme. de Courteille, a very rich widow, had married her only daughter to the Comte de Rochechouart. She lived with her son-in-law and their two daughters in a large and beautiful mansion in the

Rue de Grenelle. Mme. de Rochechouart had been an intimate friend of my mother's, and I had passed my childhood with her two daughters, who were from two to four years older than myself. The elder had married, at the age of fifteen, the Duc de Piennes, since Duc d'Aumont. She was an amiable girl with an agreeable face, without being precisely pretty. Her husband, according to the usage in high society at that time, was the avowed and declared lover of Mme. de Reuilly, which made his wife very unhappy.

I was more intimate, however, with Rosalie, the younger sister. She had been married at the age of twelve years and one day with the grandson of the Maréchal de Richelieu, the Comte de Chinon, who then was only fifteen years of age. At this time she was still a nice little girl, but thin and very delicate, while he was a disagreeable boy whom in our children's parties we could not endure. This marriage was celebrated before the death of my mother, and I was present. Immediately after the dinner, which was given at the Hôtel de Richelieu, the bridegroom set out with his tutor for a European tour. Leaving thus at the beginning of the year 1782, he did not return to France until about seven years later. He had then become a large and fine young man and an excellent fellow.

At the Hôtel de Rochechouart every one was delighted at his return, except his poor wife who was far from participating in this joy. In completing her growth she had become, at the age of fourteen, a complete hunchback, and she was afraid that her

LE MARQUIS DE LALLY-TOLLENDAL

1751 - 1830

husband would detest her on account of this de-
formity. To add to the misfortunes of this poor man,
he found upon his return two sisters, born of a second
marriage of his father, who were deformed in the
same manner as his wife. These three hunchbacks
gave him a feeling of horror for his native country.

At the first indications of the coming Revolution,
he emigrated and went to Russia, where he gained
much glory in the war between the Russians and the
Turks, during the course of which he served as a
volunteer in the army of Catherine II with MM. de
Damas and de Langeron.

Returning to France under the Consulate, he left
almost immediately for Russia whence he did not
return until after the Restoration.

I think that it was during the spring of the year
1789 that the Duke of Dorset, the English Ambassador, who had just been replaced by Lord Gower
and his charming wife, Lady Sutherland, gave a fine
ball on the eve of his leaving Paris. At the bottom
of the invitations he had placed very cavalierly:
"Les dames seront en blanc." This order displeased
me. By way of protest, I ordered a charming robe
of blue crêpe, trimmed with flowers of the same
color. My gloves and my fan were also adorned with
blue ribbons. In my coiffure, arranged by Léonard,
were blue feathers. This piece of childish folly had a
great success. Everybody kept remarking: "Oiseau
bleu, couleur du temps." The Duke of Dorset himself was amused at this pleasantry and said that the
Irish were pig-headed!

[65]

In the midst of our pleasures we approached the month of May, 1789. Now that a long life permits me to pass in review the events which I saw unroll before me, I am confounded by the profound blindness of the unfortunate King and of his Ministers. Every one insisted upon the necessity of modelling the new Constitution of France upon that of England, which few persons understood. Monsieur de Lally, afterwards the Marquis de Lally-Tollendal, in spite of his pretensions fully to understand the English Constitution, was himself ignorant of its details, although he passed for an oracle. The force of his speech filled with delight the ladies who listened to him. He had turned the head of my aunt who had no doubt of his success in the States-General.

Monsieur de Lally had just been elected Deputy to the Assembly by the nobility of Paris. I was present at one of the first meetings of this Assembly. With twenty or thirty ladies I was concealed behind the curtains of the tribunes which had been arranged in the windows of the hall. The first two names taken from the election urn, of persons nominated for Secretaries of the Assembly, were those of Monsieur de Lally and Monsieur d'Espréménil, the President of the Parliament of Paris. Now it so happened that Monsieur d'Espréménil was the person who had made the report upon the sad affair which had sent General de Lally to the scaffold in 1766. Before the different courts where Monsieur de Lally, his son, had pleaded for the rehabilitation of the memory of his father, Monsieur d'Espréménil had pleaded on the other side and in such a furious manner that a profound hatred had arisen between the two men. Therefore when these two were proclaimed as the Secretaries of the Assembly, and they left their places at the end of the hall to seat themselves side by side at the desk, there was heard a murmur of very marked interest in favor of Monsieur de Lally. When, a few moments later, he addressed a few brief words to the Assembly to thank them for his nomination, and stated that all private misunderstanding should disappear before the public interest, every one present enthusiastically applauded him.

At the beginning of the spring of 1789, which followed a terrible winter that had been very hard upon the poor, the Duc d'Orléans (Egalité) was very popular in Paris. He had sold, the previous year, a large part of the pictures of the splendid gallery of his palace, and it was generally stated that the eight million francs received from this sale had been devoted to relieving the misery of the people during the rigorous winter which had just ended. On the other hand, nothing was said, rightly or wrongly, of the charities of the Princes of the Royal family and of the King and Queen. This unfortunate Princess had become entirely devoted to the Polignac family. She no longer went to the theatre in Paris, and no one ever saw her or her children. The King also never appeared in public. Shut up at Versailles, or hunting in the surrounding woods, he suspected nothing, foresaw nothing, believed nothing.

The Queen detested the Duc d'Orléans, who had spoken harshly of her. He had wished to marry his son, the Duc de Chartres, afterwards King Louis-

Philippe, with Madame Royale, the daughter of the King. But the Comte d'Artois, afterwards Charles X, also desired the hand of this Princess for his son, the Duc d'Angoulême, a match which the Queen preferred. The demand of the Duc d'Orléans was therefore refused, and he was mortally offended. His visits to Versailles were very infrequent, and I do not recall ever having met him in the Queen's room at the hour that the Princes came there just before the mass. As he never was in his *appartement* at Versailles, I had not been officially presented to him. This, however, did not prevent me from being present at the suppers which he gave at the Palais-Royal, which during this winter were very brilliant.

I was present at the supper he gave at which was employed for the first time the beautiful silver service which he had ordered of Arthur, the great jeweller of the epoch. If I am correct in my recollection, the service appeared to me too light and too English. But this was the fashion. It was necessary that everything should be English — from our Constitution to our horses and our carriages. I was often envied because in public places I had the good fortune to evoke the exclamation, "Voilà une Anglaise!"

Since I have spoken of Monsieur de Lally at the moment that he became a marked man, it is well to tell the story of his origin, as well as the remarkable history of that illegitimacy from father to son which has perhaps never been encountered in any other family.

Gérard Lally, the great-grandfather of the Lally

of whom I am speaking, was a poor little Irish gentleman who had taken the side of James II. I think that
he came originally from the estate of my ancestor,
Lord Dillon.

The daughter of my great-great-uncle, Lord Dillon,
had been seduced by this Gérard Lally, who was
probably handsome and attractive. A son was born
of their relations, and Lord Dillon demanded that
Gérard should wed his daughter and legitimatize the
child: first case of bastardy.

The natural son of Gérard Lally distinguished
himself during the troubles and wars of James II,
who made him a baronet and permitted him to
recruit troops on the estate of his ancestors. He accompanied James II to France and died, if I am not
mistaken, at Saint-Germain. Although he was never
married, nevertheless he also left a natural son by a
lady of Normandy, whose name I have never known:
second case of bastardy.

The natural son of Sir Gérard Lally became the
General Lally who was condemned to death and
executed in 1766 and whose name was rehabilitated
in 1781.

At seventeen years of age he entered the Army and
distinguished himself in all the wars of Louis XV.
He accompanied Prince Charles Edward in the
glorious campaign of 1745, which ended in the unfortunate defeat of Culloden in 1746.

It is said that on his return to France he became
very much enamored of my grandmother. But this
is certain, that he formed a very tender friendship
for Mlle. Mary Dillon, elder sister of my great-uncle,

the Archbishop of Narbonne. Mlle. Mary Dillon was never married and died in 1786 at Saint-Germain-en-Laye, at a very advanced age.

She was on bad terms for a long time with her brother, the Archbishop. This misunderstanding, caused originally by some family disagreement, was perpetuated by the troublesome interference of my grandmother, Mme. de Rothe, who feared the influence on the Archbishop of Mlle. Dillon, whom she detested. It so happened that I never saw Mlle. Dillon until the year before her death. She had then become reconciled with my uncle, and we frequently went to see her at Saint-Germain.

But to return to Lally and the third case of bastardy, to which the family seemed to be condemned. Before General de Lally was sent to India as Governor of the French possessions, he had had an *intrigue amoureuse* with a Comtesse de Maulde, née Saluces, wife of a Flemish lord of the environs of Arras or of Saint-Omer, and aunt of the Saluces whom we knew at Bordeaux. As a result of this liaison he had a son whom he caused to be brought up under another name at the Jesuit College of Paris. A dramatic event was destined to have a dominant influence upon the future of this child.

As I have already said, Mlle. Mary Dillon, who was a great friend of General de Lally, was his confidante in the matter of the intrigue with the Comtesse de Maulde and looked after this child, who was ignorant of his origin and of the name of his father. After the execution of General de Lally, an Irish officer named Drumgold was entrusted by

Mlle. Dillon with the details of the allowance of this young boy and went to see him. Drumgold no sooner found himself alone with the child than this lad of twelve years began to speak to him of the execution of Monsieur de Lally which had taken place the previous day. He approved of the sentence, and, to justify it, repeated all the arguments which he had heard at the Jesuit College. Drumgold, unable to remain silent upon hearing such language from the mouth of the son of the person who had just been executed, cried: "Malheureux, il était ton père!" At these words young Lally fainted and remained unconscious several hours. A severe illness followed, and it was during his convalescence that he formed the resolution to consecrate his life to the rehabilitation of the memory of his father. From this moment all his readings, all his studies, all his thoughts tended to this end.

General de Lally had recognized his son in his will. The boy took his name, and at eighteen years of age he commenced the work of rehabilitating his father by composing pleadings and memoirs which were models of close reasoning and eloquence. During a period of twenty years this was his sole occupation and his only thought. Having received very little money from the inheritance of his father, he lived with Mlle. Dillon at Saint-Germain-en-Laye and was protected by Maréchal de Noailles and by Maréchal de Beauvau, both friends of Mlle. Dillon. When, in 1785, my great-uncle became reconciled with his sister, we saw at her *appartement* at Saint-Germain, Monsieur de Lally whom I had not previously known. He was then about thirty-five years of age and had a very handsome face but an effeminate air which did not please me. After having pleaded before three Parlements, he had succeeded in gaining his cause, and had acquired a great reputation for eloquence and a well-merited standing, from the constancy with which he had carried his case to success. It would be only just to attribute a great part of the honor of his conduct to Mlle. Dillon. A person of distinguished spirit, of very superior character, she had gained an absolute empire over Monsieur de Lally, and in the solitude in which she lived at Saint-Germain, she was entirely devoted to his interests. She died in 1786, leaving him by her will all the property of which she was able to dispose. More than this, she had arranged that he should have the reversion of the *appartement* which she occupied at Saint-Germain and which was the one given by Louis XIV to her father when he arrived at this château with James II. She had been born there, as well as her four sisters and five brothers, of whom the youngest was the Archbishop of Narbonne. My father deeply regretted, when he returned from the Islands, that she had disposed of this lodging — the cradle of the family in France. Monsieur de Lally would have shown more delicacy in not accepting, among the objects which were left him, many of the family souvenirs, which were without value to him, but which my father and I highly esteemed on account of their origin.

CHAPTER NINE

1789

FALL OF THE BASTILLE

Mme. de Genlis.— Education of the Young Orléans Princes.—
Paméla.— Horse Races at Vincennes.— First Popular
Meetings.— Residence at Versailles.— Session of the Opening of the States-General.— Attitude of the King and
Queen.— Feebleness of the Court.— Departure of Monsieur Necker. — The 14 July 1789.— Return of Mme.
de La Tour du Pin to Paris.— The Waters of Forges.

THE winter of 1789, which was cold and disastrous for the people, in society was as
brilliant as usual with spectacles and balls.
During this time circumstances led me to make a
very curious acquaintance. Mme. de Genlis was *gouverneur* of the young Orléans Princes and of their
sister Louise. This unusual title of *gouverneur* was
one which the Duc d'Orléans had wished to give her.
On his demanding permission of the King, Louis XVI,
the latter replied, shrugging his shoulders and turning on his heel: "Gouverneur ou Gouvernante! vous
êtes le maître de faire ce qu'il vous plaira; d'ailleurs,
le Comte d'Artois a des enfants."

Mme. de Genlis lived in a pavilion of the Convent
of Belle-Chasse, which was situated at the end of the
Rue de Belle-Chasse, in the Rue Saint-Dominique.
This pavilion, which was very small, was composed
of a *rez-de-chaussée*, which you entered immediately

from the street, after having mounted several steps covered by an *auvent* under which carriages could penetrate if the coachman was not too maladroit. A vestibule, where the servants remained, served as an antechamber. Mme. de Genlis occupied this small pavilion with Mlle. d'Orléans who was then thirteen years of age. She had with her Paméla, afterwards Lady Fitz-Gerald, of whom I shall speak later on, and Henriette de Sercey, both of whom were being brought up with the Princess. The Princes themselves did not sleep in the pavilion. They were brought there at an early hour of the morning and returned in the evening after supper, with their *sous-gouverneur*, to sleep at the Palais-Royal. As I had often met them, and as I was very friendly with Mme. de Valence, the daughter of Mme. de Genlis, Mme. de Montesson invited me to come to see her when the young Princes were there. Mme. de Genlis had taken a great fancy to me, and wished to have me present at the little soirées dansantes which she gave once a week during this winter. The dances always finished before eleven o'clock and were not followed by a supper.

The Duc de Chartres, afterwards King Louis-Philippe, had commenced to go out in society, that is to say, he was sometimes present at the suppers at the Palais-Royal. He had entered the Army and had the cordon bleu. He was a fat boy, very awkward and uncouth, with pale and hanging cheeks, an air at once sly, serious and timid. He was said to be well informed and even learned. It would be unjust to assert, nevertheless, that Mme. de Genlis' system of education had not its good side, especially when you compared it with the one adopted for his two pupils by the Duc de Sérent, *gouverneur* of the children of the Comte d'Artois. No one ever saw them, and they remained as great strangers to France as if they were to reign in China. The Orléans Princes, on the other hand, devoted their promenades and their recreations to everything which could instruct them. They learned at the same time that they were amused. This rendered them popular, and events have shown that the one of the three who survived profited by his experience.

Since I have mentioned the name of Paméla, let us speak a moment of her origin. Mme. de Genlis let people understand that she had found the child in England, but everybody thought that she was the daughter of herself and the Duc d'Orléans (Egalité). Strangely enough, however, I have reason to believe that the assertion of Mme. de Genlis was the truth. My aunt, Lady Jerningham, had known intimately in Shropshire, where her husband had a large estate, a clergyman who was also acquainted with Mme. de Genlis. This clergyman stated that he had received a letter from Mme. de Genlis asking him to find for her a young girl whom she wished to adopt. The Curate said that he had found such a child and that he had sent her to a place in London which had been indicated to him, and Lady Jerningham had no doubt but that this child was Paméla.

At the age of fifteen, when I knew her, you could not imagine anything more delicate than her face, which had not a defect nor even an imperfection.

She was as beautiful as a young goddess. All of her movements were graceful; her smile was angelic; her teeth like pearls. In 1792, at the age of eighteen, she turned the head of Lord Edward Fitz-Gerald, fifth son of the Duke of Leinster, who married her and took her to Ireland, where he was head of the insurgents — "United Irishmen." On the death of her husband she returned to the Continent and established herself at Hamburg, where she married the American consul, Mr. Pitcairn. I shall speak of her later on.

In the spring of 1789, after the winter which had been so cruel for the poor, and after the opening of the States-General, never had people shown themselves more disposed to amusement, without being embarrassed in any way by the public misery. There were races at Vincennes, where the horses of the Duc d'Orléans ran against those of the Comte d'Artois. It was when returning from the last of these races with Mme. de Valence in her carriage that, in passing through the Rue Saint-Antoine, we came upon the first of the public Assemblies of this epoch.

The elections being terminated, every one made arrangements to establish himself at Versailles. All the members of the States-General searched for apartments in the city. Those who were attached to the Court, arranged to occupy the apartments reserved for them in the Château. My aunt had her lodging there and I lived with her. Her quarters were located very high, over the Gallery of the Princes, and were situated in the wing of the Château fronting on the Parterre du Midi and the Terrasse de l'Orangerie. The room which I occupied looked out on the roofs, while that of my aunt faced the terrace and had a very fine view. We occupied these lodgings Saturday nights only. Monsieur de Poix, as Governor of Versailles, had at his disposal a charming little house with a pretty garden at the Ménagerie, which was a small isolated château situated in the Grand Parc at the extremity of one of the arms of the canal, opposite the Trianon. He loaned this to my aunt, and here we settled with our servants, her horses and mine, that is to say, my saddle-horses and my English groom. This lodging was very agreeable. All of our acquaintances were established at Versailles, and we attended with pleasure, and without anxiety, the opening of this Assembly which was to regenerate France. When I reflect now upon this blindness, I can only conceive it as possible for young people like myself. As for men of affairs, and the Ministers, the thing seems inexplicable.

My husband was so put out because he had not been elected Deputy to the States-General that he did not wish to be present at the opening of the session. The spectacle was magnificent, but as it has been so often described in the memoirs of the time, I shall not speak of it. The King wore the costume of the "cordons bleus" and all the Princes the same, with the difference only that the King's costume was more richly ornamented and covered with diamonds.

This good Prince had no dignity of carriage. He held himself badly and waddled; his movements were brusque and ungraceful, and his shortsightedness, inasmuch as it was not customary then to wear glasses, caused him to squint. His speech, although very short, was given in a resolute tone. The Queen was remarkable for her great dignity, but you could see by the almost convulsive movements of her fan that she was very much moved.

The address of Monsieur Necker, Minister of Finance, bored me to death. It lasted more than two hours and, to my nineteen years, seemed eternal.

The first of June my husband and the other Colonels rejoined their regiments. He was in garrison at Valenciennes, and consequently was not connected with the troops which had been assembled at the gates of Paris, under the command of Maréchal de Broglie. Owing to the fatal feebleness which was always shown at the moment when firmness was necessary, the Government did not employ these troops at the opportune moment. The Queen showed only discontent without ever deciding to act.

Meanwhile there was no material change in the system of etiquette which enveloped the Court. Every day I wrote my husband the news which I had gathered. These letters, which would have been of great assistance to me in writing these souvenirs, I did not preserve.

The first event which seemed to me serious was the withdrawal of Monsieur Necker from the Ministry. It was the extraordinary conditions of his departure, rather than the consequences, which struck me. I had made a visit to the *Contrôle-Général* the eve of the day that we were to set out, my aunt and I, to visit the Maréchal de Beauvau at his country house of Le Val, at the end of the terrace of Saint-Germain. While we were taking luncheon in the pavilion in the garden, a valet de chambre arrived very much troubled and inquired of the Maréchal if he knew where Monsieur Necker was. He added that the evening before, on returning from the Council, the Minister had gotten into a carriage with Mme. Necker, saying that he was going to take supper at Le Val, and that since then he had not been seen, and no one knew where to find him. This disappearance very much disturbed us, and my aunt wished to return to Versailles, or rather to the Ménagerie, where we were established. On arriving there the mystery was unveiled. The horses of Monsieur Necker had returned to Versailles after having conducted their master to Bourget. From this place he had taken the post to go to Switzerland by way of the Low Countries. His intention, in so leaving the Ministry, was to avoid testimonials of his popularity which his departure could not have failed to evoke.

Mme. de Montesson, who was at Paris, had formed the plan of going to Berny to pass the summer. Loving the world as she did, she would doubtless have preferred to establish herself for the season at Versailles, which was then the centre of society and affairs. But her position with regard to the Court did not permit this. Berny was not very far from Versailles and she could go there in two hours by the Sceaux road. She therefore decided to establish herself there with Mme. de Valence and invited me to come and pass a month or six weeks.

The thirteenth of July therefore I sent off my saddle-horses, with my English groom, who hardly spoke French, and ordered him to go by way of Paris in order to secure certain articles which were necessary. I relate this little incident as proof that no one had the least idea of what was to happen in Paris the following day. The little army which was assembled in the Plain of Grenelle and the Champ-de-Mars reassured the Court, and although there were desertions every day, no one was disturbed.

When you remember that my personal position put me in the way of knowing everything; that Monsieur de Lally, an influential member of the Assembly, lived with my aunt and myself at the little house of the Ménagerie; that I went every day to supper at Versailles with Mme. de Poix, whose husband was Captain of the Guards and a member of the Assembly, and saw the King every evening, you will be very much surprised at what I am going to relate.

Our security was so profound that the 14 July at noon we had no idea, my aunt and myself, that there was the slightest tumult at Paris, and I got into my carriage with a maid, and a domestic on the box, to go to Berny by the highway to Sceaux which traverses the Bois de Verrières. It is true that this route, that of Versailles to Choisy-le-Roi, does not pass through any villages and is very solitary.

I recall that I had dined at an early hour at Versailles so as to arrive at Berny in my apartment before supper, which in the country was served at nine o'clock. On arriving at Berny, I was surprised, after having entered the first court, to see no one and to find the stables deserted, the doors closed and the same solitude in the court of the château. The concierge, who knew me well, on hearing the carriage came out on the step and cried with a troubled air: "Eh! mon Dieu, madame! Madame n'est pas ici. Personne n'est sorti de Paris. On a tiré le canon de la Bastille. Il y a eu un massacre. Quitter la ville est impossible. Les portes sont barricadées et gardées par les Gardes Françaises qui se sont révoltés avec le peuple."

You can conceive of my astonishment — greater even than my anxiety; but as unforeseen circumstances, in spite of my youth, did not greatly disconcert me, I ordered the carriage to turn around and conduct me to the *poste aux chevaux* of Berny, where I knew the master to be a worthy man, very devoted to Mme. de Montesson and her friends. I told him of my desire to return immediately to Versailles. He confirmed to me the story of the concierge. My hired coachman, however, declared that he would not return to Versailles for anything in the world. I then arranged to have hitched up four post horses with two postilions, for whom the master vouched as determined fellows, and we set out at a full gallop to return to Versailles. I arrived there at eleven o'clock. My aunt, who had a headache, was already in bed. She had not seen Mme.

de Poix, and Monsieur de Lally had not returned. She therefore knew nothing. On seeing me at her bedside she thought that she had a bad dream or that my head was turned. As for myself, I confess that the fate of my English groom and my three horses worried me more than anything else.

The next morning at an early hour we were at the Château. My aunt went to look for news, while I hastened to my father-in-law, from whom I learned everything that had passed: the taking of the Bastille; the revolt of the regiment of the French Guards; the deaths of MM. de Launay and Flesselles and of many others who were more obscure; the use-less charge upon the Place Louis XV of the squad-ron Royal-Allemand, commanded by the Prince de Lambesc. The following day a deputation of the people forced Monsieur de La Fayette to place him-self at the head of the National Guard which had been instituted.

Seven or eight days after the 14 July, Monsieur de La Tour du Pin arrived *en secret* at Versailles from his garrison, as he was much disturbed regarding his father and myself. The Ministry of War did not dis-approve of this slight infraction, and a leave of absence was given him at the request of his father who was glad to have his son beside him. Neverthe-less, after the visit of the King to Paris, which had been required by the Commune, and the return of Monsieur Necker, who had been brought back in the hope of calming the excitement, my husband, who did not think that his father should accept the position of Minister of War, which had been offered him, wished to leave Versailles in order not to influence his father in his determination.

I had been ordered to go to the Springs of Forges in Normandy, and the month which we spent there is one of the periods of my life which I recall with the greatest pleasure. Having sent our saddle-horses, we made long promenades every day in the beautiful woods and pretty country which surround this little city. We had brought with us a great variety of books and my husband, an indefatigable reader, read them to me while I occupied myself with embroidery and other handiwork.

CHAPTER TEN

1789

VERSAILLES INVADED BY THE MOB

Monsieur de La Tour du Pin Père, Minister of War.— Official
Dinners.— Commencement of the Emigration.— Ruin of
the La Tour du Pin Family.— The *Contrôle-Général* and
Mme. de Staël.— Organization of the National Guard of
Versailles.— Monsieur de La Tour du Pin, Second in Command.— The National Guard of Paris and Monsieur de
La Fayette.— Banquet of the Gardes du Corps at the
Château.— Day of the 5th of October.— The King at the
Hunt.— Paris Marches on Versailles.— Arrangements for
the Defence.— The Women of Paris at Versailles.— Revolt
of the National Guard of Versailles.— Plan for the Departure of the Royal Family for Rambouillet.— Invasion
of the Offices of the Ministry.— Hesitation of the King.—
Monsieur de La Fayette with the King.— Calm Re-
established.— Day of the 6th of October.— An Armed
Band Invades the Château.— Massacre of the Gardes du
Corps.— Attempted Assassination of the Queen.— Presence
of the Duc d'Orléans.— Departure of the Royal Family
for Paris.— The King Confides the Guard of the Palace
of Versailles to Monsieur de La Tour du Pin.— Mme. de
La Tour du Pin Takes Refuge at Saint-Germain.

SEVERAL days after the events which I have
just recounted, my husband received a courier
announcing the nomination of his father as
Minister of War. We immediately set out for Versailles. This was the commencement of my public
life. My father-in-law took up his quarters in the

War Department, which was installed in that part of the Palace forming the southern wing of the Cour des Ministres. He put me at the head of his mansion to do the honors, together with my sister-in-law, who was also lodged at the Ministry, but who, at the end of two months, was obliged to leave us. With my husband I occupied a fine apartment on the first floor. I had become so accustomed at Montpellier and Paris to state dinners that my new situation did not in any way embarrass me. There were two dinners a week of twenty-four covers, to which were invited all the members of the Assembly in turn. Their wives were never invited. Mme. de Lameth and I were seated facing each other, and we had beside us the four individuals of the most importance, chosen always from the different parties. Inasmuch as we were at Versailles, the men, without exception, were always in full dress at these dinners, and I remember Monsieur de Robespierre, in an apple-green costume, with a mass of white hair which was well dressed. Mirabeau was the only one who did not come and was never invited. I often went out to supper — sometimes to the houses of our colleagues, and sometimes to those of persons established at Versailles during the period of the National Assembly.

Two days after the taking of the Bastille, the fourteenth of July, the Comte d'Artois, with his children, left France and went to Turin to his father-in-law, the King of Sardinia. Several persons of his household accompanied him, among others, Monsieur d'Hénin, the Captain of his Guards. The Queen, thinking that the popular feeling might compromise the security of the Polignac family, arranged for them also to leave France. Mme. de Polignac took with her her daughter, the Duchesse de Gramont, and I saw her for the last time on the eve of her departure.

Everything in France follows the custom, and that of emigration commenced at this time. All began to raise money upon their property in order to carry away a large sum. Nobody at that time foresaw the consequences that would follow this action.

Nevertheless, the motion adopted the night of the fourth of August, which destroyed feudal rights, should have proved to the most incredulous that the National Assembly would not stop at this beginning of robbery. My father-in-law was ruined, and we have never recovered from this blow to our fortune. Entire spoliation was not decreed at this time; they only settled the rate at which property could be re-acquired; but before the expiration of the date fixed for the payment of this sum, it was decided that such payment could not be made. In fine, everything was lost. By a stroke of the pen we were ruined. Since then we have been obliged to live by expedients, from the proceeds of the sale of what remained to us.

At this time I did not realize that my grandmother, who during the past six months had retired to Haute-fontaine with my uncle, the Archbishop, was also to entirely deprive me of my fortune, upon which I had every reason to count. I could not foresee that my uncle, who still enjoyed an income of over 400,000 francs, of which he could not spend one fourth part, in the retreat where he lived, would leave, when he departed from France the following year, nearly two million francs of debts in which my grandmother was compromised.

We did not at once realize all the consequences of the ruin which had come to us. My father-in-law as Minister received a salary of 300,000 francs, besides his income as Lieutenant-General and Commander of a province. However, he was obliged to keep up an expensive establishment, and besides the two state dinners a week of twenty-four covers, we gave two elegant suppers to which I invited twenty-five or thirty ladies.

Mme. Necker, the wife of the *Contrôle-Général*, or to speak more correctly, of the Prime Minister, lived on a footing similar to our own. But as she rarely went out, she received every day at supper the Deputies and the savants, together with the admirers of her daughter, who was then in the full flush of her youth, interested at the same time in politics, science, intrigue and love. Mme. de Staël lived with her father at the ministerial residence at Versailles, and it was at this period that she was the most involved with Alexandre de Lameth, who at the time was still the friend of my husband. This friendship, which dated from their youth, disturbed me. I had a very poor opinion of the morality of this young man, and my sister-in-law shared my feeling in this respect. Therefore, when several months later my husband completely broke with him and his brother Charles, we were delighted. Although I was on a footing of intimate relations with Mme. de Staël, these never went so far as confidence in her.

This woman was a strange mixture of good and bad qualities, of which I have often endeavored to explain the connection. Her good qualities were tarnished by the passions to which she easily gave way. Nevertheless, it would be wrong to think that I considered her as really a licentious person. In spite of everything, she always exacted a certain delicacy of sentiment, and she was susceptible to passions which were very strong and very ardent as long as they lasted. Thus it was that she passionately loved Monsieur de Narbonne, who abandoned her in a very unworthy manner.

At this time the National Guard was being organized throughout the kingdom on the model of that of Paris, of which Monsieur de La Fayette was Generalissimo. The King himself desired that that of Versailles should be formed and that all the clerks and employés of the Ministry should become members. In the Comte d'Estaing a bad choice was made for the Commander. My father had served under his orders at the beginning of the American war and had the most positive proofs that the Comte was lacking not only in ability but in courage. However, on his return he was loaded with praise, whereas my father, to whom he owed his first success, as it was the Dillon Regiment which took Grenade, received after the war only neglect. It was due to the request of the Queen that Monsieur d'Estaing was named as Commander-in-chief of the National Guard of Versailles. My father-in-law appointed his son as second in command, which was equivalent to the real command, as Monsieur d'Estaing never occupied himself with his duties except when he was unable to avoid it. Monsieur Berthier, who was later Prince de Wagram, a very distinguished officer of the General Staff, was named as Major-General. He was a worthy man who had talent as organizer, but the feebleness of his character left him open to all kinds of intrigues.

The day of Saint-Louis it was customary for the magistrates and officers of the city of Paris to bring their felicitations to the King. This year the National Guard wished also to take part in this function, and the Generalissimo, Monsieur de La Fayette, went to Versailles with his staff, at the same time as Monsieur Bailly, the Mayor of Paris, and all of the municipal officers. The fish-women also came as usual to bring a bouquet to the King. The Queen received them all ceremoniously in the *salon vert*, adjoining her bedchamber. The ordinary etiquette of these receptions was followed. The Queen, as usual, wore a dress which was very much trimmed and covered with diamonds. She was seated in a large fauteuil with a kind of small stool at her feet. At right and left, seated upon stools, were several Duchesses in full dress, and behind them, all the ladies and gentlemen of the household.

The usher announced: "La ville de Paris!" The Queen expected that the Mayor would kneel as he had done in previous years, but Monsieur Bailly, on entering, only made a deep bow, to which the Queen responded by a nod of the head which was not very cordial. He delivered a short address, very well written, in which he spoke of devotion, of attachment and also a little of the fear of the people regarding the shortage of food, with which they were menaced every day.

Then Monsieur de La Fayette advanced and presented the Staff of the National Guard. The Queen turned red, and I saw that her emotion was very great. She stammered several words in a trembling voice and then dismissed them with a nod of the head. They went away very much displeased with her, as I have since learned. This unfortunate Princess never considered the importance of the circumstances in which she found herself. She was influenced by the feelings of the moment, without considering the consequences. These officers of the National Guard, whom a gracious word would have won, went away in bad humor and spread their discontent throughout Paris. All this increased the ill-feeling which they had towards the Queen and of which the Duc d'Orléans was the first author.

The National Guard of Versailles, like the other troops of the kingdom, wished to have flags, and it was decided that these should be solemnly consecrated at Notre-Dame-de-Versailles. A deputation of the principal officers, with Monsieur d'Estaing at their head, came to request me to interest myself in the ceremony of this benediction. If any one had told me, at the time, that the modest Major of the National Guard, Berthier, whose father was steward of the War Department, would become the Sovereign Prince of Neufchâtel and that he would wed a German Princess, I should have laughed at such a tale; but we have seen others even more remarkable!

VERSAILLES INVADED BY THE MOB

I was present at this very brilliant and very solemn ceremony where there were deputations from all the military corps present at Versailles. During this high mass, which was very long, I had time to reflect upon the march of events. Hardly fourteen months before, I had been present the day of Pentecost in the Chapel of Versailles, at a meeting of the chapter of the cordons bleus, at which were present the King and all the Princes of the Royal House, of whom several had already left France.

The regiment of Flandre-Infanterie, of which the Marquis de Lusignan, a Deputy, was Colonel, had been ordered to Versailles. At this time the Gardes du Corps wished to offer a dinner to the officers of this regiment of Flanders and to those of the National Guard. They requested that for this purpose they should be allowed to use the large Salle des Spectacles de la Cour, at the end of the gallery of the Chapel. This superb hall could be converted into a ball-room by placing over the parterre a floor on a level with the boxes, and the permission was given them. The dinner commenced rather late and the theatre was brilliantly illuminated, which would have been necessary under any circumstances, as there were no windows.

My sister-in-law and I went, towards the end of the dinner, to view the scene which was really magnificent. Toasts were being proposed, and my husband, who came to meet us and to conduct us to one of the first tier boxes, had time to tell us very low that the officers were very much excited and that inconsiderate words had been uttered.

All at once it was announced that the King and Queen were coming to the banquet — a very imprudent step which had the worst possible aftereffect. The sovereigns appeared in a box with the little Dauphin who was about five years of age. There were enthusiastic cries of: "Vive le Roi!" A Swiss officer approached the box and asked the Queen to confide to him the Dauphin, in order to make the round of the hall. She consented and the poor little fellow was not at all afraid. The officer put the child on the table and he made the round very boldly, smiling and not at all frightened by the cries which he heard around him. The Queen was not so calm, and when the child was brought back to her, she embraced him tenderly. We left as soon as the King and Queen had retired. The next day the opposition journals, of which several were already in existence, did not fail to give a description of the "orgy" at Versailles.

The fourth of October there was a shortage of bread at several bakers in Paris and a great deal of tumult. One of these bakers was hung, in spite of the efforts of Monsieur de La Fayette and the National Guard. Nevertheless, at Versailles no one was alarmed. They thought that this revolt was similar to those which had already taken place and that the National Guard, of whose loyalty they felt sure, would be able to control the people. Several messages which came to the King and to the President of the Chambers were so reassuring that the fifth of October, at ten o'clock in the morning, the King set out for the hunt in the wood of Verrières, while I myself, after déjeuner, went to rejoin Mme. de Valence who had come to Versailles. We went for a drive in the garden of Mme. Elisabeth at the end of the Grande Avenue. As we descended from the carriage to traverse the *contre-allée*, we saw a man on horse-back pass near us at full gallop. It was the Duc de Maillé, who cried out to us: "Paris is marching here with cannon!" This news greatly frightened us, and we returned at once to Versailles, where the alarm had been given.

My husband had gone to the Assembly without knowing anything. We were not in ignorance of the fact that there was a great deal of tumult in Paris; but we were not able to learn anything more, because the gates had been closed and no one was permitted to go out. Monsieur de La Tour du Pin, in searching in the corridors for a person with whom he wished to speak, passed behind a large man whom he did not at once recognize, who was saying: "Paris is marching here with twelve pieces of cannon." This personage was Mirabeau, then strongly allied with the Duc d'Orléans. My husband hastened to his father, who was already in conference with the other Ministers. The first thing that they did was to send in every direction where they thought the hunt might have led the King, to warn him to return. My husband occupied himself in assembling the National Guard, in whom he was far from having confidence. He ordered the Flanders Regiment to take their arms and to occupy the Place d'Armes. The Gardes du Corps saddled their horses. Couriers were sent out to call the Swiss from Courbevoie. Messengers were sent out at every moment on the highway to obtain news of what was going on. It was learned that an innumerable mob of men with many women were marching upon Versailles; that after this kind of advance guard came the National Guard of Paris with their cannon, followed by a large troop of individuals marching without order. There was no longer time to defend the bridge of Sèvres. The National Guard of that city had already given it up to the women and had fraternized with the Guard of Paris. My father-in-law wished to send the Flanders Regiment to cut off the road from Paris, but the National Assembly had declared itself in a permanent session, the King was absent, and there was no one present to take the initiative in any hostile demonstration.

During this time the drums beat the call to assemble the National Guard. They came together on the Place d'Armes and were placed in battle order with their backs to the railing of the Cour Royale. The Flanders Regiment had its left wing on the Grande Écurie and its right on the railing. The post of the interior of the Cour Royale and that of the Chapel were occupied by the Swiss, of whom there was always a strong detachment at Versailles. The gates everywhere were closed. All the outlets of the Château were barricaded, and the doors, which had not turned on their hinges since the days of Louis XIV, were closed for the first time.

Finally, at about three o'clock, the King and his suite arrived at full gallop by the Grande Avenue.

This unfortunate Prince, instead of stopping and addressing a kind word to this fine Flanders Regiment, before which he passed, and which cried: "Vive le Roi!" did not say a single word to them. He went to shut himself up in his apartment, from which he did not come out. The National Guard of Versailles, which was making its first campaign, commenced to murmur and to declare that it would not fire upon the people of Paris. There were no cannon at Versailles.

The advance guard of two or three hundred women commenced to arrive and to spread out in the Avenue. Many entered the Assembly and said that they had come to look for bread and to take the Deputies to Paris. Night came on, and several gun shots were heard. They came from the ranks of the National Guard and were directed against my husband, their commander, whom they had refused to obey, by remaining at their post. My husband escaped by a miracle and, realizing the fact that his troop had abandoned him, he went to take a place in front of the Gardes du Corps, who were drawn up in battle order near the Petite Écurie. But these troops, which comprised only the company of Gramont, were so few in number that any idea of defence was thought impossible.

At this moment, my father-in-law and Monsieur de Saint-Priest offered the advice that the King should retire to Rambouillet with his family and await there any propositions which might be made to him by the insurgents of Paris and by the National Assembly. The King at first accepted this plan. At about eight or nine o'clock a company of the Gardes du Corps was ordered to the Cour Royale, which they entered by the gate of the Rue de la Sur-Intendance, now the Rue Gambetta. From here they passed by the Terrasse de l'Orangerie, under the windows of the apartments of Queen Marie-Antoinette, traversed the Little Park and gained, by the Ménagerie, the Grande Route to Saint-Cyr. There was left of this troop at Versailles only sufficient men to relieve the posts in the apartments of the King and Queen. The Suisses and the Cent-Suisses guarded their own posts.

It was at this moment that two or three hundred women, who for an hour had been hovering around the gates, discovered a little door opening upon the Rue du Grand-Commun, which was a prolongation of the Rue de la Chancellerie. This door gave access to a secret staircase which ended under that part of the building where we had our quarters in the Cour des Ministres. Some traitor had probably shown them this entrance. They entered in a crowd, knocking down the Swiss guard posted at the top of the stairway, then spread through the court and gained the quarters of the four Ministers which were located in this part of the building. My husband returned at this moment to bring news to his sister and myself. Very much disturbed to find us in such bad company, he accompanied us into the Château. My sister-in-law had taken the precaution of sending her children to the house of a deputy, one of our friends, who was lodged in the city. Guided by Monsieur de La Tour du Pin, we ascended to the Gallery where we found

ANNE-LOUISE NECKER

Baronne de Staël-Holstein

1766 - 1817

already gathered a number of persons living in the Château, who had come from their apartments to be nearer the source of news.

During this time the King, still hesitating as to what decision to make, was no longer willing to depart for Rambouillet. He consulted everybody. The Queen, equally undecided, could not make up her mind to this flight by night. My father-in-law went down on his knees to the King to implore him to put himself and his family in a place of security. The Ministers would have remained to treat with the insurgents and the Assembly. But the King, repeating continually, "I do not wish to compromise any one," thus lost a precious period of time. At one time it was thought that he was going to yield, and the order was given to prepare the carriages for departure. For two hours they had been ready waiting in the Grande Écurie. No one seemed to think that the people of Versailles would oppose the departure of the Royal family. This, however, is what happened. The moment that the crowd of people from Paris and Versailles who were assembled on the Place d'Armes saw the gate of the court of the Grande Écurie opened, there was a unanimous cry of fear and fury: "Le roi s'en va!" At the same moment they rushed upon the carriages, cut the harness and led the horses back, so that it was necessary to bring word to the Château that the departure was impossible. My father-in-law and Monsieur de Saint-Priest then offered our carriages, which were hitched up outside the railing of the Orangerie, but the King and the Queen rejected this proposition, and every one, discouraged, frightened and fearing the greatest misfortunes, remained in silence and suspense.

In this Gallery, witness of all the splendors of the monarchy since Louis XIV, every one walked up and down without exchanging a word. The Queen remained in her room with Mme. Elisabeth, the sister of Louis XVI, and the wife of the Comte de Provence. The Salon de Jeu, hardly lighted, was full of women who were talking in low tones — some seated on stools and others upon the tables. As for myself, my agitation was so great that I could not remain for a moment in the same place. Every few minutes I went to the *œil-de-bœuf*, from which one could see those who entered and who came out of the King's apartment, in the hope of encountering my husband or my father-in-law and of learning from them some news. The wait to me seemed intolerable.

Finally at midnight, my husband, who had been in the court for some time, came to announce that Monsieur de La Fayette had arrived before the gate of the Cour des Ministres, with the National Guard of Paris, and requested to speak with the King. He added that a part of this Guard, composed of the former Régiment des Gardes, was manifesting much impatience and that the least delay might lead to trouble and even danger.

The King then said: "Have Monsieur de La Fayette come up." In an instant Monsieur de La Tour du Pin was at the gate, and Monsieur de La Fayette, dismounting from his horse, and so fatigued that he was hardly able to stand upright, ascended to the King's apartment accompanied by seven or eight persons, mostly from his staff. Very much moved he addressed the King in these terms: "Sire, j'ai pensé qu'il valait mieux venir ici, mourir aux pieds de Votre Majesté, que de périr inutilement sur la Place de Grève." To these words the King replied: "Que veulent-ils donc?" La Fayette said: "Le peuple demande du pain, et la Garde désire reprendre ses anciens postes auprès de Votre Majesté." The King said: "Well, let them do so."

These words were immediately reported to me. My husband descended with Monsieur de La Fayette, and the National Guard of Paris, composed almost exclusively of the Gardes Françaises, resumed at once their former posts. Thus it happened that at every outer door where there had been a Swiss guard, a member of the Guard of Paris was posted, and the rest, made up of several hundred men, were sent to bivouac, as usual, upon the Place d'Armes, in a long building comprising several large halls constructed and painted in the form of tents.

During this time the people of Paris had left the vicinity of the Château and had dispersed in the city and the cabarets. The women, who had invaded the offices of the Ministry, were sleeping everywhere on the floor. The principal leaders of the women had taken refuge in the hall of the National Assembly where they remained during the night mingled with the Deputies, who were being relieved in order to keep up the permanent session.

I think that Monsieur de La Fayette, after having established his posts of the National Guard, went to the Assembly, whence he returned to the Château with Mme. de Poix, whose quarters were near the chapel in the gallery of that name. As for Monsieur d'Estaing, he had not appeared during the whole day and had remained in the cabinet of the King, taking no more responsibility for the National Guard of Versailles than as if he had not been their commander-in-chief. Monsieur de La Tour du Pin had brought together a small number of the officers of his staff, upon whom he thought he could count, among whom was Major Berthier. But the majority of the officers at this advanced hour had retired to their own quarters or to the houses of persons of their acquaintance.

The King, to whom they had reported that the most absolute calm reigned at Versailles, which at that moment was really true, dismissed all the persons who were still present in the *œil-de-bœuf* or in his cabinet. The ushers came to the Gallery to tell the ladies who were still there that the Queen had retired. The doors were closed, the candles extinguished, and my husband escorted us back to the apartment of my aunt, which was situated above the Galerie des Princes, at the top of the south wing of the Château. He did not wish to take us back to our rooms in the Ministry on account of the women who were sleeping in the antechambers and who caused us great disgust.

After having placed us in security in this apartment, he redescended to find his father and pray him to go to bed, saying that he himself would watch during the night. He went to his room to put on an overcoat over his uniform, for the night was cold and damp; then, taking a round hat, he descended to the court and proceeded to visit the posts. He went through the courts, the passages and the garden to assure himself that it was quiet everywhere. He did not hear the least noise, either around the Château or in the adjacent streets. The different posts were relieved with vigilance, and the guard which was installed in the large tent upon the Place d'Armes, and which had placed the cannon in form of battery before the gate, was performing its service with the same regularity as before the 14 July.

Such is the exact account of what passed at Versailles the fifth of October.

Monsieur de La Tour du Pin, having heard nothing of a nature to lead him to fear the least disorder, returned after his nocturnal round to the office of the Minister of War in the south wing of the Cour des Ministres. However, instead of going to the cabinet or to his room, which, like my own, faced the Rue du Grand-Commun, he remained in the dining-room and placed himself at a window to have the air for fear of going to sleep. It is well to explain here that the Cour des Princes was then closed by a gate near which was stationed a garde du corps, for here was the first post of the guard of the King's person, a service which particularly devolved upon the Gardes du Corps and the Cent-Suisses. In the interior of this little court there was a passage which communicated with the Cour Royale. This had been arranged so as to enable the Gardes du Corps, who were stationed in the Cour Royale at the corner of the Cour Marbre, when the posts were changed, to go out by the gate at the middle of the Cour Royale and reënter by that of the Cour des Princes. It will be seen in a moment how necessary the knowledge of this passageway was to the assassins.

Day was commencing to break. It was almost six o'clock, and the most profound silence reigned in the court. Monsieur de La Tour du Pin, leaning out of the window, thought he heard the steps of a great crowd of people which seemed to ascend the *rampe* that led to the Cour des Ministres, from the Rue de la Sur-Intendance. Then, to his great surprise, he saw a mob of miserable creatures enter by the gate, although it had been closed and locked. The key had been obtained by an act of treason. The crowd was armed with axes and sabres. At the same moment my husband heard a gun-shot. During the time that he took to descend the stairway and to have the door of the Ministry opened, the assassins had killed Monsieur de Vallori, the garde du corps posted at the gate of the Cour des Princes, and had rushed through the passage of which I have just spoken to fall upon the Corps de Garde of the Cour Royale. Some of the crowd, who were not more than two hundred in number, rushed to the marble staircase, while another part hurled themselves upon the garde du corps whom his comrades had abandoned without defence. This unfortunate man, after having fired one shot, with which he killed the nearest of his assailants, was immediately cut down by the others. This task accomplished, the invaders rushed to rejoin the other part of the band which, at this moment, had forced aside the guard of the Cent-Suisses posted at the top of the marble staircase.

The proof that no extra precautions had been taken, is found in the fact that the assassins, arrived at the top of the staircase, and certainly guided by some one who knew the route to follow, turned into the Queen's Guardroom and fell suddenly upon the only guard who was posted in this place. This guard rushed to the door of the Queen's bed-chamber, which was closed on the inside, and having rapped several times with the cross of his *mousqueton*, he cried: "Madame, save yourself! They are coming to kill you!" Then, resolved to sell his life dearly, he placed his back against the door, discharged his *mousqueton*, and defended himself by his sabre, but was quickly cut down by these miserable creatures who fortunately had no fire-arms. He fell against the door, and his body hindered the assassins from breaking it in. His body was pushed aside into the embrasure of the window, which saved his life.

During this time my sister-in-law and I were sleeping in one of the apartments of my aunt, Mme. d'Hénin. My fatigue was so great that my sister-in-law had considerable trouble in awakening me. As neither of us was undressed, we both rushed to the room of my aunt, which looked out upon the park, and where she was unable to hear anything. Her fright was equal to our own. We immediately called our servants. Before they were awakened, my good and devoted Marguerite came running to us, pale as death, and tumbling upon the first chair, she cried: "Ah! mon Dieu! nous allons tous être massacrés." This exclamation was far from reassuring us.

Marguerite stated that she had left her room with

the intention of coming to ascertain whether I had
need of her services, but in descending the staircase, she had discovered a large number of very
ordinary people and had seen arriving a Monsieur,
with boots covered with mud, and a whip in his hand,
who was no other than the Duc d'Orléans, whom she
recognized perfectly, as she had often seen him; furthermore, that these miserable creatures surrounded
him and showed their joy at seeing him by crying:
"Vive notre roi d'Orléans!"

Marguerite had hardly finished this moving recital
when my husband arrived. He told us that on seeing
the assassins penetrate into the Cour Royale, he had
immediately rushed to the *grand'garde* stationed
upon the Place d'Armes to have the drums beat the
alarm. We also learned from him that the Queen had
been able to save herself by going to the King's
apartment through a little passage, arranged under
the room known as the *Œil-de-Bœuf*, which formed the
means of communication between her bedroom and
that of the King. He persuaded us to leave my aunt's
apartment, which was too near, in his opinion, to
those of the King and Queen, and counselled us to
rejoin Mme. de Simaine, who was lodged near the
Orangerie. The Abbé de Damas came to find us and
conduct us there.

At the end of two hours, which seemed to me
centuries, my husband sent a valet de chambre to
inform me that they were leading the King and
Queen to Paris, that the Ministers, the Administration and the National Assembly were quitting Versailles, where he himself had the order to remain to

save the Château from pillage after the departure of
the King. He added that for this purpose they were
leaving him a Swiss battalion, the National Guard of
Versailles, of which the commander-in-chief, Monsieur d'Estaing, had sent in his resignation, and a
battalion of the National Guard of Paris. For the
moment he forbade me absolutely to issue from my
refuge. I remained alone for several hours, as my
aunt had gone to Mme. de Poix, who was also
leaving for Paris, and my sister-in-law had left me
to go in search of her children and her husband.
He had just arrived from Hénencourt and wished to
have her leave at once for the country. I do not
think that I ever in my life passed hours more
cruel than those of this morning. The death-cries
by which I had been awakened still resounded in my
ears. The least noise made me tremble. My imagination conjured up all the dangers which my husband
could run. My maid, Marguerite, who could have
encouraged me, was also absent. She had returned
to the Ministry to assist my servants in packing our
effects, which were to go to Paris by the wagons of
my father-in-law.

About three o'clock Mme. d'Hénin returned to
look for me and announced that the sad cortège had
set out for Paris, the carriage of the King preceded
by the heads of the Gardes du Corps, which their
assassins were carrying on the ends of their pikes.

In getting into his carriage, Louis XVI had said
to Monsieur de La Tour du Pin: "Vous restez
maître ici. Tâchez de me sauver mon pauvre Versailles." This injunction was equivalent to an order,

which he was firmly resolved to obey. He took measures to carry out this order with the commander of the battalion of the National Guard of Paris who had been left with him — a man who was very determined and who showed the best good-will — this was Santerre!

I left my refuge with my aunt and returned to the Ministry. A frightful solitude then reigned at Versailles. The only noise which was heard in the Château was that of the doors, the blinds and the window-shutters which were being closed for the first time since the reign of Louis XIV. My husband made all arrangements for the defence of the Château, being convinced that as soon as night arrived, the strange and sinister figures which he saw roaming around the streets and the courts would come together to pillage the Château. Alarmed for my safety, in view of the disorder which he foresaw, he insisted that I should leave with my aunt.

We were not willing to go to Paris, because of the fear that the gates would be closed upon us and that I would find myself separated from my husband without the power of rejoining him. My wish would have been to remain at Versailles, as, near to my husband, I had no fear. But he said that my presence would paralyze the efforts which it was his duty to make to show himself worthy of the King's confidence. Finally he persuaded me to set out for Saint-Germain and to await events in the apartment of Monsieur de Lally, at the Château. This apartment was that of my family, which my great-aunt, Mlle. Dillon, had left him entirely furnished.

We made the trip in a wretched cariole, my aunt and I, accompanied by a femme de chambre, originally from Saint-Germain. The horses and carriages of my father-in-law had been sent to Paris, and it was impossible to find at Versailles any other means of transport, no matter what sum was offered. The trip took us three long hours.

CHAPTER ELEVEN

1789–1790

VISIT TO SWITZERLAND

Residence of Mme. de La Tour du Pin at Paris.— The Minister
of War at the Hôtel de Choiseul.— Birth of Humbert.—
Kindness of the Queen for Mme. de La Tour du Pin.— The
Fête of the Federation.— The Garrison of Paris.— Com-
position of the National Guard.— Monsieur de La Fayette.
— Talleyrand, Bishop of Autun.— The Spectacle at the
Champ-de-Mars.— The Royal Family.— Excursion to
Switzerland.— An Adventure at Dôle.— Four Days of
Captivity.— Departure from Dôle.— The Lake of Geneva.
— Revolt of the Garrison of Nancy.— Monsieur de La Tour
du Pin Sent as *Parlementaire*.— Suppression of the Revolt.
— Sojourn at Lausanne.— Return to Paris via Alsace.

A T the end of two weeks I left for Paris where
I stayed with my aunt, Rue de Verneuil,
until the Hôtel de Choiseul, which had been
set apart for the War Department, was ready. My
father-in-law was temporarily quartered in a house
which belonged, I think, to the *Menus plaisirs* near
the Louvre. Every day I went there to dine with
him and to do the honors of his salon.

My aunt had persuaded Monsieur Lally, over
whom she exercised an absolute control, to abandon
the National Assembly after the Revolution of the
sixth of October. She also forced him to leave France
with Monsieur Mounier. They both retired to

Switzerland. This was a very false move. It was to desert their post on the eve of battle. However this may be, she followed M. Lally to Switzerland, and it was at this time that she persuaded him to marry his former mistress, Miss Halkett, niece of Lord Loughborough, who was then Lord Chancellor of England. It was only for the purpose of legitimatizing the daughter whom he had had by this woman several years before, that he decided to espouse her, for he had for her neither esteem nor love. But at the moment of leaving Lausanne to rejoin Miss Halkett at Turin, he was taken ill with a terrible attack of smallpox, of which he nearly died. The marriage was therefore adjourned and did not take place until the following year.

At the beginning of winter we went to take up our quarters at the Hôtel de Choiseul. It was a superb mansion, in which I had a charming apartment entirely distinct from that of my father-in-law, with which it was connected, however, by a door into one of the salons. A fine separate staircase led to my quarters, which were like a separate house, with a view upon the gardens, which today are all built up. My husband, who was entrusted by his father with many important matters, was very much occupied. I saw him only at luncheon which we took together, and at dinner.

My father-in-law ceased to give large dinners when we were at Paris. The dinner hour was four o'clock. An hour after dinner, after having chatted in the salon with several persons who came for coffee, according to the custom at Versailles, my father-in-law returned to his cabinet. I then went back to my own apartment, whence I went out to take part in social functions.

On arriving in Paris the Queen had given up her theatre boxes, and this act of spite, which was natural but also very ill-advised, had still further turned the Parisians against her. This unfortunate Princess had no tact, or did not wish to employ it. She openly showed her dislike to those whose presence displeased her. In giving way in this manner to feelings of which she did not weigh the consequences she injured the interests of the King. Although endowed with great courage, she had very little *esprit*, no address, and, above all, a lack of confidence, generally unwarranted, with regard to those who were the most disposed to serve her. After the sixth of October, failing to appreciate that the terrible danger which had menaced her was the result of a plot woven by the Duc d'Orléans, she let her resentment fall upon all of the inhabitants of Paris indiscriminately and avoided every occasion to appear in public.

I missed very much the privilege of using the Queen's boxes, and, fearing the crowd, I was not present at any performances during the winter of 1789 and 1790. I often brought together eight or ten persons in my apartment for little suppers, in which my father-in-law did not take part, for he retired at an early hour and arose very early in the morning.

It was during the first months of 1790 that the demagogues employed all their means to corrupt the Army. Every day bad news was received, and my poor father-in-law was nearly overwhelmed with the labor caused by these reports. Many officers left France without leave, and this example of indiscipline, of which the other officers took advantage, encouraged the revolt.

The nineteenth of May was born my eldest son, who was baptised in the Parish of Saint-Eustache and received the name of Humbert. My aunt, Mme. d'Hénin, who had come from Switzerland, was the godmother, and my father-in-law was the godfather.

At Paris the Court was still conducted in accordance with the customs of Versailles, with the exception of the mass, which had been abandoned. Dinner was served as at Versailles. As soon as I was able to leave the house, I paid a visit to the Queen, in full costume, and was received by her with great kindness. In leaving for Switzerland, Mme. d'Hénin had resigned her position, and the question came up as to whether I should take her place in the Queen's service. The Queen, however, was not in favor of this, because there was already talk of appointing my husband Minister to Holland, and as I would naturally accompany him, the Queen did not think it was worth while, if my service was to be interrupted so soon. "Besides," said she, "who knows that I may not expose you to dangers like those of the fifth of October?"

I no longer recall the reasons which inspired the idea of having all the military corps of the State fraternize, as they called it then, by sending to Paris the oldest of each grade to be present the fourteenth of July, the anniversary of the taking of the Bastille. The National Guards, which had been organized throughout the kingdom during the year, were to send deputations composed of the officers of the highest rank. The preparatory work for receiving them was begun at the end of June. The Champ-de-Mars, facing the École Militaire, at this time presented the appearance of a well-levelled lawn, on which were held the exercises of the pupils of the school and the manœuvres of the regiments of the Gardes Françaises.

At that time there was no garrison, either at Paris or in the environs. The Gardes Françaises were the only body of troops in the city, and their number did not exceed, I think, two thousand men at the most. They furnished a detachment at Versailles which was changed every week. At Courbevoie there was quartered the regiment of Swiss Guards, which was never seen at Paris. The Gardes du Corps were composed of four companies, of which only one was in service at Versailles. The others occupied the neighboring cities: Chartres, Beauvais and Saint-Germain. No other body of troops ever appeared either at Versailles or at Paris, where the only uniforms you saw were those of the *sergents recruteurs* for the different regiments.

My husband had been instructed by his father to look after all the deputations and to arrange for their board and lodging, as well as their amusements, for all the theatres had orders to reserve free places for the old soldiers and boxes for the officers. A large

PRINCESSE D'HÉNIN

1749 - 1826

number were lodged in the Invalides and the École Militaire. The people of Paris took part enthusiastically in the work undertaken at the Champ-de-Mars. All was finished in two weeks.

Finally on the evening of the thirteenth of July, my sister-in-law, who had just arrived at Paris, and myself went to take up our quarters at the École Militaire, in a little apartment looking out upon the Champ-de-Mars, so as to be on hand the following morning. My father-in-law had sent in a fine repast, and provisions, so as to offer a substantial déjeuner to the soldiers who might have the intention of coming to see us during the ceremony. This precaution was all the more necessary, because at the Tuileries they had forgotten to bring anything for the King's children, and the Dauphin was very glad to share our collation. The poor little Prince wore the uniform of the National Guard, to which nearly every one at that time belonged. In society all the men under fifty years of age had had their names inscribed, and performed very faithfully their service.

Monsieur de La Fayette, who has been so much condemned, did not then think of a republic for France, whatever may have been the ideas as to this kind of government that he had brought back from America. He desired as much as any of us the establishment of a wise liberty and the abolition of abuses, but I am certain that he had not at that time the least idea or desire of overturning the throne, and that he never had such a thought. The unbounded hatred which the Queen had for him, and which she showed every time that she dared, nevertheless

[113]

caused him as much chagrin as was possible in the case of a character which was soft even to foolishness. Yet La Fayette was not weak, as his conduct under the Empire has well proved. He resisted all the approaches, all the offers and even the cajolery of Napoleon. The Restoration showed itself very unjust towards him. The Duchesse d'Angoulême had inherited from her mother the hatred which the Queen bore him.

But to return to the *Fédération* of 1790. The altar had been erected in the Champ-de-Mars, and a mass was celebrated by the least respectable of the French priests. The Abbé de Périgord, since Prince Talleyrand, had been designated as Bishop of Autun when Monsieur Marbœuf was transferred to the diocese of Lyon. The King, however, justly offended by his ecclesiastical conduct, refused to confirm the appointment. In this refusal the King showed a firmness very different from his ordinary character, but aroused on this occasion by his conscience. However, when the Comte de Talleyrand, father of the Abbé, was upon his deathbed and demanded as a last favor this appointment, which the King had previously refused, he no longer made any opposition, and the Abbé de Périgord was appointed Bishop of Autun. It was he who celebrated the mass of the *Fédération* of 1790.

No words can give any idea of this pageant. The troops, arranged in order in the middle of the arena, the multitude of different uniforms, mingled with those of the National Guard, brilliant from their newness, — all this constituted one of the most surprising spectacles which you could possibly see, and which I enjoyed from the windows of the École Militaire, where I was located. In front of the middle balcony had been constructed a fine tribune, highly decorated. The unfortunate Royal family this day comprised the King, the Queen, their two children, Mme. Elisabeth, the sister of the King, and the Comte and Comtesse de Provence. As I was still very weak, I did not descend to the Royal tribune. Nevertheless, I was near the Queen when she passed, and, accustomed for a long time to the expression of her face, I saw that she was making great efforts to conceal her ill-humor, without succeeding well enough either for her own interests or for those of the King.

Towards the end of July, 1790, my health was quite well reëstablished. My aunt wished to return to Lausanne, and my husband, knowing my desire to see Switzerland, gave me permission to make a trip of six weeks. Mme. de Valence was at this time at Sécheron, near Geneva, with Mme. de Montesson, who passed the summer there. It was arranged that I should join her and pass some time with her in a little house which was separate from that of my aunt. I left my son with his nurse and Marguerite at the Hôtel de la Guerre. As my maid could not accompany me, I took with me only one servant. I travelled by a little *chaise de poste*, for *calèches* were not then known.

My aunt and I were furnished with all possible passports for the civil authorities, as well as for the National Guards and the military authorities. An act of imprudence on the part of my aunt nearly cost us very dear. The post where we were to change horses at Dôle was outside the city upon the route to Besançon. Accordingly, we passed through the city by a quiet street without any trouble. Arrived at the post, my aunt inquired of the *maître de poste* if this route led to Geneva. He replied that to take the route to Geneva, that of the *Rousses*, it was necessary to recross the city. In vain I suggested to my aunt that our passports stated that we were to leave France by Pontarlier. She said that that was of no importance, and as soon as the horses were attached, gave the order to turn back and recross the city to gain the route of *Rousses* under the pretext that she had given a rendez-vous at Geneva to Monsieur Lally.

Accordingly, we reëntered the city. We were ignorant of the fact that it was necessary to pass through the market, which was being held upon a large square. Forced to go at a walk, in order to avoid the market baskets and the persons in the street, we were received with abuse. Suddenly a voice exclaimed: "C'est la Reine!" At once we were stopped, our horses were unhitched, our courier was dragged from his horse, and there were cries of "A la lanterne!" They opened the door of the carriage and ordered us to descend, which we did, not without fear. I stated that I was the daughter of the Minister of War and demanded that they should take me to the commander of the place or send to look for him. My aunt said that she had a letter from Monsieur de La Fayette for the commander of the National Guard.

"There is his house," cried some one, and we saw two sentinels at a door over which floated a large tricolored flag. It was only a few steps away, and my aunt and I entered the house, where the crowd of people did not dare to follow us. We went through an ante-chamber, without finding any one. From there we entered a dining-room where there was a table laid out with seven or eight covers. The guests had left precipitately, and two or three over-turned chairs testified to the haste with which they had disappeared. My aunt refused to go farther, but rang a bell, which she had noticed, in the hope that some one would appear. As we had had no déjeuner, we sat down at the table and commenced to eat the dinner which had been abandoned. An excellent meal satisfied our hunger, while we laughed over our adventure and the cowardice of the chief of the National Guard.

Finally, after waiting three hours, there entered a grave personage, a kind of fat bourgeois, accompanied by two or three other men. This individual addressed my aunt and demanded her name. Then, pointing to me, he said: "This young lady is your daughter?" She replied that I was the daughter-in-law of the Minister of War; that I knew that there was a regiment of cavalry in garrison at Dôle; that I wished to speak to the commander who would arrange, without doubt, with the President of the Cummune that we should be set at liberty. The person who had approached us stated that he himself was the President of the Commune. My aunt, seeing that they wished to keep us prisoners, suggested, as a means of clearing the matter up, that a servant should be sent as a courier to Paris, and demanded that while awaiting his return we should be authorized to establish ourselves at an inn. One of the members of the Commune who accompanied the President, proposed to take us to his house. This asylum seemed more certain than an inn, where we might be insulted by the people. Upon our consenting, he offered me his arm, and leaving this inhospitable house, where we had eaten our dinner without invitation, we were conducted by our host to a mansion where we were lodged in rooms which, although common, were quite good. Here we were rejoined by the maid and our three servants.

We at once wrote to Paris about our misadventure, my aunt to Monsieur de La Fayette and I to my husband. Our host advised us not to attempt to go out, and we resigned ourselves to remaining in this dismal lodging on the ground floor, looking out on a very small garden where the sun hardly penetrated at midday.

The next morning two members of the Commune came to interrogate us. They asked a thousand questions and examined our papers and writing portfolios. They demanded an account of everything we had in our *chaise de poste*, also why I had so many new shoes, if I was only going to pass six weeks in Switzerland, as I had stated, and hundreds of other similar absurdities which caused me to laugh in their faces. Finally the thought occurred to me to say to them that the officers of the city sent to Paris to the *Fédération*, and who ought to be back with their regiment, having probably dined with my father-in-law, would recognize me. This idea appeared to them a brilliant one and they went to look for the officers.

Towards the end of our first day of seclusion there arrived the officers of Royal-Étranger who offered me the services of their protection. I prayed the officers to conceal their dissatisfaction, but I could not prevent them from coming every day to call, one after another. At the end of the fourth day the members of the Municipality made up their minds that they had made a foolish mistake in arresting us and gave us permission to set out. It required several hours to repack our carriages, and as we wished to stop for the night at Nyon, we resolved not to set out before the next morning at five o'clock. The next day, with many thanks to the officers for their politeness, we took the road for the Jura.

Our triumph came that very evening. The President of the National Assembly wrote the Mayor, or President of the Commune, by a courier sent expressly, a very strong reprimand on account of our arrest. Monsieur de La Fayette also sent a message to the commander of the National Guard. My father-in-law entrusted our safety to the Lieutenant-Colonel commanding the place. For our part, we were glad to escape by a prompt retreat from the honors which they wished to shower upon us to make up for our unjust detention.

We arrived at Nyon at midnight after having passed the frontier without difficulty. My aunt did not find Monsieur Lally there. He was at Sécheron, where it was arranged that we should go the next morning.

The next day we arrived at Sécheron, where we found Monsieur Lally and Monsieur Mounier. Here I received letters from my husband, who seemed to be disturbed by the revolt of several garrisons in Lorraine — in particular of that of Nancy. This news, however, did not arouse my anxiety. Monsieur Mounier persuaded my aunt to make a visit to Chamonix, and we set out the next day and did not return to Geneva before the end of five or six days. On our return to Sécheron, I found a letter from my husband which had been forwarded to me from Lausanne, where he thought I was with my aunt. He announced his departure for Nancy to carry orders from the King to Monsieur de Bouillé. Their tenor was that he should unite several French and Swiss regiments and march on Nancy.

At Rolle, where we stopped to refresh our horses, we learned at the inn that Monsieur Plantamour of Geneva was there and that he was en route for Nancy. My aunt asked to speak to him in private. In a few minutes he entered the room where I was, and I observed that he was very much troubled, which increased my anxiety. He told me that there had been fighting at Nancy, but that details were lacking. We continued our route to Lausanne, and on arriving there Monsieur Lally, who had preceded us, gave me several letters from my husband, written after his return to Paris. In these letters he told me everything which had occurred at Nancy. As these details belong to the domain of history, I shall not relate them here.

While these events were happening at Nancy, I

was at Lausanne, where I passed two weeks and enjoyed myself very much. Here I encountered a celebrated person — Mr. Gibbon — whose grotesque face gave me such a desire to laugh that it was difficult to control myself. There were also many émigrés at Lausanne. As I did not enjoy myself in their society, as soon as Mme. Montesson was established at Pâquis, near Geneva, I hastened to rejoin her, and went to lodge with Mme. Valence in a little house distinct from that of Mme. Montesson.

The inn of Sécheron was then very popular. Many of the émigrés whom I knew were settled there for the summer. Several young men, after having accompanied the Comte d'Artois to Turin, already tired of Piémont, had come to Switzerland.

Fortunately I remained only three or four weeks at Geneva, or rather Pâquis. My husband came to join me and take me back to Paris. As he was in a hurry and wished to return by way of Alsace, in order to meet Monsieur Bouillé, we left Geneva at an early hour in the morning so as to have several hours to visit Berne and Bâle. Monsieur Bouillé came to meet us between Huningue and Neuf-Brisach, and I waited patiently in the carriage while my husband talked with him in walking up and down the highway. After a morning devoted to Strasbourg, we passed the night at Saverne and from there went to Nancy. From Nancy we made the trip to Paris without stopping, and upon my return I found my dear boy in good health and looking well and handsome.

CHAPTER TWELVE

1791–1792

RESIDENCE IN HOLLAND

Sojourn at Paris.— Monsieur de La Tour du Pin Leaves the
Ministry of War.— His Son Refuses the Post.— Is Named
as Minister to Holland.— Residence at Rue de Varenne.—
The Flight of the Royal Family.— Departure for Holland.—
The Lameth Family.— Life of Pleasure at The Hague.—
Recall of Monsieur de La Tour du Pin.—Decree against
the Emigrés.— Flight of La Fayette.— Mme. de La Tour
du Pin Returns to France.

I RESUMED my life at Paris, at the Hôtel de la
Guerre. Nearly every morning I rode on horseback accompanied by my cousin, Dominique
Sheldon. I often went to the theatre with young Mme.
de Noailles, whose mother, Mme. Laborde, did not
go out. Every day my father-in-law became more
disgusted with the Ministry. Nearly all the regiments
of the army were in a state of revolt. The greater part
of the officers, instead of opposing the efforts of the
Revolutionists with consistent firmness, sent in their
resignations and left France. Emigration became a
point of honor. The officers who remained with their
regiments received letters from those who had emigrated, reproaching them for cowardice and lack of
attachment to the Royal family. They endeavored to
make them see that it was their duty to abandon
their sovereign. They promised them the interven-

tion of enormous armies of foreigners. The King, whose feebleness was equal to his goodness, hesitated to arrest this torrent. It thus happened that every day saw the departure of some members of his party or even of his household.

My father-in-law, who was powerless against the intrigues of the Assembly, and who did not find in the King the firmness which he had the right to expect, resolved to leave the Ministry. This he did on the fifteenth of November, 1790. It was proposed that my husband should succeed him. He had just finished a plan for the reorganization of the Army, which was entirely his own work. The King himself felt that the author of this plan was capable of putting it in operation. My husband refused. He did not wish to succeed his father for fear that the matter would be misinterpreted.

It was at this time, in the last days of December, 1790, that he was given the place of Minister Plenipotentiary to Holland. It was arranged, however, that he should not join his post before the King had accepted the Constitution, which the National Assembly expected to finish before the end of the winter.

Having left the Hôtel de la Guerre, we went to live in the house of my aunt, Mme. d'Hénin, Rue de Varenne, near the Rue du Bac. She had had transported here all the furniture from the Rue de Verneuil, where she had given up her lease. This house was very convenient. We lived here with my sister-in-law, Mme. de Lameth, her two children and my father-in-law. My husband kept the saddle-horses and a coupé horse for himself. My father-in-law did

not wish to have any carriage. He kept only two
carriage horses for my sister-in-law and myself. Mme.
de Lameth hardly ever went out in the evening, but
she went every morning to the sittings of the Assembly, which were held in the Riding School of the
Tuileries. The National Assembly had taken up its
quarters in this place at the time it was transferred
from Versailles to Paris.

I occasionally went to meetings which I thought
would interest me, but not regularly like my sister-
in-law. My mornings were employed more usefully.
I had a master of design, one of singing, one for
Italian and, if the weather was good, I rode horseback from three o'clock to nightfall. When my cousin
Sheldon was able to accompany me, I went to the
Bois de Boulogne, but more often I went by the Plaine
de Grenelle to the Bois de Meudon, and those days I
rode a thoroughbred who was very lively and whose
manners pleased me very much. But it was difficult
to manage him in the Bois de Boulogne, because he
would not allow another horse before him and was
always ready to run away.

In the spring of 1791 my husband made his preparations to leave for Holland. We packed up our
effects, and our boxes were sent to Rotterdam by sea.
We sold our saddle-horses and set out with our son
and his nurse for Hénencourt where my sister-in-law
was staying. Monsieur de La Tour du Pin came to
pass some time there and then returned to Paris to
finish up his business. At Paris he was informed by
Monsieur Montmorin that the King did not wish
him to leave for his post until the day after the

Constitution, which was to be presented to him, had received the royal sanction. My husband therefore remained at Paris. I went to rejoin him for several days to see the indecent funeral procession of Voltaire when his remains were taken to the Panthéon.

I was living quietly at Hénencourt with my sister-in-law, when my negro servant, Zamore, entered my room at about nine o'clock one morning in a state of great excitement. He informed me that two strangers had passed in front of the gate who stated that the evening before, the King, his children, the Queen and Mme. Elisabeth had left Paris and that it was not known where they had gone. This news troubled me very much, and I wished to speak with these men. I ran to the gate of the court, but they had already disappeared, and no one knew what had become of them.

My anxiety was very great, as I was afraid that my husband might be compromised. Therefore I decided to send Zamore to Paris as a courier to obtain some definite news. An hour later he set out, but before he returned I received by mail a word from my husband which confirmed the news. My brother-in-law returned from Amiens, where he was at the time, and we passed two days in a state of agitation which nothing can describe. Ignorant of the outcome of this adventure, the days seemed like centuries. My brother-in-law would not allow us to go to Amiens for fear that they might close the city gates and that we would not be able to return to the country. We hoped that the King had passed the frontier, but we did not dare to calculate the effect that this event would cause in Paris. My anxiety for my husband was intense, but I did not dare to go to rejoin him because he had forbidden me to do so. On the third day, at evening, we learned by a man who had come from Amiens that the King had been arrested and taken back as a prisoner to Paris. An hour later Zamore arrived bringing a long letter from my husband, who was in despair.

I will not attempt to relate the details of this unfortunate flight, so badly organized. The memoirs of the time have recounted all the circumstances. This whole affair, originated by Monsieur Fersen, who was a fool, was one succession of mistakes and imprudences.

It was only after a seclusion of two months that the King decided to accept the Constitution which had been presented to him. My husband had drawn up a long memorandum, written entirely in his own hand but not signed, in which he implored the King to refuse to sign. This memorandum, which was handed by my husband, personally, to the King, was found after the tenth of August in the famous *Armoire de Fer*. The King had written at the top: "Handed me by Monsieur G—— to advise me to refuse the Constitution." Later it was generally supposed that the initial was that of Monsieur Gouvion who was killed in one of the first combats of the war.

After the acceptance of the Constitution, during the session of the Legislative Assembly there were several months of respite, and I am persuaded that if war had not been declared, if the émigrés had returned as the King seemed to desire, the excesses of the Revolution would have been arrested. But the King and Queen believed in the good faith of the Powers. Every party was deceived, and France saw and found glory in the defence of its territory. As Napoleon said to Sieyès: "Si j'avais été à la place de La Fayette, le roi serait encore sur le trône, et vous, l'abbé, vous seriez trop heureux de me dire la messe."

We set out for The Hague at the beginning of October, 1791. My sister-in-law accompanied us with her two sons and their tutor. My sister-in-law's health was very bad, for the consumption of which she died the following year had already made much progress. As she was very fond of society, the thought of spending the winter alone at Hénencourt was insupportable. She no longer had an establishment at Paris. Until the Revolution she had lived with her whole family at the Hôtel de Lameth, Rue Notre-Dame-des-Champs. There the mother of the four Lameth brothers, who was a sister of Maréchal de Broglie, had brought up her children. The Maréchal had placed the boys in four different regiments, and the three youngest had taken part with distinction in the American war, in which one of them, Charles, had been severely wounded. My husband's brother-in-law, the eldest of the four, had retired to the country, after having resigned as Colonel of the regiment of the Couronne-Infanterie. The second brother, Théodore, also left the army and is still living at the time these lines are written (1841). The third, Charles, had married Mlle. Picot, the only daughter and heir of a planter of Saint-Domingue and lived at Bayonne.

In 1787 the French embassy had been driven from

Holland, and the Comte de Saint-Priest had retired to Antwerp. France was only represented at The Hague by a chargé d'affaires, Monsieur Caillard, who was a consummate diplomat. He was very useful to my husband, who until then had never occupied himself with diplomacy, except in reading history which was his favorite study.

When we arrived at The Hague, in the month of October, 1791, the Stadtholder was at Berlin where he had gone to attend the marriage of his eldest son to the young Princess of Prussia. He returned to The Hague several months later, and then there began a series of fêtes, balls and suppers, and diversions of every kind, which were very pleasant for my twenty-one years. I had brought many elegant things with me from France and I soon became very much in vogue. They tried to copy me in everything. I danced very well and my success at the balls was very great. I enjoyed it like a child. No thought of the morrow bothered me. At all the social reunions I was the first. The Princesse d'Orange did not object to being dressed like me and to have her hair dressed by my valet de chambre. In short, this life of success, which was to last so short a time, intoxicated me.

When Dumouriez was appointed Minister of Foreign Affairs in the month of March, 1792, his first care was to avenge himself for I know not what personal discontent which had been caused him by my father-in-law during the time he was Minister. He therefore recalled my husband under the false pretext that he had not shown sufficient firmness in demanding reparation for a pretended

insult made to the National flag of France. As soon
as we received the news of our recall, we at once
leased a pretty little unfurnished house, for ourselves, my sister-in-law and her children. She did
not wish to return to France and preferred to remain
with me at The Hague. During the day all the furniture which belonged to us, and which we did not wish
to sell, was transported to this house. The rest of
our effects, as well as the wines, the service of porcelain, the horses and carriages, remained at the Hôtel
de France to be placed on sale after the arrival of
the new Minister, in case he did not wish to acquire
them from us. As my husband had no secretary of
legation, because Monsieur Caillard had been sent
to Pétersbourg as chargé d'affaires, he placed the
archives in the hands of his own private secretary,
who was none other than Monsieur Combes, my
former instructor.

Monsieur de La Tour du Pin then left for England
to see my father who had just arrived there, in order
to persuade him to rejoin us at The Hague. From
there he went to Paris, whence he wrote me by every
mail letters which were more and more alarming.

Monsieur de Maulde, who had been appointed
Minister to The Hague, arrived at his post about the
tenth of August and was very badly received. No
one paid any visits to him, except the Ambassador
of England, which power was not yet at war with
France. He did not wish to buy any of our effects,
and sent his secretary to notify me of his refusal to
allow us to have the auction sale of our things held

in the salons of the ground floor of the Hôtel de France.

As the weather was fine, I obtained permission to have the sale of our things held upon the Petit Voorhout, a charming promenade before the door of the Embassy. This auction was an event at The Hague. All my friends were present, and the smallest things were sold at a very high price. I received a sum of money which was more than double what everything had cost us. The proceeds of the sale were put in the hands of Monsieur Molière, a trustworthy Dutch banker. He took care of the money, and later on sent it to me in America.

Mme. d'Hénin, my aunt, had emigrated to England and was very anxious to have me come there and join her, but the health of my sister-in-law was visibly declining and I did not wish to leave her. On the other hand, my father-in-law was thinking of joining us in Holland. My husband passed several days at The Hague between the tenth of August and the massacres of September, 1792. Then his father recalled him to London to be with him.

During the last days of November, 1792, the Convention adopted a decree against the émigrés and fixed a short term in which they could return to France, under pain of confiscation. My excellent father-in-law was in England and was thinking of joining us at The Hague where his daughter and I were awaiting him with impatience. But the news of this decree changed his plans. He wrote us that he was not willing to injure the interests of his children on account of any personal consideration and that he should return to Paris.

I do not know why I neglected to speak of the flight of Messieurs de La Fayette, Alexandre de Lameth and de La Tour-Maubourg. All three secretly left the *corps d'armée* commanded by Monsieur de La Fayette, to pass into foreign territory, with a foolish confidence which it would be difficult to explain. Having presented themselves at the advance posts of the Austrians, they were at once arrested. The Austrians wished to use them as hostages to guarantee the safety of the King and his family, who had been confined in the Temple since the day of the tenth of August. Monsieur Alexandre de Lameth had permission to write to his sister-in-law who was then with me at The Hague, as I have already said, in order to ask for money. Monsieur de La Fayette, for his part, wrote to Mr. Short, the American Minister at The Hague. A man named Dulong, who had been for many years in the service of the French Legation, had undertaken to arrange the escape of Monsieur de La Fayette who was imprisoned at Liège. For this purpose it was necessary for him to have at least 25,000 francs. Mr. Short, although he was a rich man, refused to advance the sum. Accordingly, Monsieur de La Fayette was transferred with his two companions to the prison of Olmutz, where he remained until the Treaty of Campo-Formio (October, 1797).

At the end of the Terror, Mme. de La Fayette went to Vienna, accompanied by her two daughters, and obtained permission from the Emperor of Austria to be shut up at Olmutz with her husband and to undergo all the rigours of his fate. Almost by a miracle, she had escaped the scaffold upon which perished on the same day, (22 July 1794), her grandmother, her mother and her sister. In her voluntary captivity, she showed a resignation and a courage which only religion could have inspired. Nevertheless, she had never been treated by her husband except with the most cruel indifference, and she certainly could not have forgotten the numerous infidelities of which he had been guilty.

My father commanded the *corps d'armée* established in camp between Quesnoy and Valenciennes. At the news of the events of the month of August 1792 at Paris — the attack on the Tuileries and the overthrow of the Monarchy — he had addressed an order of the day to the troops, prescribing the renewal of the oath of fidelity to the King which he himself took at the same time. The result of this noble profession of faith was his removal, the 23 August, 1792, with the order to report at Paris. My endeavors to prevent this remained fruitless and my fears were only too well justified. I have always reproached myself because I did not go to find him and force him to return with me to The Hague. God had decided otherwise! Poor father! He perished on the scaffold, 13 April, 1794.

As I owned a house at Paris, occupied by the Swedish Ambassador, and had an income from the State, or from the City of Paris, my husband was afraid that my name would be put upon the list of émigrés which was about to appear. He therefore sent to me at The Hague a very faithful valet de chambre to accompany me on my return to Paris and charged him to tell me that I would find at the Belgian frontier, several leagues from Antwerp, a former aide de camp of my father, provided with an order to secure my safety, and that this man would escort me if necessary. I made my adieux to my poor sister-in-law, who died two months later, and set out in company with my son, aged two years and a half, my faithful Marguerite, a valet de chambre and my negro, Zamore. The winter which had just commenced rendered the journey very disagreeable.

The first day of December, 1792, buried in the back of an excellent *berline*, well enveloped with furs and bear skins, I left The Hague, to pass the first night, I think, at Gorkum. During the whole day we heard the noise of cannon. My valet de chambre thought that this noise must come from the French who were besieging the city of Antwerp, but that it would take them a long time to capture the city as the garrison was very strong and the city well provisioned. The next day, at Bréda, a city situated also in Holland, there was the same noise of cannonade. As no alarming news was published, I set out, nevertheless, without fear and found, at the Austrian frontier of the Low-Countries, Monsieur Schnetz, a brave officer and friend of my father's whose presence gave me great pleasure. Arrived there the evening before, he had been astonished that there was no news from Antwerp. He said laughingly, but without really believing it, that perhaps the city had been taken. However, about midday, the noise of the cannon having ceased, he then declared that this rampart of the Austrian power had capitulated, which was indeed true. On arriving at the French post, at the exterior gate of the city, we learned that the French were masters of this great fortress. On arriving at the Hôtel du Grand Laboureur upon the large Place Meir, we had much trouble in obtaining a room. It was only due to the intervention of a general, whose name escapes me, that an officer gave up for me the room in which he was already installed, from which he had his baggage taken out with rather bad grace.

In the morning Monsieur Schnetz informed me that we must set out for Mons, where we were to pass the night, as had been arranged. I was so upset by the events of the previous day, that I did not venture to request the privilege of passing the next night at Brussels, which would have permitted me to see my aunt, Lady Jerningham, who was then in this city with her daughter. It was therefore arranged that we should only change horses at Brussels.

In leaving Antwerp, I was struck by the originality of a spectacle new to me. Between the advance lines of the fortifications and the first post, at Contich, we passed through the entire French army, which was in bivouac there. These conquerors, who had already caused the armies of Austria and Prussia to tremble, had all the appearance of a horde of bandits. The greater part were without uniforms. The Convention had had manufactured in haste for the soldiers caps of cloth of the most varied colors, for which they had requisitioned the material from all the shops of Paris and the large cities. The officers

return from England. The house which he occupied was named La Tuilerie. It was isolated and situated between Auteuil and Passy. Fortunately we could go there by byways where we never encountered any one. An old cabriolet and a wretched horse conducted us to Paris, without the necessity of letting the public coachmen into the secret of our retreat.

Every day after our déjeuner, I went to Paris with my husband who was occupied with his own affairs and those of his father. We nearly always took our dinner in the city, either with my father or with Mme. de Montesson whose house was always open to us.

My father who was living in a furnished hotel in the Chaussée-d'Antin was giving all his time to the service of the King, endeavoring to organize the party which was later known as the Girondins. To them he pointed out that their best interests lay in preserving the life of the King, of arranging his escape from Paris, and then of guarding him as hostage in some city of the interior where he would not be able to communicate either with foreign powers, or with the Royalists, who were then commencing to organize in the Vendée. But the party of Terrorists was too strong for any human efforts to thwart its terrible intentions.

My unfortunate father made his strongest efforts with Dumouriez, who came to Paris about the middle of January, but was deceived by the latter with vain promises. Dumouriez was entirely committed to the party of Egalité and his son of whom he boasted that he was the military tutor. His trip to Paris had no other end than that of serving the Orléans Princes.

I will not attempt to relate all of the series of

anxieties and discouragements through which we passed during the month of January, 1793. These events belong to the domain of history and have been related by the historians in the light of their own opinions. My only idea is to clear the memory of my father from the odious imputations with which they have not hesitated to tarnish his honorable character. He only saw the judges of Louis XVI with the hope of saving, if not the liberty, the life of the King; and the very morning of his sentence, he thought it certain that a vote of imprisonment until the end of the war was assured. During this memorable meeting, we remained at home in a state of anxiety which no words can express. When the sentence was known and we had left my father, we still hoped that an insurrection would break out.

The morning of the twenty-first of January, the gates of Paris were closed with orders to make no reply to those who demanded the reason. We understood the meaning of this only too well, and my husband and I, leaning out of the window of our house, which overlooked Paris, listened for the sound of musketry which would bring to us the hope that so great a crime would not be committed without opposition. In a state of stupor, we hardly dared to address a word to each other. Alas, the greatest silence continued to reign in the regicidal city. At half-past ten, the gates were opened and everything resumed its ordinary course. A great nation had stained its annals with a crime for which the centuries would reproach it, and not even the course of life had been changed.

FLIGHT TO BORDEAUX

We set out on foot for Paris, and, taking care not to traverse the Place Louis XV, we went to the house of my father, then to that of Mme. de Montesson, and later to Mme. de Poix.

Returning at an early hour to Passy, we found at our house Mathieu de Montmorency and the Abbé de Damas. Both of them had been on the place of execution with their battalion of the National Guard. Having compromised themselves by some remarks, they had left Paris from the fear of being arrested and had come to demand that we should conceal them until they could leave or return home. They were afraid of a *visite domiciliaire*, the first sign of trouble, which generally preceded by some months the arrest of people who were suspected. In these visits papers of every kind were seized and taken to the Section, where often the most secret correspondence served as a pastime for the young members of the National Guard who were on duty that day.

About the middle of March, my father-in-law was arrested at La Tuilerie and conducted to the Commune of Paris. After answering many questions, he was released. Being more disturbed over the fate of his son than over his own danger, he decided that we ought to retire to Le Bouilh, whence my husband would be able to reach Vendée or with us to escape to Spain. This plan seemed the more feasible, as our excellent friend, Monsieur de Brouquens, had been living at Bordeaux during the past year. In this city, as Food Director, he was in charge of the supplies for our army which was waging war in Spain. We therefore resolved to set out. I left my father with the most profound emotion, although I was far from thinking that I was embracing him for the last time. The difference between our ages, hardly nineteen years, was so little, that he seemed to me more like a brother than like a father. He had an aquiline nose, a very small mouth, large black eyes and light chestnut hair. His tall figure, his handsome face and his superb form gave him all the appearance of youth. No one could have had more noble manners, nor a greater air of *grand seigneur*. He was my best friend and at the same time the comrade of my husband.

My father-in-law was impatient to have us far from Paris and urged us to set out as soon as possible. The first day of April, 1793, we were on our way. It had been decided that we should make short journeys on account of the state of my health.

We finally arrived at Le Bouilh towards the middle of April, and I experienced great joy in finding myself in this place so dear to my poor father-in-law. He had diminished his fortune by the embellishments which he had made and by the buildings which he had constructed. The four months which we passed there have remained in my memory, and above all in my heart, as the pleasantest of my life. There was a fine library and my husband, who could read for hours without fatigue, consecrated our evenings to a course of history and literature which was as interesting as it was instructive. Our happiness was without a cloud and more complete than at any other moment of our past life together.

FLIGHT TO BORDEAUX

The city of Bordeaux, controlled by the Girondins, was in a state of semi-revolt against the Convention. Many of the Royalists had taken part, in the hope of leading the Departments of the Midi, and above all those of the Gironde, to join in the movement which had broken out in the Departments of the West. But Bordeaux was far from possessing the energetic courage of the Vendée. There had been organized in the city an armed troop of eight hundred or one thousand young men of the first families. The instigators of this movement had only one end in view, namely: to declare their independence of Paris and of the Convention and establish on the model of the United States a federal government in the south of France. Monsieur de La Tour du Pin went to Bordeaux where he saw the chiefs of this projected federation and returned disgusted with his interview.

At the end of the summer, we began to be disturbed by the municipality of Saint-André-de-Cubzac. The possibility of a *visite domiciliaire* or the establishment of a garrison in the Château frightened my husband. My father-in-law had just been arrested. Seals had been placed upon the Château of Tesson near Saintes, and the Department of Charente-Inférieure had arbitrarily taken possession for their offices of the fine mansion which we possessed at Saintes. Under these conditions it seemed to us prudent to accept the proposition of our excellent friend, Monsieur de Brouquens, to go and settle in a small house which he possessed at a quarter of a league from Bordeaux. This house, named Canoles, offered every kind of security. It was isolated in the midst of a vineyard surrounded on three sides by parish roads leading in different directions, and on the fourth side by an extensive moor. No village was to be found in the environs, and all this part of the country, called Haut-Brion, comprised an agglomeration of properties, larger or smaller, planted with vines and almost all contiguous. Accordingly, on the first of September, 1793, we went to establish ourselves at Canoles. Here Monsieur de Brouquens came to dine with us every day.

If it had not been for the delicate state of my health, we would have perhaps set out for Spain. Admitting, however, that this departure was possible it would have been necessary for us to pass through the entire French army.

The morning of the thirteenth of September, the Revolutionary Army entered Bordeaux. Less than an hour later all the federal chiefs were arrested and imprisoned. The Revolutionary Tribune immediately began its sessions, and during a period of six months there was not a day passed which did not see the death of some innocent person. A guillotine was permanently established upon the Place Dauphine.

During the course of these events was born my little girl who was named Séraphine, after her father. An hour after her birth my husband was obliged to leave us to seek a place of safety.

Monsieur de Brouquens had hardly returned to his house in Bordeaux when they came to arrest him and conduct him to prison. He protested that he was charged with the details of the administration of the supplies for the army fighting in Spain, that his arrest would greatly compromise this service and in consequence would be strongly disapproved of by the general-in-chief. These good reasons determined the representatives of the people to place him under arrest in his own house. It was indeed a kind of imprisonment, because he was not able to go out, but he had the liberty of a house, which was very large, with several means of escape in case the danger became too imminent. The twenty-five men of the *garde bourgeoise* stationed at his door were almost all from his quarter and under some kind of obligation to him. His goodness and kindness were very great and he was adored in Bordeaux.

It was necessary, however, for him to board these twenty-five men the whole time that he was under arrest, which was during the greater part of the winter. Every day the guards were changed.

The night following the arrest of Monsieur de Brouquens, about midnight, when he was about to go to bed, a municipal officer, followed by the chief of his section and several guards, presented themselves at his house and summoned him to follow them to Canoles where they wished to examine his papers. His trouble and embarrassment were extreme. He knew that my name, my rank in the world, the situation of my father-in-law who had just been confronted with the Queen at Paris, were so many motives for proscription. My fate seemed to him certain, and he was in despair in thinking of my husband who had confided me to his care and whom he tenderly loved. He could not think of any means of avoiding the fate with which I seemed to be menaced. Fortunately, among the members of his guards there was one who was very much attached to him. Divining his perplexity, of his own accord, he came to give the alarm.

I was sleeping quietly when suddenly I felt myself shaken by a faithful old woman, who, in tears and as pale as death cried: "Here are the *coupe-têtes* who are coming to search and attach the seals. We are all lost!" In saying these words, she pushed under my pillow a large packet and disappeared as suddenly as she had come. I felt of the package and recognized that it was a sack containing five or six hundred louis, of which Monsieur de Brouquens had spoken to me, and which he kept in reserve, in case of urgent necessity, either for himself or for Monsieur de La Tour du Pin or me. This bag of money was not reassuring. Nevertheless, I did not dare, in taking it from its hiding place, to let it be seen by the girl who was caring for my child. Not only was I suspicious of her, but the physician had discovered that she was playing the rôle of a spy.

A half an hour later, the visitors arrived. After carefully examining the exterior of the house, they entered the salon. The blood froze in my veins when I thought of all the dangers to which I was exposed. Every moment I expected to hear a hand placed upon my door. Finally, I distinctly heard some one ask: "Who is in this room?" Monsieur de Brouquens replied in a whisper and I could not hear the words.

Later he explained to me that the inspiration had come to him to state that a young girl, whom some friends had confided to him, was in the room and that she was in a delicate condition and very ill. No one entered my room, and at the end of two hours, after having drunk and eaten everything there was in the house, they went away, taking their prisoner with them.

I remained alone at Canoles with my worthy physician, who commenced to feel reassured, although all danger had not passed.

Every evening upon my request the good doctor read the papers to me. The news then was something terrible, and became even more so for me when we found the report of the confrontation of my worthy father-in-law with the Queen. In these reports was described the wrath of Fouquier-Tinville when Monsieur de La Tour du Pin continued to name her "The Queen," or "Her Majesty," instead of "Femme Capet," as the public prosecutor wished. My fear reached its height when I learned that in answer to the question as to where his son was, Monsieur de La Tour du Pin had replied with simplicity that he was on his estate, near Bordeaux. The result of this reply was an order, sent the same day, to Saint-André-de-Cubzac, to arrest my husband and send him to Paris.

He was at Le Bouilh, and there was only an hour to save him. Fortunately, in anticipation of this eventuality, and under the pretext of having a farm to visit, he kept quite a good horse ready in the stable. Disguising himself as well as possible, he set out with the intention of gaining the estate of Tesson, near to Saintes, and concealing himself in the Château. The house was under sequestration but was in charge of an excellent care-taker and his wife. He was not short of money as he had from 10,000 to 12,000 francs in *assignats*. He rode all night long. The weather was terrible. The rain fell in torrents and the thunder did not cease to rumble. The flashes of lightning blinded and frightened his horse who was quite a lively beast.

In leaving Saint-Genis, upon the route from Blaye to Saintes, a man who was standing before a small house addressed him. "What weather, citizen! Would you like to enter and let the storm pass?" Monsieur de La Tour du Pin consented. He dismounted and tied his horse to a little shed, situated fortunately for him, as you will see later on, very near to the door. He entered the house where he found an old man occupying the corner of the fire-place. A quarter of an hour passed in conversation upon the dearness of grains and cattle. At this point the individual who had been seated near the fire issued from the house and returned ten minutes later wearing a scarf. It was the Mayor. "Citizen, you undoubtedly have a passport," he said to my husband. "Why certainly," replied the latter. "No one travels without that." So saying, my husband produced a false passport in the name of Gouvernet, of which he had made use in going and coming between Saint-André and Bordeaux. "But," declared the Mayor, after examination, "your passport has no visé to go into Charente-Inférieure. Remain here until morning. I will consult the Municipal Council." Then he resumed his place.

My husband felt that he was lost if he did not take his courage in both hands. During this conversation the master of the house, who appeared to be very much bored, had approached the opened door, and now remarked in a loud tone, as though speaking to himself: "Ah! the weather has all cleared up." My husband at that time was only thirty-four years of age, was extremely quick, and could rival in point of address the most practised horseman. After hearing the above remark of the master of the house, he arose quietly and approached the door which had remained open. Extending his arm out in the obscurity of the night, he unfastened the bridle of his horse. In a single bound he was on the back of the horse and, putting the spurs to him, had escaped before the poor Mayor had had the time to leave his seat beside the fire and reach the door of the house.

Monsieur de La Tour du Pin did not dare to pass through Pons where there was a fair during the day. He stopped at Mirambeau with the former groom of his father, who inhabited this locality and in whom he had confidence. This man had a little inn and conducted a stage which went to Saintes once a week. Têtard, which was his name, offered to conceal him, but he had young children, and was afraid of their indiscretion. He therefore proposed to my husband to demand an asylum with his brother-in-law, a rich locksmith, who was married but had no children. The latter consented, upon the payment of quite a large sum, and the bargain was concluded. My husband was hidden at the house in a closet without windows, connected with the bedroom which was also used as a kitchen.

I have since visited this horrible hole. A thin flooring alone separated it from the shop where the employés worked and where were situated the forge and bellows. When the locksmith and his wife left their room they always took away the key, and it was necessary for my husband to remain stretched upon his bed and not make the slightest noise. They had also recommended to him not to have any light from fear that it might be perceived from without, but, as soon as the shop was closed, my husband descended to supper with the man and his wife. The groom often brought news, frequently newspapers and also books which he went to Tesson to obtain.

It was in this way that my poor husband passed the first three months of our separation. The postmaster of Saintes, upon whose devotion he could count, advised him to go to Vendée, but aside from the extreme difficulty of passing through the lines of the Republican troops, my husband was not willing to go there under an assumed name, and, by rejoining openly the Vendéens, he would have only made certain the death of his father and myself.

CHAPTER FOURTEEN

1793–1794

LIFE AT BORDEAUX

The Seals at Le Bouilh.— Refuge at Bordeaux with Bonie.—
The Pain de la Section.— The Queue at the Door of the
Butchers and Bakers.— Arrest of the English and Americans.— A Belle Grisette.— Unexpected Protection.— Mme.
Tallien.— Interview with Tallien.— Monsieur de La Tour
du Pin Takes Refuge at Tesson.— New Flight.—Return
to Tesson.— The Cartes de Sûreté.

A MEMORANDUM had been presented to
the municipality of Saint-André-de-Cubzac
going to show that the estate of Le Bouilh
was a royal domain. Without any further information, the commissioners were sent to Le Bouilh
where they placed the seals with such prodigality
that there was not a single door which could be
opened. However, an excellent girl whom I had left
at the Château had already concealed the most
valuable effects which I had there, in the way of
linen and so forth, and brought them to me at
Bordeaux each week in small packets.

About this time I began to fear that my prolonged
sojourn with Monsieur de Brouquens was attracting
too much attention. Above all, I feared that my
presence at his house would end by compromising
him. This situation was often the subject of my

[151]

conversations with a relative of Monsieur de Brouquens, Monsieur de Chambeau, who was himself
suspected and obliged to hide. He had found a very
retired place of refuge with an individual who kept
a little obscure hôtel, Place Puy-Paulin. This individual, young and active, a widower with a single
child whom he had confided to his mother-in-law,
lived entirely alone in this hôtel with a single domestic.
This man, whose name was Bonie, pretended to be
a furious demagogue. He wore a vest of coarse plush,
called *carmagnole*, sabots and a sabre. He went to the
meetings of the Section, to the Jacobins' Club and
"thoued" every one.

Monsieur de Chambeau spoke to him of my anxieties. I did not know where I could retire. My husband was in flight, my father and father-in-law were
prisoners, my house had been seized and my only
friend, Monsieur de Brouquens, was under arrest at
his own house. At twenty-four years of age, with two
little children, what was to become of me?

Bonie came to see me at Canoles and was interested
in my sad situation. He proposed that I take refuge
with him. His house was vacant and Monsieur de
Brouquens advised me not to reject his offer. I therefore accepted. He gave me an apartment which was
very sombre and very dilapidated, with an outlook
upon a little garden. Here I installed myself with my
two children, their nurse and my dear Marguerite,
who was continually tormented by a fever which
nothing seemed to cure. My negro, Zamore, passed
for a free black who was awaiting the moment to
join the army.

The location of my own apartment enabled me to enjoy my music, without the danger of being overheard. As I was alone a great deal of the time, this was a great distraction for me. I knew a very good music teacher named Ferrari, of Italian origin, who had stated and also proved to me that he was an agent of the Royal Princes. He was very *spirituel* and original and had much talent.

My room which was quite large was reached through a kind of wood-house in which I had had piled up a large lot of wood which had been brought from Le Bouilh, unknown to the guardian there. This wood was brought by our peasants who took it in my interest. A woman of the country, who was entirely devoted to us, also came to Bordeaux twice a week to sell vegetables. She led a donkey which bore paniers half-full of linen and clothing which were covered with cabbages and potatoes. She was adroit enough to make the employés of the *octroi* believe that these objects had been taken from enemies of the people. Sometimes she made them a present of some articles and brought the rest to me.

My husband found means of writing me, by a boy who came to Bordeaux each week. His letter, which was without address, was concealed in a loaf of bread which the child brought to the Place Puy-Paulin ostensibly for the nurse. As he arrived at a fixed hour, the cook awaited him at the time of high tide. This poor child, fifteen years of age, was ignorant of the subterfuge. They had simply told him that there was a nurse in the house whom the physician had forbidden to eat the bread of the Section.

This *pain de section* was composed of all kinds of flour, was black and sticky, and one would hesitate now to give it even to the dogs. It was delivered hot from the furnace, and every one was forced to place himself in line to obtain it. It was a very singular thing, however, that the people found a sort of pleasure in this assemblage. As the terror under which they lived hardly permitted them to exchange a word with those whom they met in the street, this "queue" represented, so to speak, an authorized meeting where they could speak with their neighbors and learn the news without being exposed to the imprudence of a question.

I do not recall under what circumstances all the English and American merchants residing at Bordeaux were arrested. This measure gave me the well-founded fear of being taken for an Englishwoman, which had often happened. Bonie was seriously alarmed and advised me no longer to wear a hat when I went out during the day but to dress myself like the women of Bordeaux. This idea of disguise was not disagreeable. I ordered some brassières which were well suited to my form, very slight at that time, and which with the red handkerchief upon my head changed me so completely that I encountered people of my acquaintance without being recognized. Monsieur de Brouquens, who was still in confinement, was very much amused at the comments of his twenty-five guardians upon the daily visits which he received from the *belle grisette*.

Nevertheless, my position at Bordeaux became more perilous from day to day, and I cannot understand now how I escaped death. I was advised to endeavor to have the *séquestre* of Le Bouilh raised, but any manifestation of my existence seemed to me too dangerous, and I was in a state of the most desperate uncertainty when Providence sent me a special protection.

Mme. de Fontenay, who was then called Thérésia Cabarrus, arrived at Bordeaux. Four years before I had met her once at Paris. Mme. Charles de Lameth, with whom she had been a pupil in a convent, pointed her out to me one evening in coming out of the theatre. She did not seem to me at the time to be more than fourteen or fifteen years of age and only left in my mind the remembrance of a child. It was said that she had divorced her husband to preserve her fortune, but it was rather to use and abuse her liberty. Having met Tallien at the Baths of the Pyrenees, he had rendered her some kind of service of which I am ignorant, which she had rewarded with an unlimited devotion which she took no pains to disguise. She had come to Bordeaux to rejoin him and was quartered at the Hôtel d'Angleterre.

On the day following her arrival, I wrote her the following note: "A lady who has met Mme. de Fontenay at Paris, and who knows that she is as good as she is beautiful, requests a moment of interview." She replied verbally that this lady could come whenever she wished. A half hour later I was at her door. When I entered, she came to me, and looking me in the face cried: "Grand Dieu! Madame de Gouvernet!" Then having embraced me with effusion, she put herself at my service. (This was her expression.) I explained to her my situation. She considered it more dangerous than I had thought it myself and declared that the only means of saving myself was to fly as soon as possible. I told her that I could not make up my mind to leave without my husband. She said, "You must see Tallien. He will advise you as to the course to adopt. You will be safe here as soon as he knows that you are the object of my interest." I determined to solicit from Tallien the lifting of the *séquestre* of Le Bouilh in the name of my children, also the permission to retire there with them. Then I left her, with a feeling of confidence from the interest she had shown, and at the same time asking myself why she was interested in me.

Mme. de Fontenay was then not more than twenty years of age. A more beautiful human being had never issued from the hands of the Creator. She was a perfect woman. All her features bore the imprint of the most regular and artistic perfection. Her hair, black as ebony, seemed made of the finest silk, and nothing detracted from the brilliancy of her complexion which was clear as ivory. An enchanting smile displayed the most admirable teeth. Her tall form recalled that of Diane Chasseresse. The least movements revealed an incomparable grace, while her voice, which was harmonious and slightly marked with a foreign accent, exercised a charm which no words can express. You could not help feeling sad when you thought that so much youth, beauty, grace and spirit was abandoned to the man who, every morning, signed the death warrant of many innocent persons.

The following morning I received from Mme. de Fontenay this message: "This evening at ten o'clock." I passed the day in a state of agitation difficult to describe. Arming myself with all my courage, at nine o'clock I took the arm of Monsieur de Chambeau, who was more alarmed than myself, without daring to show it. He conducted me to the door of Mme. de Fontenay where he left me with the promise to walk up and down on the boulevard until the moment when I came out.

Tallien had not yet arrived and the moment of waiting was full of anguish. Mme. de Fontenay could not talk with me as there were several persons present whom I did not know. Finally we heard the carriage, and it was impossible to be mistaken, for it was the only one which rolled in the streets of this large city. Mme. de Fontenay went out and returned in a moment. She took my hand saying: "He awaits you." If she had announced to me that the executioner was there, I could not have had a different feeling. She opened a door upon a little passageway, at the end of which I saw a lighted room. As I hesitated involuntarily, Mme. de Fontenay gave me a push in the back, and said: "Go ahead! Do not act like a child." Then she turned and went away, closing the door. It was necessary for me to advance, but I did not dare to raise my eyes. Nevertheless, I walked to the corner of the chimney-piece, upon which there were two lighted candles. Without the support of the marble I should have fallen. Tallien was leaning on the other corner. He said in a voice that was quite soft: "What do you wish of me?" Then I stammered the request to be allowed to go to our country estate of Le Bouilh and that the seals which had been placed there by error should be taken from the property of my father-in-law, with whom I had resided. Brusquely he replied that all this was none of his affair. Then he said: "But you are then the daughter-in-law of this man who was confronted with the woman Capet? . . . And you have a father? . . . What is his name? . . . Ah! Dillon, the General? . . . All the enemies of the Republic will pass like this," he added, making at the same time with his hand the gesture of cutting off a head. I was overcome with indignation which gave me back all my courage. I raised my eyes to look at this monster whom I had not yet regarded. Before me I saw a man of twenty-five or twenty-six, with a fine face which he endeavored to render severe. A mass of blond curls escaped from all sides under a large military hat covered with varnished cloth and surmounted by a tricolored plume. He was dressed in a long tight overcoat of coarse blue cloth, over which hung a sabre by a shoulder belt which was crossed by a long silk scarf of the three colors. "I have not come here, citizen," said I, "to hear the sentence of death of my family, and since you cannot accord me what I have demanded, I must not trouble you longer." At the same time I gave him a slight salute with my head. He smiled as if to say: "You are very rash to talk to me in this manner." Then I went out by the door by which I had entered without going again to the salon.

On my return home, I felt that my position was

aggravated rather than helped. If Tallien did not help me, my fate appeared to me certain.

Towards the middle of the winter, the locksmith with whom my husband was concealed arrived at Bordeaux to purchase iron. He came to see me and I showed him my appreciation and my confidence. I also let him see my children so that he would be able to tell their father that he had found them in good health. He was a good peasant of Saintonge, but very simple and ignorant and understanding nothing of the state of the country. He could not comprehend why they were able to eat excellent white bread at Mirambeau, while that which they had given him that morning at Bordeaux was so black that his dog would have refused it. While waiting for the tide to turn, so that he could return to Blaye, he walked in Bordeaux, and unfortunately passed the Place Dauphine where executions were taking place. A lady mounted the scaffold and he demanded what was her crime. "She is an aristocrat," they replied. Soon he saw a peasant like himself called upon to submit to the same fate. Again he demanded the reason and it was explained that this man had given asylum to a nobleman and that for this reason only he was condemned to die with him.

The poor man forgot what had brought him to Bordeaux. He set out to return on foot, and on his arrival home during the night, he at once announced to my husband that he could not guard him for another hour, as his own life and that of his wife were in danger. He ran to wake up his brother-in-law, the groom, who could not succeed in reassuring him. It was decided that they should attach a horse to a little chariot, at the bottom of which they put some straw in which my husband was concealed. Then they departed, through round-about roads, for Tesson, the château of my father-in-law, upon which the seals had been placed, but to which the concierge Grégoire and his wife had a secret entrance. One of the windows of the pavilion which they occupied looked out upon the road. The groom rapped at a shutter, which they opened, and my husband entered by this window, and was received by these worthy people with exclamations of pleasure. He was installed in a room adjoining their own, with a chimney in common. This permitted them to have a fire every day without attracting attention without, which was very much appreciated by my husband who was very chilly.

At Tesson there was an excellent library. The inventory of this and also of the furniture of the Château had not yet been taken. The seals had been placed only upon the exterior doors, so that it was possible to go anywhere in the house as long as the Venetian blinds were not opened. My husband therefore had access to all the books he wished to read. He even found means of withdrawing papers and old correspondence of his father, the publication of which would have been disagreeable. However, he was not destined to enjoy this retreat, which was comparatively comfortable, without trouble.

At the end of seven or eight days orders arrived at the municipality of Tesson that they should at

Le Conventionnel TALLIEN

1767 - 1820

once proceed with the inventory of all that was contained in the Château, which was large and very well furnished. The father of my husband had inherited this property from Monsieur de Monconseil, his father-in-law, who had lived there for forty years and had furnished it in a sumptuous and magnificent manner of the time of Louis XIV. This inventory would take about two days and it was impossible to expect that any corner of the Château would escape the vigilance of the visitors.

Grégoire did not disguise his fears from my unfortunate husband. He declared that he did not know a place where he could conceal him, or a person in the village or the neighborhood who would be willing to receive him. It was therefore agreed that Grégoire should go to Saintes to see Boucher, the postmaster, a former *écuyer* of Monsieur de Monconseil, who was very much attached to my husband, whom he had known when very young at his grandfather's, and request him to receive the fugitive at his house. Grégoire set out early in the morning on foot in very bad weather, although he was over seventy years of age. He did not find Boucher at home, but his sister, who was equally devoted to our interests, consented to receive my husband and conceal him during the absence of her brother. Grégoire accordingly returned to Tesson without having taken any rest. That very night he again set out with my husband for Saintes, a locality where there were no walls and which was consequently accessible by byways known to Grégoire.

I have omitted to say before that I had sent my

husband, during the time that he was at Mirambeau, a complete costume of a peasant of the Revolutionary period, in which he could hardly recognize himself.

Mlle. Boucher received him very well but with an exaggeration of precautions from which he drew the conclusion that the shorter the time he remained in the house the better she would like it.

The inventory at Tesson having been finished at the end of three days, it was possible for my husband to return.

CHAPTER FIFTEEN
1794
DECISION TO LEAVE FRANCE

Alarming Situation of Mme. de La Tour du Pin at Bordeaux and of Her Husband at Tesson.— Certificates of Residence with Nine Witnesses.— Decision to Leave for America.— The American Vessel "Diane."— Preparations for Departure.— On the Arm of Tallien.— Passport of the Citizen Latour.— Anxiety over the Delay.— Return of Monsieur de La Tour du Pin.— How He Came Back from Tesson.

HOWEVER, the situation became more alarming from hour to hour. Not a day passed without executions. I was lodged sufficiently near the Place Dauphine to hear the drum, the roll of which marked each head that fell. I could count them before the evening papers told me the names of the victims. The window of my room looked out on the garden, the end of which touched an old church in which was established the Club of the *Amis du peuple*, and when the evening session was animated, the applause and vociferations of the miserable creatures who were present reached even to my room.

The news which I received of my husband depicted his situation at Tesson as most precarious. At every moment Grégoire was menaced with the establishment in the Château of a body of troops, or a military hospital, or something similar, which would have obliged my husband to flee again.

I did not know of any other place where he could be in greater security. I could not think of recalling him to Bordeaux, near me, on account of the girl who took care of my child. I had been told again that it was impossible to trust her. Nevertheless, I did not dare to send her away for fear of worse.

Another circumstance had proved to me that I was not forgotten at Bordeaux, as much as I had hoped. My man-of-affairs had written me from Paris that a law had just been adopted requiring *certificats de résidence* with nine witnesses, and that it was necessary to renew these *certificats* every three months under pain of the confiscation of the property which you possessed in the communes where you did not reside. I had a house at Paris, occupied by the Swedish Ambassador, and an income from the State which had already been reduced by a third. It was therefore necessary for me to obtain this certificate. Bonie took charge of getting together the nine witnesses, none of whom had ever seen me in their lives, but who were willing to believe his word. By arrangement, we went to the municipality one morning. Here I was seated near the fire while Bonie had the act drawn up and obtained the signatures of the witnesses. Finally the moment for me to sign arrived and the municipal officer, with a kind of respect which astonished me, gave me a chair to use while signing. Then to my great alarm the certificate was read from one end to the other in a loud voice, and at the name of Dillon, one of these rascals interrupted by saying: "Ah! ah! the citizeness is apparently sister or niece of all the émigrés of this name whom we have upon our list?" I was going to reply in the negative, when the head of the Bureau said brusquely, "You do not know what you are talking about. She is not even their relative." I looked at him in surprise, and he said to me in a low tone, while giving me the pen to sign: "You are the niece of the Archbishop of Narbonne. I am from Sorèze." I thanked him with a slight inclination of the head, but I thought as I went away that it was necessary to leave Bordeaux since I was so well known.

I felt at the end of my resources. I saw that Bonie was disturbed over my fate. Several means of escape had been recognized as impossible. Every day some one was executed who had thought he was in safety. My nights were passed without sleep, as I thought at every noise that they were coming to arrest me. I hardly dared any longer to leave the house. I was afraid of falling sick at the moment when I never had had greater use for my health, in order to be strong enough to act, if this was found necessary. Finally, one morning, going to see Monsieur de Brouquens, who was still under arrest at his house, I was leaning pensively upon the table, when my eyes were mechanically drawn to a morning paper which was open. Here I read under the commercial news: "The ship 'Diane' of Boston, 150 tons, will leave in eight days in ballast with the permission of the Minister of Marine." Without saying a word, I immediately got up and was leaving when Monsieur de Brouquens raised his eyes and said: "Where are you going then so quickly?" "I am going to America," I replied as I went out.

I went directly to see Mme. de Fontenay whom I advised of my resolution. She approved of my plan, especially as she had just had bad news from Paris. Tallien had been denounced there by his colleague and was likely to be recalled at any moment. This recall she thought would probably be the signal for a new outbreak of cruelty at Bordeaux, where she herself did not wish to remain if Tallien left. There was therefore not a moment to lose if we wished to be saved.

I returned to my house and called Bonie, to whom I said that it was necessary to find me a man in whom he had confidence, to go in search of my husband. He did not hesitate a moment. He said: "The commission is perilous, but I know a man who can undertake it, and that man is myself." He assured me that he would succeed, and I had confidence in his zeal and his intelligence. He hazarded his life, which would have been sacrificed with that of my husband if they had been discovered; but as in this case my own would not have been spared, I did not feel any scruples in accepting his proposition.

I did not lose an instant. I went to find an old ship-owner, a friend of my father's, who was also a ship-broker. He was very devoted to me and agreed to go and arrange passage on the "Diane" for myself, my husband and our two children. I should have liked to take Marguerite with me, but for a period of six months already she had had a double intermittent fever, and no remedy seemed to cure her. I was afraid that a sea voyage at this bad season of the year, as we were in the last days of February, might be fatal to her. I therefore resolved to leave without her. When I returned to see Monsieur de Brouquens, having already arranged everything, his surprise was very great. He then told me that he had just been restored to liberty by an order from Paris and that he was counting on leaving in several days. He proposed to me to go the following day to Canoles for luncheon, to which place he had not returned since the *visite domiciliaire.*

Once more at my own residence, I placed my confidence in my good Zamore, for the most difficult thing was to arrange to pack our effects without the knowledge of the maid, who would immediately have denounced us to the Section. She slept with my little girl, then six months of age, in a long room lined with wardrobes in which I had placed all the things which had been sent me from Le Bouilh, as well as those which I had brought from there myself, when I came to take up my residence at Canoles. This room was between my own and that of Marguerite. The latter had an exit on a little staircase which descended to the cellar. Fortunately, having no confidence in this maid, I had always kept the wardrobes closed. I therefore arranged with Zamore that on the following morning, while I was at Canoles, where I would take with me the maid and the children, he should get out all my things and take them down to the cellar by the little stairway, and there pack them in the boxes which he would find. I especially charged him not to leave on the floor even a piece of thread, the sight of which might reveal to the maid that the wardrobes had recently been opened. He executed this commission with his usual intelligence.

The next day I went in company with Monsieur de Chambeau to luncheon at Canoles at the house of Monsieur de Brouquens. While we three were at the table the gate of the garden opened and we saw Mme. de Fontenay enter on the arm of Tallien. My surprise was very great as she had not told me of her plan. Brouquens was stupified but soon recovered himself. As for myself I endeavored to conceal my emotion at the sight of a man who had entered behind Tallien. He had placed a finger upon his lips on looking at me, and I immediately turned my eyes away. This was Monsieur de Jumilhac, whom I knew well, and who, concealed at Bordeaux under another name, accompanied Tallien. The latter, after a polite remark to Brouquens regarding the liberty which he had taken to pass through his garden to go to the house of the Swedish Consul, came to me with the polite bearing of a *seigneur* of the *ancienne cour*, and said to me in the most gracious manner: "I am told, Madame, that I am in a position to-day to repair my faults with regard to you. I am entirely at your disposal." Accordingly, laying aside the air of cold disdain which I had formerly assumed towards him, with an expression sufficiently polite, I explained that having some pecuniary interests at Martinique, I desired to go there to look after my affairs, and that I would like to ask him for a passport for myself, my husband and my children. He replied: "But where then is your husband?" I said, laughing, "Permit me, citizen representative, not to tell you." "As you wish," said he, gayly. The monster was very amiable. His beautiful mistress had threatened to see

[168]

him no longer if he did not save me, and this menace had enchained his cruelty for the moment.

After several minutes of conversation, they spoke of going to the house of the Swedish Consul. I excused myself from going under the pretext that I must look after my children whom the maid had brought to Canoles. But Mme. de Fontenay, looking at me with her big black eyes, said: "Venez donc!" and I understood with horror what was about to happen. She herself took the arm of M. de Brouquens and Tallien offered me his. I do not know how to express what I felt at this moment. If only my own life had been in question, and if that of my husband had not depended upon my taking the arm which he offered me, I should have refused. I therefore accepted and took advantage of the moment to arrange my affair definitely.

The poor Swedish Consul and his charming daughter were more dead than alive at receiving this amiable visit from the representative of the people. We entered the billiard room, where Tallien played two or three games, including one with poor Brouquens, who missed nearly all his strokes, although he was a very good player.

Finally Tallien declared that he had an engagement and that he was obliged to leave. He took out his watch and looked at the time. "You have there a pretty watch," said Mme. de Fontenay. "Yes," he replied. "It is one of the new watches of Breguet and is worth from seven to eight thousand francs. Would you like to have it?" he added in offering it to her. "Ah! merci!" she said, as if he had offered her a flower, and taking the watch she put it in her bag.

This incident caused me a profound disgust, for it was the act of a corrupted *courtisane*.

This visit finished, we returned, Brouquens and I, to Canoles, for Monsieur de Chambeau had concealed himself upon the arrival of Tallien. When we were alone, the alteration in the face of Brouquens struck me. He threw himself upon a sofa in a great state of agitation, and in a reply to my question as to the cause of his trouble, he said: "Alas, you saw the watch which was given by Tallien to Mme. de Fontenay. Well, it belonged to poor Saige! (The name of the former Mayor of Bordeaux, an intimate friend of Brouquens, and one of the first victims of The Terror at Bordeaux.) When he was condemned he placed this watch upon the desk of the tribunal, saying: 'Take it, I do not wish to have the executioner profit by it.' And Tallien took it and put it in his pocket."

It is easy to comprehend the repulsion which this recital inspired in me. I would like to believe that the citizeness Thérésia was ignorant of this fact when she accepted the present.

Two hours after my return to Bordeaux, Alexandre, the secretary of Tallien, brought me the order enjoining upon the municipality of Bordeaux to deliver a passport to the citizen Latour and his wife with two young children, to go to Martinique on board the ship "Diane." Once furnished with this precious paper, it only remained for me to recall my husband to Bordeaux, for the American captain would not have been willing to take him on board if these papers had not been in order.

DECISION TO LEAVE FRANCE

This journey from Tesson to Bordeaux was full of difficulties and dangers. As I have already said above, Bonie did not hesitate a moment and set out for Blaye with the falling tide. He had already procured a regular passport for himself, for without that he could not leave the department and enter that of Charente-Inférieure, in which was located Tesson, ten leagues from the frontier of the Gironde. But as soon as he returned to the Gironde, a simple *carte de sûreté* would be sufficient for him to travel anywhere in the department. Bonie had indeed his personal *carte de sûreté*, but it was necessary to procure one for my husband. He therefore went to find one of his friends, who for the moment was sick, and under the pretext that he had mislaid his own card, he borrowed the card of his friend for several days. Bonie set out that evening.

I had calculated the moments that would be necessary to accomplish this perilous journey, and the third day, towards nine o'clock in the evening, I thought that the boat which came every day from Blaye with the tide would bring to me the travelers so anxiously awaited. The fever of impatience which devoured me would not permit me to remain in the house. With Monsieur de Chambeau I went upon the Chartrons to the place where I knew the Blaye boat should arrive. The darkness was so profound that it was impossible to see the water in the river. I did not dare to ask for any information, as I knew that all the points on the river were observed by numerous police spies. Finally, after a long wait, we heard the clock strike the hour of nine-thirty, and Monsieur de Chambeau, who had no *carte de sûreté*, remarked to me that we had only a half hour to return to the house without danger. Having lost all hope for that day, I returned to the house where I passed the night in imagining with anguish all the obstacles which might have delayed Bonie and his unfortunate companion.

While I was trembling thus with anxiety and impatience, my husband was sleeping quietly upon a comfortable bed prepared for him by Bonie before his departure, in one of the unoccupied rooms of the house. In the morning the maid, when she came to dress my little girl, said to me, with an indifferent air: "A propos, madame, Monsieur Bonie est là qui demande si vous êtes levée." I made a prodigious effort not to cry out, and the reader can understand that my toilette was not long. Bonie then entered and informed me that they had arrived too late at Blaye to take the ordinary boat, upon which my husband also might have been recognized. He had chartered a fishing bark, and the wind being favorable and very strong, he had set out with his companion and soon overtaken and then passed the ordinary boat. They had therefore already arrived when I was waiting for them in a state of despair upon the bank of the river.

I was dying with impatience to enter the room where my husband was concealed, but Bonie advised me to dress as if I were going out, so as to deceive the maid. Finally, a half hour later, I went out under the pretext of doing some shopping, and Bonie having rejoined me, he conducted me by a secret staircase to my husband's room. It was thus that we met after six months of the most painful separation.

CHAPTER SIXTEEN

1794

VOYAGE TO BOSTON

Delivery of the Passport.— The Visé by Ysabeau.— Monsieur de Fontenay and His Wife's Diamonds.— Final Preparations.— Adieux to Marguerite.— Monsieur de Chambeau Accompanies Us.— Embarkment on the "Diane."— The Boat and Its Equipment.— Off the Azores.— The Pilot.— The Port of Boston.— Joy at Arriving.

I HAVE already related how I took out, two months before, a certificate of residence with nine witnesses under the name of Dillon Gouvernet. It was now necessary to go and obtain a passport under the name of Latour, and to avoid the name of Dillon which was too well known at Bordeaux, I decided to replace the name of Dillon with that of Lee, which my uncle Lord Dillon had added to his own when he received the inheritance of Lord Lichfield, his great-uncle. It was impossible to draw back. The bureau of passports was closed at nine o'clock and we went there at eight-thirty. The date was the eighth of March, 1794. My husband walked quite a distance ahead with Bonie. I followed, accompanied by a friend of the latter, who carried in his arms my little girl, six months of age, and led by the hand my son who was not then four years old. On account of the English or American name which I wished to take, I was dressed as a lady, but very badly gotten up and wearing an old straw hat. We entered the hall of the Hôtel de Ville which was full of people. I was trembling with fear lest some inhabitant of Saint-André-de-Cubzac or of Bordeaux should recognize us. We therefore took care, Monsieur de La Tour du Pin and I, to keep as far apart from one another as possible and to avoid the lighted part of the hall.

Furnished with this card, we ascended to the bureau of passports, and as we entered we heard the employé cry out: "That is enough for today, the rest tomorrow." Any delay would have cost our lives, as you will see. Bonie rushed up to the desk and said: "If you are tired, citizen, I will write for you." The other consented and Bonie made out the collective passport for the Latour family.

As soon as the passport was signed, we took it with keen satisfaction, although we were still very far from being saved. It had been arranged, in order that we should not both be found in the same house, and to avoid the necessity of passing through Bordeaux the following morning in full daylight, that Monsieur de La Tour du Pin should pass the night with the Consul of Holland, Monsieur Meyer, who lived in the last house of the Chartrons, and who was entirely devoted to us. Monsieur de Brouquens was waiting for us in the street and conducted my husband there. As for myself, after having taken the children back to the house, I went to see Mme. de Fontenay, where I expected to see Tallien who had to visé our passport. I found her in tears. Tallien had received the order of his recall and had already left two hours

MADAME TALLIEN

née Thérésia Cabarrus

1773 - 1835

before. She herself was to leave in the morning and she did not conceal from me her fears that the ferocious Ysabeau, the colleague of Tallien, would refuse to visé our passport. But Alexandre, the secretary of Tallien, assured us that he would obtain the visé. He said that Ysabeau always signed on leaving the theatre, and that as he was in haste to have his supper, he hardly regarded the papers which were presented to him. Providence in its kindness had wished that Ysabeau should demand of Tallien to leave with him his secretary Alexandre, who not only was very useful to him but had also the address to render himself necessary.

At the moment that I entered the house of Mme. de Fontenay, Alexandre left to go and get the signature. He took the passport and slipped it in between a number of others. Ysabeau who was very much taken up that day with the arrival of his new colleague, whom he looked for in the morning, signed without paying any attention, and as soon as Alexandre was at liberty to leave, he ran to Mme. de Fontenay's where I was waiting more dead than alive. I was not there alone, for a person whom I did not know had entered. This man was no other than Monsieur de Fontenay. At this moment, Alexandre arrived holding the passport unfolded in his hand. He was so out of breath that he fell on a chair without being able to articulate more than the words "Le voilà!" Mme. de Fontenay and I embraced him with all our hearts, for he was our real *sauveur*.

Alexandre was getting ready to leave and, as it was nearly midnight, I also prepared to leave with him. Mme. de Fontenay kept me for a moment by saying that she would have me escorted, but that before I left she wished to show me something very pretty. I followed her into her bedroom where Monsieur de Fontenay, who was still silent, accompanied us. From a drawer she took out a handkerchief and laid it upon the table. Then opening a handsome jewel-case, she took out a collection of diamonds of the greatest magnificence and threw them upon the handkerchief pell-mell. When she had thus emptied all the drawers of the jewel-box, without leaving the least thing, she tied up the ends of the handkerchief and handed it to Monsieur de Fontenay with these words: "Prenez tout." And he indeed took all and went out without opening his mouth. I showed my great surprise and she replied to my thought by saying: "He had given me a part; the rest came from my mother. He also is leaving tomorrow for America."

All of our baggage had now been on board for three days, without my spy having imagined that all the wardrobes and all the drawers were empty. I paid the most tender adieux to my maid, Marguerite, whom I left under the protection of Monsieur de Brouquens. Finally, on the tenth of March, taking my daughter Séraphine in my arms and my son Humbert by the hand, I said to the nurse that I was going to take them to the Allées de Tourny, which at this time was still the usual promenade for children, and that I would be back in an hour or two. Instead of returning, I walked towards the Glacis du Château-

Trompette, where I rejoined Monsieur de Chambeau, to whom I had given rendez-vous. He had also obtained passage on our boat, as it was necessary for political reasons for him to leave the city with the shortest possible delay. I found him at Château-Trompette accompanied by a boy carrying his portmanteau which was very light. He took the hand of Humbert and when we arrived at the end of the Chartrons, and saw the boat of the "Diane," we both of us experienced a feeling of joy such as one does not often have in this life.

Monsieur Meyer, with whom my husband had passed the night, was awaiting us. We found, already at luncheon, the good Brouquens, Mme. de Fontenay and three or four other persons. In spite of all of our efforts, the famine at Bordeaux was so great that we had been able to procure very few provisions. Several sacks of potatoes and of beans, a small box of preserves and fifty bottles of Bordeaux wine comprised all our riches. Captain Pease had several casks of biscuits, but they were eighteen months old, as he had brought them from Baltimore. Monsieur Meyer gave me a little bag of fresh biscuits which I kept to make soup for my little girl. But of what importance was all that compared to the fact that the life of my husband was saved!

Mme. de Fontenay was overjoyed at her success. Her beautiful face was bathed with tears of joy when we entered the boat. She has since told me that this moment, thanks to our expressions of gratitude, was one of the pleasantest of which she had preserved the memory.

When the captain was seated at the helm and cried "Off!" a feeling of indescribable happiness overcame me. Seated before my husband whose life I was saving, with my two children upon my knees, nothing to me seemed impossible. Poverty, work, misery, nothing was difficult with him.

The boat "Diane" had descended with the preceding tide as far as Bec d'Ambez, where we were to rejoin it. We had received orders from headquarters to hail a ship of war stationed as a sentinel in the middle of the river at the entrance of the port. Our captain prepared to submit his papers and our passports. This was a dangerous moment. We did not dare to speak French, nor to look up towards the bridge of the war vessel. The captain alone went on board. He did not know a word of French although he had spent a year at Bordeaux. A voice from the bridge cried: "Have the woman come up to serve as interpreter." I was struck with a mortal terror. But our captain leaned over the rail and told me not to answer. I did not raise my eyes. At this moment a French boat in great haste and full of men in uniform approached. The captain took advantage of this diversion, seized his papers, jumped into the boat and we rowed away as fast as possible.

At last we found our little vessel the "Diane" and settled ourselves on board as well as possible. The second falling tide took us in front of Pauillac. There we had again to receive the visit of two other guard vessels. The officers who came on board were very polite, but very inquisitive.

As the wind was absolutely contrary and showed

no signs of changing, the captain proposed to us to go on land for dinner, where we might have a chance to buy some articles to add to our provisions. Here we had a narrow escape from being recognized by a servant who served the dessert and who thought she recognized my husband. It was therefore with a feeling of relief that we found ourselves once more in the cabin of the "Diane." Fortunately the wind changed and the following day we left behind us the Tour de Cordouan.

The little brig upon which we had embarked was only of 150 tons, that is to say a large bark. As the cargo was composed solely of our twenty-five boxes or trunks, the boat rolled horribly. My maritime apprenticeship was very painful.

We had agreed with the captain regarding our board, but he, as unfortunate as ourselves, had not been able to procure provisions other than those which had been furnished by the marine stores.

At the time of our departure from Bordeaux, one of the four sailors had had a terrible fall from the top of the mast into the hold and was out of service. Only three sailors remained to manœuvre the boat. The crew therefore consisted only of these three sailors, a cabin boy who acted as servant, the captain, who was a young man without much experience, the mate, who like himself was from Nantucket, and an old sailor of much experience named Harper whom the captain consulted on every occasion.

The captain had a little room which he occupied alone. He had given a cabin to my husband and to myself and another to Monsieur de Chambeau. My husband did not leave his bed for thirty days. He suffered terribly from sea-sickness and also from the poor food.

At the time, the Americans were at war with the Algerians, who had already captured several of their vessels. Our captain was in such great terror of these pirates that at two leagues from the Tour de Cordouan he set his course towards the north and declared that nothing in the world would reassure him before he was to the north of Ireland.

One day the sailor who was on watch upon the deck cried out: "French man-of-war ahead." The captain rushed on deck and at the same time ordered us not to appear. A cannon shot was heard. It was the commencement of a conversation upon which depended the question of our life or death. The vessel announced itself as French by displaying its flag. We also showed our flag, and after the usual questions, we heard our captain reply, for we were not able to distinguish the questions from the French boat: "No passengers; no cargo." To which the "Atalante" replied: "Come on board." Our captain said that the sea was too rough. Then the conversation terminated with a word from the French vessel: "Follow," and we set our only sail and with submission followed in the wake of the French vessel. The captain on descending said to us gayly: "In another hour it will be night, and there is a fog coming on." Never was a fog hailed with greater joy. We soon lost sight of the frigate in the darkness, and as we were making as little sail as possible, she continued to gain upon us.

The frigate had signalled to us that she was going into Brest and wanted us to follow. As soon as night fell, we took the route directly contrary, and, the wind being very strong and favorable, with all sails set, we laid our course to the northwest, without caring whether or not it was the route to Boston, where we were to go.

This incident threw us completely out of our course, and we experienced thick fogs which did not enable us to take an observation for a period of twelve or fifteen days. Provisions commenced to run short and we were put upon a ration of water. We encountered an English vessel coming from Ireland and our captain went on board and returned with a bag of potatoes and two small pots of butter for myself and children. Having compared his position with that of the English captain, he found that we were fifty leagues to the north of the Azores. On learning this, my husband prayed him to put us on the shore of the Azores, from which we might have been able to gain England, but the captain was unwilling to do so.

Ten days followed in which we were unable to take an observation, and the fog was so dense that even upon our little boat we could not see the bowsprit. The captain did not know where he was. Old Harper assured us that he felt land breezes, but we thought that he was endeavoring to cheer us up. Finally, the twelfth of May, 1794, at daybreak, as the weather was warm and the sea calm, we were on deck with the children to breathe the fresh air. The fog was still very dense, and the captain declared that the land was still at a distance of at least fifty or sixty leagues. I could not help remarking, however, the nervousness of the dog — a black terrier, of which I was very fond and who had taken a great fancy to me. The poor beast rushed forward barking and then at once returned to me and licked my hands, and then repeated the same action. This singular performance had already lasted for an hour when a little pilot boat appeared near to us and a man cried in English: "If you do not change your direction, you are going to run onto the Cape." A cord was thrown to him and he sprang on board. It is impossible to describe the joy we felt upon seeing this pilot from Boston. We had arrived without knowing it at the entrance of this magnificent harbor, of whcih the finest lake in Europe can give no idea. Leaving the open sea, where the waves were breaking with fury over the rocks, we entered by a narrow passage, where two vessels could hardly pass at the same time, into a body of water as quiet and smooth as a mirror. A light breeze came up from the friendly land which was to receive us.

The transports of my son cannot be described. For a period of sixty days he had heard us talk of the dangers from which, thanks to Heaven, we had escaped. The remembrance of good white bread and of the good milk of other days often troubled his young imagination. When he saw from this straight passage by which we were entering, the green fields, the trees and flowers and all the beauty of the most luxuriant vegetation, his joy was unbounded. Our own, although more reasonable, was not less intense.

SECOND PART

CHAPTER ONE
1794
ARRIVAL IN AMERICA

Adieux to the "Diane."— Joy of Being in a Friendly Country.—
Temporary Residence at Boston.— Mr. Geyer.— General
Schuyler.— Sale of Superfluous Articles.— Departure for
Albany.— Mme. de La Tour du Pin Learns of the Death
of Her Father.— The Inn at Lebanon.— Arrival at Albany.
— Friendly Reception by General Schuyler and the Van
Rensselaer Family.— Mrs. Van Rensselaer.— Talleyrand
in America.

IT is probably very presumptuous on my part to
continue to write these memoirs at the age of
nearly seventy-three years. But having to-day
finished the task of copying the part which I had
already written upon loose sheets, I warn you, my
dear son, Aymar, that you shall have the rest if God
permits, as long as I retain a little strength and
reason and eyes to guide my hand. An enterprise of
this kind demands, above all things, memory, and
it seems to me that I have not entirely lost mine.

But abandoning preambles, let us return to our
entrance into the port of Boston. Our ecstacy, I
admit with shame, was entirely concentrated upon
an enormous fresh fish which the pilot had just
caught and which, with a pitcher of milk, fresh
butter and white bread, composed what the captain

called "a welcome breakfast." While we were eating with voracious appetites, we were advancing, towed by our boat, up this magnificent bay. At two cables' length from the land, our captain dropped the anchor and then left us with the promise to return in the evening after having found us a lodging.

We did not have a single letter of introduction, and we awaited his return with patience. Fresh provisions arrived from all sides. Several Frenchmen also came, who were impatient to have news. They assailed us with questions to which we could reply only very imperfectly. One wished to know what was going on at Lille, another at Grenoble, a third at Metz, and all were surprised and almost angry to obtain replies only regarding Paris or France in general. Most of them were very common people: ruined merchants, or workmen who were looking for positions. They left us in very bad humor, and we were not troubled by them during the rest of the time that we were at Boston.

The remainder of the day was passed in putting our things in order. The captain returned in the evening. He had found a little lodging upon the Market Place, and his ship-owner had charged him to offer us his services. My husband resolved to go to see him the following day on landing. The captain told us that he was a rich man and highly considered, and that we were fortunate to be under his protection.

You may well believe that daybreak the following morning found me already awake. I made my adieux to all the members of the crew individually by "shaking hands" with them. These worthy fellows had been full of attention for us. The cabin-boy shed tears on separating from my son. Every one expressed his regret at parting, and I for my part was very sorry not to be able to take the dog "Black" who was much attached to me. I had consulted my friend Boyd to learn whether the captain would willingly let me have her. Boyd assured me that the request would be refused, and I therefore did not dare to make it.

Our good captain conducted us first to one of the best inns, where he had ordered prepared an excellent luncheon, and we found everything of which we had been deprived for so long a time. After this, we went to the little lodging house chosen by the captain, where my husband left me to go and see the owner of our ship.

Mr. Geyer was one of the richest proprietors of the city of Boston. Although he had returned after the peace to enjoy his fortune in his native land, he had been counted among the partisans of England, and had taken no part in the Revolution against the Mother Country. Following the example of many other Boston merchants, he had even taken his family with him to England during the war. My husband was received by Mr. Geyer with a charming cordiality.

I omitted to say that at Pauillac we were moored alongside a vessel which was waiting for a favorable wind, like ourselves, and which was bound for England. I had written a few words in haste to Mme. d'Hénin, then living at London, to beg her to write us at Boston, in care of Mr. Geyer whose address had been given me by the captain. The length of our voyage had permitted my aunt to reply, and we found, on landing, letters which settled the place in the United States which we were to inhabit. I will return to this later.

The house, in which were located the rooms found for us by the captain, was inhabited by three generations of ladies: Mrs. Pierce, her mother and her daughter. The house was situated upon the Market Place, the locality the most frequented and most animated in the city. Our lodging comprised, on one side, a little sitting-room lighted by two windows looking out on the Market Place; on the other side, at the top of a little stairway, a comfortable bedchamber allotted to my husband, my children and myself. This room had a view over an isolated dockyard where ship carpenters were working. Beyond that extended the neighboring country. You will see later why I enter into these details.

We arranged for board with some excellent people, who nourished us well in the English fashion. The evening of the first day found us settled as if no grief or inquietude had ever troubled our life.

Towards the middle of the night I was awakened by the barking of a dog and by a scratching at the door of the kitchen which opened out on the dockyard. This bark was not unknown to me. I got up and opened the window. By the moonlight I could recognize the dog "Black." I at once descended and opened the door for her. As soon as she had entered my room, I saw that the poor beast was so wet that she certainly must have remained a long time in the water. The following morning, I found that she had been kept chained on board during the day, but that at ten o'clock in the evening, the sailor thinking that it would be all right to release her, had done so, and she had immediately jumped into the sea. As the "Diane" was at anchor about a mile from the quay, it is certain that the good beast must have swum this entire distance and then have searched through the city until she discovered exactly the door of the house which was nearest to the room where we were sleeping. The captain felt a sort of superstition that he must not oppose an attachment so clearly shown. "Black" never left us again and returned with us to Europe.

The morning of the day after our arrival, Mr. Geyer came to see me with his wife and daughter. He spoke French quite well, but the ladies did not know a single word. They were delighted to find that their language was as familiar to me as it was to themselves.

Mr. Geyer offered to put at our disposal a farm which he owned about eighteen miles from Boston. Perhaps we should have done well to accept his proposition, but my husband wished to be as near as possible to Canada, where he would have liked to settle. He spoke English with difficulty, although he understood it perfectly, and the thought that French was, as it still is, the language which is usually spoken at Montreal, gave him the desire to live in the vicinity of that city.

In the letters which we had received from England, Mme. d'Hénin, while regretting that we had not been able to rejoin her in England, sent us letters from an American who was one of her friends. This lady, Mrs. Church, recommended us to a family residing at Albany. She was a daughter of General Schuyler who had gained a great reputation during the War of Independence. Until a short time before the surrender of General Burgoyne, at Saratoga in October, 1777, he had commanded the American army which opposed the forces led from Canada by General Burgoyne to reënforce the English army which was in possession of New York. Since the peace, General Schuyler, a Hollander by origin, lived upon his estate with all his family. His eldest daughter had married the head of the Van Rensselaer family which was settled at Albany and possessed a large fortune in the county.

Mrs. Church, seeing the great maternal interest and tender friendship which animated our aunt, wrote to her relatives, and we received on our arrival in Boston very pressing letters from General Schuyler in which he urged us to come without delay to Albany, where he assured us we would easily be able to establish ourselves. To this end he offered us all of his support. We therefore made up our minds to accept his proposition. Having sent all of our baggage by sea to New York, whence it would be forwarded to Albany by the Hudson River, we waited at Boston for the news of its arrival at destination before setting out by land. We preferred to make in this way the trip of two hundred miles, as it would permit us to see the country and would not be more expensive.

It was a simple opening through the trees which had been cut off at the foot and thrown to the right and left to leave a free passageway.

About midway, we stopped for luncheon at an inn recently erected, in the middle of these immense woods. In America, as soon as a rustic house is built in the forest, if it is near a road, even if only one person passes during the course of the year, the first expenditure of the owner is the purchase of a sign, and the first task is the erection of a post to attach it. Then he nails to the post below the sign a letter-box, and this locality, where the road is hardly laid out, is at once designated upon the map of the country as a city.

The wooden house where we stopped had reached the second degree of civilization, as it was a frame house, that is to say, a house provided with sashes and panes of glass.

At the end of the dinner which we took together, the master of the house rose, removed his cap, and, with a respectful air, pronounced these words: "We will drink the health of our beloved President." You would not then have found a cabin, no matter how buried it was in the depths of the woods, where this act of love for the great Washington did not terminate every meal. Sometimes there was also added a toast to the "Marquis," Monsieur de La Fayette, who had left a well-loved name in the United States.

At Lebanon there was an establishment of sulphureous baths which was already quite important. The inn was very good, and above all was perfectly neat. But the luxury of white bed-linen was then unknown in this part of the United States. A request for it would only have appeared fantastic and would not have been understood.

The city of Albany, the capital of the state, had been almost entirely burned two years before by an insurrection of negroes. Slavery was not yet entirely abolished in the state of New York, except for children to be born during the year of 1794, and only when these had reached their twentieth year. This very wise measure, which obliged the owners of the slaves to raise them, gave, on the other hand, to the slave the time to make good to his master, by his work, the cost of his education. One of these "blacks," a very worthless character, who had hoped that the act of the legislature would give him his liberty without conditions, resolved to be revenged. He enrolled several miserable fellows like himself, and on a fixed day arranged to set fire to the city, which at this time was constructed mainly of wood. This atrocious plan succeeded beyond their expectations. Fires were started in twenty places at once, and houses and stores, with their contents, were destroyed, notwithstanding the efforts of the inhabitants, at the head of whom labored the old General Schuyler, and all his family. A little negress, twelve years old, was arrested at the moment she was setting fire to a store with straw from the stable of her master. She revealed the names of her accomplices. The next day a court assembled upon the still smoking ruins, and condemned the black chief and six of his accomplices to be hung, which sentence was executed at once.

LE BATEAU "LA DIANE"
1794

The Van Rensselaer and Schuyler families set the example of great activity in repairing the disaster. Cargoes of merchandise, of brick, and of furniture were brought up from New York, and a charming new city sprang from the ashes of the old. Houses of stone and especially of brick were erected, which were covered with plates of zinc and tin, and when we arrived at Albany there was no longer any trace of the fire.

The house of General Schuyler and that of his son-in-law, Mr. Van Rensselaer, each being isolated in the midst of a garden, had been spared. It was there that we received a welcome which was as flattering as it was hospitable. General Schuyler, in seeing me, said: "Now I shall have a sixth daughter!" He entered into all of our plans, our desires and our interests. He, as well as all his family, spoke French perfectly.

When we arrived in America the head of the Van Rensselaer family, which was divided into a large number of branches, all of which were rich, was married to the eldest daughter of General Schuyler. By the people he was called the "patroon," a Holland word which means *seigneur*. The very day of our arrival at Albany, towards evening, we took a walk in a long and very fine street, at the extremity of which we discovered a tract of ground enclosed by a simple palisade, painted white. This was a very well-kept park, planted with fine trees and flowers, and surrounding a handsome mansion of very simple architecture with no pretentions to art or exterior beauty. Behind, were to be seen a number of outbuildings which gave to the whole establishment the air of a very fine and well-kept farm. I asked of a young boy, who opened the gate to permit us to descend to the edge of the river, who was the proprietor of this large mansion. He replied with an air of surprise that it was the house of the "patroon." On my saying that I did not know what he meant by the word "patroon," he was filled with astonishment.

Two days later we were received in this house with a kind attention and friendship which in the future never failed us. Mrs. Van Rensselaer was a woman of thirty years who spoke French very well. She had learned the language while accompanying her father to the general headquarters of the American and French armies. She was endowed with a superior mind and with an extraordinary clearness of judgment regarding men and things. For years she had not gone out of the house, where she was confined to her chair by the state of her health for months at a time, the beginning of a malady which led her to the tomb a few years later. By reading the papers she had kept informed as to the state of parties in France, the mistakes which had brought on the Revolution, the vices of the higher class of society, and the folly of the medium classes. With an extraordinary perspicuity she had penetrated the causes and the effects of the troubles of our country better than we ourselves. She was very impatient to make the acquaintance of Monsieur de Talleyrand, who had arrived at Philadelphia, having been dismissed from England on very short notice. With his usual quickness of apprehension, he had made up his mind that France had not yet finished the different phases of the Revolution. He brought for us important letters from Holland which Mme. d'Hénin had confided to him. She wrote me, among other things, that Monsieur de Talleyrand had come to pass, in a country of real liberty, the period of cruel folly from which France was suffering. Monsieur de Talleyrand asked where he could find me at the end of a trip to the interior of the country which he was thinking of making in company with Monsieur de Beaumetz, his friend, and a millionaire Englishman who had just arrived from India.

CHAPTER TWO

1794

THE FARM NEAR ALBANY

En Pension with the Van Burens.— Mme. de La Tour du Pin's
Father-in-Law.— Apprenticeship as Farmer.— Purchase of
a Farm.— Temporary Residence at Troy.— A Log House.
— Unexpected Visit of Monsieur de Talleyrand.— News
of the 9 Thermidor.— An Appreciation of Monsieur de
Talleyrand.— Mr. Law.— Alexander Hamilton.— Begin-
ning of Winter.— First Encounter with the Indians.—
Purchase of the First Negro, Minck.— Repairs of the
Farmhouse.— Activity of Mme. de La Tour du Pin.

AS we did not wish to remain at Albany,
General Schuyler took charge of finding us
a farm which we could buy in the neighborhood. He advised us in the meantime to arrange for
three months to live with a family of his acquaintance
which was located not far from the farm which his
brother, Colonel Schuyler, occupied with his twelve
children. Our sojourn at Albany, therefore, was not
prolonged beyond several days. After this, we went
to live with Mr. Van Buren to learn American
manners, as we had made it a condition of living
with this family that they were not to change in
any way the customs of the house. It was also arranged that Mrs. Van Buren should employ me in
the housework the same as if I were one of her
daughters. Monsieur de Chambeau at the same time

began an apprenticeship with a carpenter of the little growing city of Troy situated at a quarter of a mile from the Van Buren farm. He set out Monday morning and returned Saturday night only to pass Sunday with us. We had just received news of the tragic end of my father-in-law who perished upon the scaffold the twenty-eighth of April, 1794. Monsieur de Chambeau had received at the same time news of the death of his own father. As I was a very good seamstress, I fashioned for myself my mourning costume, and my good hostess, having thus learned to appreciate the skill of my needle, found it very pleasant to have a seamstress at her command without cost, when she would have been obliged to pay a dollar a day and board if she had hired one from Albany.

My husband visited several farms. We were awaiting the arrival of the funds which had been sent us from Holland before purchasing the farm which we expected to acquire. General Schuyler and Mr. Van Rensselaer advised my husband to divide his funds into three equal parts: A third for the purchase; a third for the management, the purchase of negroes, horses, cows, agricultural implements and household furniture; and a third part, added to what remained of the 12,000 francs brought by us from Bordeaux, for a reserve fund to meet unexpected circumstances, such as the loss of negroes or cattle and also for living expenses the first year. This arrangement became our rule of conduct.

Personally, I resolved to be in a position to fulfill my duties as manager of the farm. I began by accustoming myself never to remain in bed after sunrise. At three o'clock in the morning, during the summer, I was up and dressed. My room opened upon a little lawn stretching down to the river. When I say "opened," I am not speaking of the window, but of the door which was on a level with the turf. Therefore, without moving from my bed, I could see the vessels passing.

The Van Buren farm, an old mansion built in the style of Holland, occupied a delightful situation upon the bank of the river. Entirely isolated on the land side, it had easy facilities of communication with the other side of the river. Opposite, on the highway to Canada, was situated a large inn where could be found all the notices, the papers, and the posters regarding sales. Two or three stage coaches passed there every day. Van Buren owned two canoes, and the river was always so calm that it was possible to cross it at any moment. No road crossed this property. It was bounded at a distance of several hundred yards by a mountain covered with fine trees belonging to the Van Burens. We often said that this farm was just what we wanted, but the value was far beyond what we were able to pay. This was the only thing which prevented us from acquiring it, for the general rule in America at this time was that no matter how attached a man might be to his house, his farm, his horse or his negro, if you offered him a third more than the value, you were assured of becoming the owner.

During the month of September my husband entered into negotiations with a farmer whose land was situated on the other side of the river, upon the road from Troy to Schenectady, a distance of two miles in the interior. The situation of this farm upon a hill overlooking a large expanse of country appeared to us agreeable. The house was new, pretty and in very good condition. The land was only partially under cultivation. There were one hundred and fifty acres sown down, as many in woods and pasturage, a small kitchen garden of a quarter of an acre full of vegetables, and finally a handsome orchard sown with red clover and planted with cider apples. These trees were ten years old and in full bearing. They asked us 12,000 francs. General Schuyler did not think the price exorbitant. The property was situated at four miles from Albany, upon a route which they were going to open up to communicate with the city of Schenectady, which was in a thriving situation.

The proprietor did not wish to move until after the snow was well packed. As we had arranged with the Van Burens, who evidently had had enough of us, for two months only, it was necessary, therefore, to look for another home from the first of September to the first of November. At Troy, we found for a moderate sum, a little wooden house in the midst of a large yard, enclosed by a board fence. Here we established ourselves, and, as it would be necessary for us to purchase some furniture for the farm, we immediately acquired what we wanted. These pieces of furniture, added to those which we had brought from Europe, permitted us to be well settled at once. I had engaged a white girl, who was quite satisfactory. She was to be married in two months and consented to enter my service while awaiting the erection of the log house which her future husband was building, where they expected to live after their marriage.

Here is what is meant by a log house. A plan better than a description would give an exact idea. A piece of land fourteen or fifteen feet square was levelled and the construction was begun by building a brick chimney, which was the first comfort of the house; then the walls were erected. These were composed of large pieces of wood, covered with bark, which were hewn in such a manner as to join exactly to each other. Above the walls was constructed the roof, with an opening for the chimney. In the middle a door was installed. You see many of these houses in Switzerland where they serve exclusively for the use of the cattle and the men who guard them. In America these houses represent the first degree of shelter and often the last, for there are always unfortunate persons, and these log houses in a prosperous city become the refuge of the poor.

One day at the end of September, I was in the yard with a hatchet in my hand, occupied with cutting the bone of a leg of mutton which I was preparing to put on the spit for our dinner. All of a sudden, I heard behind me a loud voice which said in French: "On ne peut embrocher un gigot avec plus de majesté." Turning quickly, I saw Monsieur de Talleyrand and Monsieur de Beaumetz. Having arrived the evening before at Albany, they had learned from General Schuyler where we were. They came on his part to invite us to dinner and to pass the following day with them at his house. These gentlemen were to remain in the city only two days. An Englishman who was one of their friends was accompanying them and was very impatient to return to New York. However, as Monsieur de Talleyrand was very much amused at the sight of my leg of mutton, I insisted that he should return the following day to eat it with us. He consented. Leaving the children in the care of Monsieur de Chambeau and Betsey, we set out for Albany.

En route we talked a great deal upon all kinds of subjects, as people do when they meet after a long time. The latest news from Europe, of which they were ignorant, owing to their visit to Niagara, from which they had only just returned, was more terrible than ever. Blood flowed in floods at Paris. Mme. Elisabeth, the sister of the King, had perished; our relatives, and our friends were counted among the victims of the Terror.

When we arrived at the house of the good General, he was on the stoop. From a distance he made signs to us and cried: "Come quickly, come quickly! There is great news from France!" We entered the sitting-room and every one of us took a paper. Here we found the news of the Revolution of the 9 Thermidor; the death of Robespierre and his followers, the end of the shedding of blood and the just punishment of the Revolutionary Tribunal.

Monsieur de Talleyrand was rejoicing especially that his sister-in-law, Mme. Archambauld de Périgord, had escaped, when, later in the evening, having taken up from the table a paper which he thought he had read, he found her name among the terrible list of victims executed the 9 Thermidor, that very morning, during the session in which Robespierre was denounced. The news of her death painfully affected him. His brother, who cared little for his wife, had left France in 1790, and as their fortune belonged to his wife, he had found it more convenient that she should remain in order to avoid confiscation. She left three children, a daughter who was later Duchesse de Poix, and two sons: Louis, who died in the army under Napoleon, and Edmond who married the youngest of the daughters of the Duchesse de Courlande. Without the news of this cruel event, our evening with General Schuyler would have been more agreeable.

Mr. Law, the travelling companion of Messieurs de Talleyrand and de Beaumetz, could have passed for the most original of Englishmen, all of whom are more or less so. He was a tall blond man, forty or forty-five years of age, with a handsome sad face. That evening upon returning to their inn, he said suddenly to Monsieur de Talleyrand:

"Mon cher, nous ne partirons pas après-demain."

"Et pourquoi? Vous avez retenu votre passage sur le sloop qui descend à New-York."

"Oh! cela est égal. Je ne veux pas partir. Ces gens de Troy que vous avez été chercher . . ."

"Eh! bien?"

"Je veux les revoir encore plusieurs fois. Demain, vous irez chez eux?"

"Oui."

"J'irai vous y prendre le soir. Je veux voir cette femme-là chez elle."

Then he became silent and they could not get another word out of him.

The following morning, after having dined with our paternal General, Monsieur de Talleyrand and my husband returned to Troy. I had preceded them during the morning, for it was necessary for me to prepare the dinner for my guests. A little negro drove the "carry-all" which could be easily procured at Albany for a dollar.

Monsieur de Talleyrand was amiable as he has always been for me, without any variation, with that charm of conversation which no one has ever possessed to a greater degree than himself. He had known me since my childhood, and therefore assumed a sort of paternal and gracious tone which was very charming. I regretted sincerely to find so many reasons for not holding him in esteem, but I could not avoid forgetting my disagreeable recollections when I had passed an hour in listening to him. As he had no moral value himself, by singular contrast, he had a horror of that which was evil in others. To listen to him without knowing him, you would have believed that he was a worthy man.

That evening Mr. Law, accompanied by Mr. Beaumetz, came to take tea. I already had a cow and gave them some excellent cream. We went for a walk, and Mr. Law offered me his arm and a long conversation followed between us. Brother of Lord Landaff, he had left while still very young for India, where, for a period of fourteen years, he had been in the employ of the Government of Patna, or some similar post. There he had married a rich Indian widow by whom he had two sons who were still children. His wife had died, leaving him a considerable fortune. Upon his return to England he had not been happy and had formed the resolution of coming to America to invest in that country in the purchase of land a part of the capital which he had brought back from India.

Two days later we were to pass the day at Mrs. Van Rensselaer's, with all the Schuylers. Monsieur de Talleyrand had been extremely impressed by the remarkable culture of Mrs. Van Rensselaer, and could not believe that she had not passed years in Europe. She had a very clear understanding of American affairs and the Revolution, of which she had gained a profound and extended knowledge through her brother-in-law, Colonel Hamilton, who was the friend and also the most intimate confidant of Washington. Colonel Hamilton was expected at Albany where he intended to pass some time with his father-in-law, General Schuyler. He had just resigned the position of Secretary of the Treasury, which he had held since the peace. It was to him that the country owed the good order which had been established in this branch of the government of the United States. Monsieur de Talleyrand knew him and had the very highest opinion of him. But he found it very remarkable that a man of his value, and endowed with talents so superior, should leave the Ministry to resume the profession of lawyer, giving as his reason for this decision that the position of Minister did not give him the means of bringing up his family of eight children. Such a pretext seemed to

Talleyrand very singular and, so to speak, even a little *naïf*.

At the end of the dinner, Mr. Law took Talleyrand by the arm and led him into the garden where they passed some time. The departure of these gentlemen was fixed for the following day, and they had formed the plan of coming to Troy in the morning to say adieu to us. After his conversation with Talleyrand, Mr. Law stated that he had letters to write and returned to his inn. Monsieur de Talleyrand then led my husband and myself to a corner of the salon where he related what Monsieur Law had said, in these terms: "My good friend, I am very fond of these people, and my intention is to lend them a thousand louis. They have just purchased a farm. It will be necessary for them to have cattle, horses, negroes and so on. As long as they inhabit the country they will not repay my loan. Besides, I would not accept it. It is necessary for me to help them in order to be happy. If they refuse, I shall fall ill. They will render me a real service in accepting my offer."

Then he added: "Cette femme, si bien élevée! qui fait la cuisine . . . qui trait sa vache . . . qui lave son linge . . . Cette idée m'est insupportable . . . elle me tue . . . Voilà deux nuits que je n'en ai pas dormi."

Talleyrand was a man of too good taste to turn to ridicule such a feeling. He asked us very seriously what reply he should make. To tell the truth we were very profoundly touched by this proposition, notwithstanding the originality with which it was made. We requested Monsieur de Talleyrand to express to his friend our very sincere thanks and to assure him that for the moment we were able to take care of all the demands of our establishment, but that later on, if, owing to some unexpected circumstance we found ourselves in need, we would promise to let him know. This promise which he received that evening quieted him a little. The following morning he came to say adieu. The poor man was as embarrassed as if he had done something wrong.

We were awaiting with impatience the first snowfall and the moment when the river would be frozen for three or four months. In order to have the ice solid, it is necessary that the freezing should take place during the twenty-four hours, and that the ice should be two or three feet thick. This peculiarity is due entirely to the locality and the immense forests which cover the large continent to the west and north of the settlements of the United States, but is not due to the latitude. It is probable that at the present writing the Great Lakes are now almost entirely surrounded by settlements, and that the climate of the region in which we lived has notably changed.

From the twenty-fifth of October until the first of November the sky was covered with a mass of clouds so thick that the day was obscured. A northwest wind, bitterly cold, blew with great violence and every one made preparations to put aside whatever could be covered up by the snow. We took out of the river the boats, the canoes and the barks, turning upside down those which had no decks. Everybody at this time displayed the greatest activity. Then the snow commenced to fall with such abundance that you could not see a man at ten paces. Ordinarily the ice formed two or three days before. The first care was to trace with pine branches a wide route along one of the banks. In the same way were marked the places where the border was not steep and where one could pass upon the ice. It would have been dangerous to pass elsewhere, for in many places the ice lacked solidity upon the edges.

We had acquired moccasins, a kind of foot-covering of buffalo-skin, made and sold by the Indians. The price of these articles was sometimes quite high when they were embroidered with dyed bark or with porcupine quills.

It was in purchasing these moccasins that I saw the Indians for the first time. They were the last survivors of the Mohawk tribe whose territory had been purchased or taken by the Americans since the peace. The Onondagas, established near Lake Champlain, also were selling their forests and disappearing at this epoch. From time to time some of them came to us. I was a little surprised when I met for the first time a man and woman practically nude promenading tranquilly upon the highway, without any one seeming to find this remarkable. But I soon became accustomed to this, and, when I was settled on the farm, I saw them almost every day during the summer.

We took advantage of the first moment that the route was traced and trodden down to commence our moving. The funds which we awaited from Holland had arrived and my grandmother, Lady Dillon, who had died the nineteenth of June, had left me a legacy of 300 guineas, although she had never seen me. With this money we bought our farm utensils. We already possessed four good horses and two work-sleds. A third served for our personal use and was called the pleasure sleigh. It could hold six persons. It was constructed in the form of a very low box. At the back was a seat, a little wider than the body of the sleigh, which was placed upon a box in which we could put small packages, and it had a back higher than your head, which broke the force of the wind. The other seats — two in number — were composed of simple planks. Buffalo-robes and sheepskins covered the feet. Two horses were attached and we were carried very swiftly.

We accordingly set out to establish ourselves on our farm, although the sellers were still occupying it. They were in no hurry to move out, and we were literally obliged to put them out of the door.

At this time we bought a negro, and this purchase, which seemed to be the most simple thing in the world, produced in my case a feeling so new that I shall remember it all my life.

A few days after our arrival, the people from whom we had purchased the farm finally went away, leaving us the house, which was dirty and badly kept. They had abandoned the property after having occupied it for several years, because it had become too small for them and they were going to take possession of another place on the other side of the river.

As soon as we were alone in the house, we spent a little money in arranging it. The house comprised only the rooms on the ground floor and was raised

COMTE ARTHUR DILLON

1750 - 1794

five feet above the earth. At the time it was built they had commenced by constructing a wall, buried six feet in the ground and rising two feet above the surface. This part formed the cellar and the milk-room. Above, the rest of the house was of wood, as you will still see frequently in Switzerland. The vacant spaces in the carpentry work were filled with sun-dried bricks which formed a wall very compact and very warm.

Monsieur de Chambeau had well profited by his four months of apprenticeship with the master-carpenter and had really become a very good work-man. Besides, it would have been impossible for him to think of idleness, for my activity admitted of no excuse. My husband and he could have applied to me those words of Talleyrand on Napoleon: "Celui qui donnerait un peu de paresse à cet homme, serait le bienfaiteur de l'univers." In short, during all the time that I lived at the farm, well or ill, the sun never found me in my bed.

CHAPTER THREE
1795
COUNTRY LIFE

Family Life at the Farm.— The Arrival of Spring.— The Indians.— Their Passion for Rum.— The Shakers.— A Visit to Their Establishment.— A Visit from Messieurs de Liancourt and Dupetit-Thouars.— Talleyrand and the Banker Morris.— Plans for a Trip to Philadelphia and New York.

MY butter had become very popular. I arranged it carefully in little rolls formed in in a mould marked with our cipher, and placed it attractively in a very neat basket upon a fine serviette. It was for general sale. We had eight cows which were well fed, and our butter did not feel the effects of the winter. My cream was always fresh. This brought me in every day quite a little money, and the sledge-load of wood also sold for at least two dollars.

Our slave, Prime, although he did not know how to read or write, nevertheless kept his accounts with such exactitude that there was never the slightest error. He often brought back some fresh meat which he had bought at Albany, and, upon his return, my husband, from his report, wrote out the sum of the receipts and expenditures.

Property like ours was generally burdened with a small rent which was paid either in grain or in money.

Our farm paid to the patroon, Van Rensselaer, twenty-two pecks of corn, either in kind or in money. All of the farms in his immense estate, which was eighteen miles wide by forty-two miles long, were held under the same conditions.

One of our neighbors at Albany, Monsieur Dejardin, had brought from Europe a complete suite of furniture, and, among other things, a fine library of a thousand or fifteen hundred books. He loaned these books to us, and my husband or Monsieur de Chambeau read to me during the evening, while I worked.

We took our déjeuner at eight o'clock, and our dinner at one o'clock. In the evening at nine o'clock we had tea, with slices of bread, our excellent butter and some fine Stilton cheese which Monsieur de Talleyrand sent us. With this consignment, he had sent, for me personally, a present which gave me the greatest pleasure. This was a very fine woman's saddle, with a bridle and other accessories complete. No gift had ever come in more à propos. We had indeed bought with the farm, and "to boot," two handsome mares, exactly similar in coat and form, but very dissimilar in character. One had the temperament of a lamb, and, although she had never had a bit in her mouth, I mounted her the very day that she was saddled for the first time. In a few days I could harness her as well as though she had been a work-horse. Her manners were very agreeable, and when you wished, she would follow you like a dog. The other was a regular devil, whom all the skill of Monsieur de Chambeau, an old Cavalry officer, could not succeed in subduing. We were able to master her only in the spring, when we made her work between two strong horses. The first time she was hitched up in this way, she was so furious that at the end of ten minutes she was wet with sweat. In time, however, she calmed down and made an excellent mare. She was worth at least twenty or thirty louis.

A propos of the springtime, it is interesting to recount with what promptitude it arrived in these parts. The latitude of forty-three degrees then made itself felt and resumed all its empire. The northwest wind, after having prevailed throughout the winter, ceased suddenly during the first days of March. The southerly breezes commenced to blow, and the snow melted with such speed that the roads were transformed into torrents during two days. As our dwelling occupied the slope of a hill, we were soon free from our white mantle. During the winter, the snow, three or four feet deep, had protected the grass and the plants from the ice. Therefore, in less than a week, the fields were green and were covered with flowers, and an innumerable variety of plants of every kind, unknown in Europe, filled the woods.

The Indians, who had not appeared during the entire winter, began to visit the farms. One of them, at the beginning of the cold weather, had asked my permission to cut some branches of a kind of willow tree which had shoots, large as my thumb and five or six feet long. He promised me to weave some baskets during the winter season. I counted little upon this promise, as I did not believe that Indians would keep their word to this degree, although I had been so informed. I was mistaken. Within a week after the snow had melted, my Indian came back with a load of baskets. He gave me six of them which were nested in one another. The first, which was round and very large, was so well made that, when filled with water, it retained it like an earthen vessel. I wished to pay him for the baskets, but he absolutely refused and would accept only a bowl of buttermilk of which the Indians are very fond. I was very careful not to give my visitors any rum, for which they have a great liking. But I had in an old paste-board box some remnants (artificial flowers, feathers, pieces of ribbons of all colors and glass beads, which were formerly much in vogue) and I distributed these among the squaws, who were delighted with them.

I had been suffering for a period of two months with a double intermittent fever. This attack which lasted from five to six hours interfered very much with my daily work. It enfeebled me and took away my appetite, and, although I never lay down, it caused me to shiver even in a temperature of eighty-five degrees, and made me incapable of any work. Under these circumstances, a young girl, my neighbor, who lived not far from us in the woods with her parents, came to my aid. She was a seamstress by trade and worked perfectly. She arrived at the farm in the morning and remained all day long, and asked no wages except her meals.

My son, Humbert, was then over five years of age,

although to judge by his size, any one would have thought he was at least seven. He spoke English perfectly — much better even than he did French. A lady of Albany, a friend of the Van Rensselaers and wife of a minister of the Church of England, had taken a great fancy to him. Several times already he had been to pass the afternoon with her. One day she proposed to me to take charge of the boy during the summer, promising me to teach him to read and write. She said that in the country I had not the time to look after him, that he would take my fever, and added several other reasons to persuade me to yield to her wish.

This lady, whose name was Mrs. Ellison, was about forty years of age and had never had any children, which had been a great grief to her. I ended by consenting to let her have Humbert, and he was very happy and very well cared for with her. This arrangement relieved me of a great deal of care. On the farm I was always afraid that he would have some accident with the horses of which he was very fond. It was almost impossible to prevent him from accompanying the negroes to the fields, and above all from mingling with the Indians, with whom he always wished to go away. I had been told that the Indians sometimes kidnapped children. Therefore, when I saw them hanging for hours around my door I imagined they were awaiting a favorable moment to take my son.

A nice wagon, loaded with fine vegetables, often passed before our door. It belonged to the Shakers,

who were located at a distance of six or seven miles.
The driver of the wagon always stopped at our house,
and I never failed to talk with him about their
manner of life, their customs, and their belief. He
urged us to visit their establishment, and we decided
to go there some day. It is known that this sect of
Quakers belonged to the reformed school of the original Quakers who took refuge in America with Penn.

After the war of 1763, an English woman set herself up for a reformer apostle. She made many
proselytes in the states of Vermont and Massa-
chusetts. Several families put their property in
common and bought land in the then uninhabited
parts of the country, but, as the clearings approached
and reached them, they sold their establishment in
order to retire further into the wilderness.

Those of whom I speak were then protected on all
sides by a forest several miles deep. They therefore
had no reason as yet to fear their neighbors. Their
establishment was bounded on one side by woods
which covered 20,000 acres, belonging to the city
of Albany, and on the other by the river Mohawk.
Without doubt, at the present writing, they no
longer live in this locality where I knew them, and
have retired beyond the Great Lakes. This establishment was a branch of their headquarters at Lebanon,
which was located in the large forest through which
we passed in going from Boston to Albany.

Our negro, Prime, who knew all the routes in our
neighborhood, conducted us to their place. At the
start we were at least three hours in the woods, following a road which was hardly laid out. Then after

having passed the barriers which marked the limits of the Shaker property, the road became more distinct and better marked. But we still had to pass through a very thick forest, broken here and there by fields where cows and horses were pastured at liberty. Finally, we came out in a vast clearing traversed by a pretty stream and surrounded on all sides by woods. In the midst was erected the establishment, composed of a large number of nice wooden houses, a church, schools, and a community house of brick.

The Shaker, whose acquaintance we had made, greeted us with kindness, although with a certain reserve. They showed Prime the stable in which he could put up his horses, for there was no inn. We had been advised that nobody would offer us anything, and that our guide would be the only one to speak to us. He first led us to a superb kitchen-garden perfectly cultivated. Everything was in a state of the greatest prosperity, but without the least evidence of elegance. Many men and women were working at the cultivation or the weeding of the garden. The sale of vegetables represented the principal source of revenue to the community.

We visited the schools for the boys and girls, the immense community stables, the dairies, and the factories in which they produced the butter and cheese. Everywhere we remarked upon the order and the absolute silence. The children, boys and girls alike, were clothed in a costume of the same form and the same color. The women of all ages wore the same kind of garments of gray wool, well kept and very neat. Through the windows we could see the looms of the weavers, and the pieces of cloth which they were dyeing, also the workshops of the tailors and dress-makers. But not a word or a song was to be heard anywhere.

Finally, a bell rang. Our guide told us that this announced the hour of prayer and asked if we would like to be present. We consented very willingly, and he led us towards the largest of the houses, which no exterior sign distinguished from the others. At the door I was separated from my husband and Monsieur de Chambeau, and we were placed at opposite extremities of the immense hall, on either side of a chimney in which was burning a magnificent fire. It was then the beginning of spring and the cold was still felt in these large woods. This hall was about 150 or 200 feet long by 50 feet wide. It was entered by two lateral doors. The building was very light and the walls, without being ornamented in any way, were perfectly smooth and painted a light blue. At each end of the hall there was a small platform upon which was placed a wooden arm-chair.

I was seated at the corner of the chimney, and my guide had enjoined silence, which was all the easier for me as I was alone. While keeping absolutely silent, I had the opportunity to admire the floor, which was constructed of pine wood, without any knots, and of a rare perfection and whiteness. Upon this fine floor were drawn in different directions lines represented by copper nails, brilliantly polished, the heads of which were level with the floor. I endeavored to divine what could be the use of these lines, which did not seem to have any connection

with each other, when at the last stroke of the bell
the two side doors opened, and I saw enter on my
side fifty or sixty young girls or women, preceded
by one who was older who seated herself upon one
of the arm-chairs. No child accompanied them.

The men were arranged in the same manner at
the opposite side, where were my husband and Monsieur de Chambeau. I then observed that the women
stood upon these lines of nails, taking care not to
cross them with their toes. They remained immobile
until the moment when the woman seated in the arm-
chair gave a sort of groan or cry which was neither
speech nor song. All then changed their places, and I
imagined that this kind of stifled cry which I had
heard must represent some command. After several
evolutions, they stopped, and the old woman mur-
mured quite a long string of words in a language
which was absolutely unintelligible, but in which
were mingled, it seemed to me, some English words.
After this, they went out in the same order in which
they had entered. Having thus visited all parts of
the establishment, we took leave of our kind guide
and entered our wagon to return home, very little
edified regarding the hospitality of the Shakers.

When the Shaker who came to sell vegetables and
fruit passed before our farm, I always bought something. He was never willing to take money from my
hand. If I remarked that the price which he asked
was too high, he replied: "Just as you please." Then
I placed upon the corner of the table the sum which
I thought sufficient. If the price was satisfactory, he
took it; if not, he climbed into his wagon, without

saying a word. He was a man of very respectable appearance, always perfectly dressed in a coat, vest and trousers of gray homespun cloth of their own manufacture.

One thing had rendered me at once very popular with my neighbors. The day that we took possession of our farm, I adopted the costume worn by the women on the neighboring places, that is to say, a skirt of blue and black striped wool, a little camisole of light brown cotton cloth, a handkerchief of the same color, with my hair parted as it is worn now, and caught up with a comb. In winter, I wore gray or blue woolen stockings, with moccasins or slippers of buffalo skin; in summer, cotton stockings, and shoes. I never put on a dress or a corset, except to go into the city. Among the effects which I had brought to America were two or three riding-costumes. These I used to transform myself into a *dame élégante*, when I wished to pay a visit to the Schuylers or Van Rensselaers, for very frequently we dined and afterwards passed the evening with them, particularly when it was moonlight, and above all, during the period of snow.

At the beginning of the summer of 1795, we received a visit from the Duc de Liancourt. He has spoken of this very kindly in his "Voyage en Amérique." He came from the new settlements formed since the War of Independence upon the banks of the Mohawk and on the territory ceded by the Oneida nation. Monsieur de Talleyrand had given him letters of introduction to the Schuylers and Van

Rensselaers. After a sojourn of a day with us, I offered to take him to Albany to present him to these two families. Had he taken seriously my woolen skirt and my cotton camisole? I do not know, but the fact is that he seemed to begin to understand that we had not entirely become beggars, when he saw me appear with a pretty robe and a very well made hat, and when my negro, Minck, brought up a fine wagon to which were hitched two excellent horses in a harness which shone brilliantly. This was the moment for me to exclaim that for nothing in the world would I take him to see Mrs. Van Rensselaer or Mrs. Schuyler, if he did not himself make a little change in his toilette. With his garments covered with mud and dust, torn in several places, he had the appearance of a shipwrecked sailor, escaped from the pirates, and nobody would have thought that in this bizarre get-up was concealed a first gentleman of the Chamber. We arranged our conditions: I agreed to take him to see Mrs. Van Rensselaer and Mrs. Schuyler, and he consented to open his trunk, which he had left at the inn in Albany, in order to clothe himself in a more conventional manner. Then I went to pay a visit in the city while waiting for him to change his costume.

After we had made our calls, he promised to return the next day to the farm, and I left Albany, taking back with me his travelling companion, Monsieur Dupetit-Thouars. As for Monsieur de Liancourt, I did not see him again. The fever with which I was suffering at the time made it impossible for me to go out. Besides, this philanthropic *grand seigneur* had

extremely displeased me, and my friends did not like him any better. The *spirituelle* Mrs. Van Rensselaer had sized him up from the first as a man who was very ordinary. Perhaps I shall be reproached with ingratitude for treating him in this way, for he spoke of me in the most flattering manner in his book.

Several days after the visit of Monsieur de Liancourt, about the month of June, we received from Monsieur de Talleyrand a letter in which he informed us of a fact that might have caused us the most serious consequences, and at the same time spoke of the important service which he had rendered us under the circumstances. The balance of the funds which we had received from Holland, 20,000 or 25,000 francs, had been deposited with the Morris Bank at Philadelphia. Monsieur de Talleyrand had offered to withdraw this money for us, and was only awaiting the formal authorization of my husband to do so. By a chance which was really providential, he learned one night through an indiscretion that Mr. Morris was going to announce his failure the next day. Without losing a moment, he went to the house of the banker, forced his door, the entrance of which had been denied him, and penetrated his cabinet. He told him that he was aware of his situation and forced him to place in his hands the Holland drafts which had only come into his possession as a depositary. Mr. Morris was constrained by fear of the dishonor which would have resulted to him from an abuse of confidence, which Monsieur de Talley-

rand would not have hesitated to proclaim. The only condition he made was that Monsieur de La Tour du Pin should sign an acknowledgement of the payment of these funds. Monsieur de Talleyrand therefore urged my husband to come to Philadelphia to arrange this matter. At the same time, he advised me to accompany my husband, for, having consulted several physicians, he said, regarding the persistency of my fever, all were of the opinion that only a journey would cure me of it.

Mr. Law possessed a charming mansion at New York, and had already urged us several times to come and make him a visit. The haying would not begin before another month, and Monsieur de Chambeau was familiar with all the details of the farm work. There was therefore nothing to stand in the way of this trip. Our neighbor, Susy, the young girl of whom I have already spoken, agreed to come and take my place to look after my little girl. As for my son, Humbert, who was still with Mrs. Ellison at Albany, he would not even know of our absence.

CHAPTER FOUR

1795

A VISIT TO NEW YORK

Fulton's Invention.— The Trip to New York.— The Hudson River.— West Point.— Sojourn at New York.— Alexander Hamilton.— The Yellow Fever.— Precipitate Departure.— General Gates.— Return to the Farm.— Death of Séraphine.— Gathering the Apples and Making Cider.— The Crop of Corn.— Ice in the River.— Recovery of a Portrait of the Queen.

STEAMBOATS had not yet been invented, although this kind of motor power was already in use in some factories. We even had, ourselves, a steam turnspit which acted perfectly, and which we used every week, in cooking either the roast beef for our Sunday dinner, or the immense brown and white turkeys, which are of a species very superior to that found in Europe. But Fulton had not yet applied this discovery to boats; and, since I have touched on this subject, I will relate at once how the thought was suggested to him.

Between Long Island and New York there is an arm of the sea a mile or more wide, which small boats can cross without interruption whenever the weather permits. Since it is not a river, there is no current, and the tide is only apparent from the elevation of the water and does not interfere with navigation. A poor sailor had lost his two legs in battle. Being still young and vigorous, he had a great deal of strength in his arms. The idea came to him to place athwart his bark canoe a round pole with wings at the two extremities, at the right and left of the boat, which he was able to turn at will while seated in the stern. This ingenious system was observed by Fulton one day when he had hired the boat to go to Brooklyn on Long Island, and this gave him the first idea of applying steam to navigation.

Trade with Albany, which was very considerable at this time, was carried on by large sloops and barks. Nearly all of these boats had good rooms, with a fine saloon at the stern, and carried passengers. The descent to New York took about thirty-six hours, as it was necessary to remain at anchor during the period of the rising tides. The boats always endeavored therefore to leave Albany at daybreak. We accordingly went on board one of these barks in the evening, and before sunrise we were already far from the point of our departure.

The North or Hudson River is extremely beautiful. The banks, covered with houses or pretty little villages, spread out on either side, until you reach the very high and steep chain of mountains which runs the length of the continent of North America and which has various names in different localities: Green Mountains, Appalachians, or Alleghanies. The river, before entering the highlands, forms a large basin over a mile wide, similar to that part of the Lake of Geneva called *Le Fond du Lac*, with this difference that here the mountains rise from the edge of the water. The opening through which the river passes, situated between two steep mountains, can be seen only when you are very close to it. The water is so deep that a large frigate could be moored to the side of this passage without danger of touching bottom. The whole morning of the day after our embarkment, we were sailing in the midst of these beautiful mountains. Then, the tide having left us, we went ashore to visit the historical place of West Point, celebrated for the treason of General Arnold and the fate of Major André.

Although I have visited many different places, and admired not a few great effects of nature, I have never seen anything comparable with the pass of West Point. Perhaps it has now lost some of its beauty, if they have cut down the fine trees which dipped their ancient branches in the waters of the river. These mountain-sides were useless for cultivation. I therefore hope, from my love of nature, that the desire of making clearings has not touched them.

We arrived at New York on the morning of the third day and here we found Monsieur de Talleyrand with Mr. Law. Their reception was most friendly. Both were alarmed at my thinness and the change in my appearance. They therefore would not hear of my proposed trip to Philadelphia, which it was necessary to make by stage. It meant that I would have to pass two nights on the way. My husband undertook the journey alone, and I was confided to the good care of Mrs. Foster, the housekeeper of Mr. Law. This good woman exhausted for my benefit all the prescriptions of her medical repertoire. Four

or five times a day she came to me with a little cup
of some kind of bouillon which she urged me to take.
I submitted willingly to this régime as I had been
much disturbed by the lamentations of Monsieur de
Talleyrand over my decline.

The three weeks which we passed in New York
have remained in my memory as a most agreeable
period. My husband returned at the end of four days.
He had much admired the fine city of Philadelphia.
But what I envied him most was the fact that he
had seen the great Washington, who was my hero.
Even to-day I cannot console myself at having
missed seeing this great man, of whom his friend,
Mr. Hamilton, had spoken to me so often. I found
again at New York the whole Hamilton family. I
had been present at the time of their arrival at Albany in a wagon driven by Mr. Hamilton himself,
when he came to resume the practice of his profession
as a lawyer, after having resigned the position of
Secretary of the Treasury. As I have already stated,
he gave up this position, to have a better chance of
leaving a small fortune to his children. Mr. Hamilton
at that time was about thirty-eight years of age. Although he had never been in Europe, he nevertheless
spoke our language like a Frenchman. His remarkable
mind, and the clearness of his thoughts, mingled well
with the originality of Monsieur de Talleyrand and
the vivacity of Monsieur de La Tour du Pin. Every
night these distinguished men, with two or three
others, came for tea. Seated upon the terrace, the
conversation which was started between them lasted
until midnight and sometimes later. At one moment,

A VISIT TO NEW YORK

Mr. Hamilton would relate the story of the beginnings of the War of Independence, of which the dull memoirs of that imbecile, Lafayette, have since rendered the details so insipid. At another, Mr. Law would speak of his sojourn in India, of his administration of Patna, where he had been Governor, of the elephants and the palanquins. Between them all, the conversation never languished. Mr. Law enjoyed these evenings so much that when we spoke of our departure, he became very sad and said to his butler, "Foster, if they leave me, I am a dead man."

Three weeks had rolled around when the news became current one evening that yellow fever had broken out in a street very near to Broadway, where we were living. That very night my husband and I were very ill; I think from having eaten too many bananas or pineapples or other fruits brought from the Islands by the same boat which had carried the fever. Fearing to be shut in by the quarantine, I resolved to leave at once, and at daybreak our trunk was packed and we had gone to reserve our places on board a sloop which was ready to set sail. We then returned to see Mr. Law and make our adieux. He decided then to leave also, under the pretext of going to visit some property in the new city of Washington, which they were beginning to build. In these purchases he compromised the greater part of his fortune. Our departure was so precipitate that I did not even see Monsieur de Talleyrand. He was not yet up when we were already far from New York.

On our return we saw with the same admiration the fine pass at West Point, and this time we made

[227]

a long promenade on land during the six hours our boat remained at anchor. We ascended the hill upon which was situated the inn which was the place of the last interview between Arnold and André. At New York I had seen the aged General Gates who had known all the French officers and loved to talk of them. I had been cautioned not to speak of the incident of Major André, a subject of conversation which was very painful to him — not because he reproached himself with the sentence, which was pronounced in conformity with rules of military justice, but because it recalled to him the terrible reprisals made by the English, who had executed a number of American prisoners.

I found my house in the best of order, although Monsieur de Chambeau did not expect us. My little girl was also in very good health. This absence of a month had appeared long to me, in spite of the very agreeable society in which I had lived. The yellow fever made great ravages that year at New York, and I congratulated myself that we had left so quickly.

I resumed with new ardor my rural occupations. My fever had departed with the change of air and my strength had returned. The work of the dairy was resumed, and the pretty designs moulded upon the butter-balls informed my customers of my return. Our orchard promised a magnificent harvest of apples, and our barn contained grain for the whole winter. Our negroes, stimulated by our example, worked with good spirit. They were better clothed and better nourished than those of our neighbors.

I was feeling very happy under these circumstances when God struck me a most unexpected blow, and, as I then imagined, the most cruel and terrible that one could endure. Alas, I have since experienced others which have surpassed it in severity. My little Séraphine was taken from us by a sudden illness very common in this part of the country — a kind of infant paralysis. She died in a few hours without losing consciousness. The physician from Albany, whom Monsieur de Chambeau had gone to bring, as soon as she began to suffer, gave us no hope that she would live and declared that this malady was then very common in the country and that no remedy was known. The young Schuyler who only the day before had been playing with my daughter during the afternoon succumbed to the same trouble a few hours later and rejoined her in Heaven. This cruel event threw us all into a state of sadness and mortal discouragement. We brought Humbert home, and I endeavored to obtain distraction from my grief in occupying myself with his education. He was then five and a half years old. His intelligence was very well developed. He spoke English perfectly and read it easily.

There was no Catholic priest either in Albany or in the neighborhood. My husband, who did not wish to have a Protestant minister called, himself performed the last rites for our child, and placed her in a little enclosure which had been arranged to serve as a cemetery for the inhabitants of the farm. It was situated in the middle of our woods. Almost every day I went to kneel upon the grave, the last resting place of the child whom I had so much loved, and it was there that God gave to me a change of heart.

Up to this period of my life, although I was far from being irreligious, I had never taken much interest in religion. During the course of my education, no one had ever spoken to me of religion. During the first years of my childhood I had had, under my eyes, the worst possible examples. In the high society of Paris, I had been witness of scandals, so often repeated, that they had become familiar to me to the point of no longer moving me. In this way every thought of morality had been benumbed in my heart, but the hour had come when I had to recognize the hand which had smitten me.

I do not know exactly how to describe the transformation which came over me. It seemed to me as if a voice cried out to me that I must change my whole being. Kneeling upon the grave of my child, I implored her to obtain from God, who had already recalled her to Him, my pardon and a little relief from my distress. My prayer was heard. God accorded me then the grace to know and serve Him. He gave me the courage to bend very humbly under the stroke which had smitten me and to prepare myself to support without complaining the new griefs, by which in His justice He deemed it proper to try me in the future. From that day the divine will found me submissive and resigned.

Although all joy had disappeared from our household, it was none the less necessary for us to continue our work, and we encouraged each other, my husband

and I, to find distraction in the obligation under which we were not to remain a moment idle. The harvest of the apples approached. It promised to be very abundant, for our orchard had the finest appearance. We could count upon the trees as many apples as there were leaves. The autumn before we had essayed what is known at Bordeaux as *une façon*. This consists in turning over with a spade a square of four or five feet around each tree, something which had never been done there before. The Americans indeed have no idea of the effect which that produces upon vegetation; but when, in the springtime, they saw our trees covered with blossoms, they looked upon us as sorcerers.

Another act brought us great reputation. Instead of buying for our cider new barrels made of very porous wood, we succeeded in finding at Albany several casks which had contained Bordeaux and also some marked *cognac* which were well known to us. Then we arranged our cellar with the same care as if it were to contain wine of the Médoc. We borrowed a cider mill to crush the apples. A horse twenty-three years old which General Schuyler had given me was hitched to it. Here is the story of this horse which I have not previously recounted:

The horse had carried him through the war, and the General wished to let him die a happy death. It seemed as though he had almost reached the end of his days, when our negro, Prime, saw him in the pasture dragging one foot after the other and reduced to skin and bones. Prime requested me to ask the General to give me the horse, which he did with pleasure. He had been a magnificent pure-blooded animal, but he no longer had any teeth. Prime had much difficulty in leading the poor beast the four miles which separated the pasture from our stable. Every day he gave him a mixture of oats and boiled corn, hay finely cut up, carrots and so on. This fodder in abundance restored to the fine animal the vigor of his youth. At the end of the month I could mount him every day, and soon at a little gallop he carried me even to Albany without making a false step. They refused to believe that he was the same horse. This display of skill greatly increased the reputation of Prime.

But to return to our apples. The cider mill was very primitive. It consisted of two pieces of channelled wood which fitted into each other, and was turned by our horse attached to a pole. The apples were fed into a hopper, and when the juice had filled a large tub, it was taken to the cellar and poured into the casks.

The whole operation was very simple and, as we had very fine weather, this harvest was a charming recreation. My son who rode the horse during the day was convinced that without him nothing could have been done.

When the work was finished, we found ourselves provided with eight or ten barrels to sell, in addition to what we had reserved for ourselves. Our reputation for honesty was so great that people had confidence that we would not put any water into our cider. This enabled us to sell it at double the ordinary price, and all was sold at once. As for that which we had reserved for ourselves, we treated it exactly as we would have done with our white wine at Le Bouilh.

The crop of corn followed that of the apples. This crop was very abundant as it is the one which succeeds best in the United States where it is indigenous. As you must not leave the ear covered with the husk more than two days, we brought together all of our neighbors to finish the harvest quickly on the spot. This is what is called a "husking bee." We began by sweeping the floor of the barn with as much care as though we were going to give a ball. Then when night arrived, we lighted several candles and the people assembled, about thirty in all, black and white, and set themselves to work. One of the party did not cease to sing or to tell stories. Towards the middle of the night we served to each one a bowl of hot milk which we had previously mixed with cider. To this mixture you add five or six pounds of brown sugar, if you are prodigal, or an equal amount of molasses, if you are not, then spices, such as cloves, cinnamon and nutmeg. Our workers drank to our very best health the contents of an immense wash-boiler filled with this mixture, with which they ate toast. At five o'clock in the morning, when the weather was already quite chilly, they left us in good spirits. Our negroes were often invited to these gatherings, but my negress never went. When all of our crops had been harvested and garnered, we commenced to work our land and to undertake the labors which precede the winter. Under a shed was piled up the wood which was to be sold. The sleds were repaired and repainted. I bought a large piece of coarse blue and white checked flannel to make two shirts for each of my negroes. A tailor was employed by the day at the farm to make them coats and well-lined caps. This man ate with us because he was white. He would certainly have refused if we had asked him to eat with the slaves, although they were incomparably better dressed and had better manners than he. But I was very careful not to express the least remark upon this custom. My neighbors acted in this way, and I followed their example and in our reciprocal relations I was always careful not to make any allusion to the place which I had formerly occupied on the social ladder. I was the proprietor of a farm of 250 acres. I lived in the same manner as my neighbors, neither better nor worse. This simplicity and abnegation gave me more respect and consideration than as if I had wished to play the lady.

I never lost a moment. Every day, winter and summer alike, I was up at dawn and my toilette did not take long. The negroes before going to their work assisted the negress to milk the cows, of which we had eight. During this time, I was busy with skimming the milk in the dairy. The days we made butter, two or three times a week, Minck remained to turn the handle of the churn, a task which was too difficult for a woman. All the rest of the making of the butter which was quite tiresome was my task. I had a remarkable collection of bowls, spoons, wooden spatulas, which were the work of my good friends the Indians, and my dairy was considered the cleanest and also the most elegant in the country.

This year the winter came very early. During the first days of November, the black curtain which announced the snow commenced to rise in the west. As we would have wished, there followed eight days of bitter cold, and the river in twenty-four hours was frozen to the depth of three feet before the snow began to fall. When it began to snow, it fell with such violence that you could not see a man at the distance of ten paces. Prudent people took care not to hitch up their sleighs to mark out the routes. This work was left to those who were more in haste, or to those whose business compelled them to go to the city or to the river. Then before venturing upon the river, we waited until the passageways to descend upon the ice had been marked by pine branches. Without this precaution, it would have been very dangerous to venture on the ice, and every year there were accidents caused by imprudence. The tide before Albany and as far up as the junction of the Mohawk rises several feet and the ice often does not remain upon the water.

Our winter passed like the preceding one. We frequently went to dine with the Schuylers and the Van Rensselaers, whose friendship never changed. Monsieur de Talleyrand, who was again living at Philadelphia, had been able to recover in a very singular manner certain articles which belonged to me: a medallion portrait of the Queen, a casket and a watch which had been left me by my mother. He knew from me that our banker at The Hague had advised me that he had placed these articles in the hands of a young American diplomat (I have forgotten his name, fortunately for him) with the request that he should arrange to send them to me. But although Monsieur de Talleyrand had done his best, he had never been able to put his hand on this person. Finally one evening, when calling upon a lady of his acquaintance at Philadelphia, she had spoken to him of a portrait of the Queen which Monsieur —— had procured at Paris and which he had loaned her to show to some of her friends. She wished to know from Monsieur de Talleyrand if the portrait was good. Hardly had he looked at it before he recognized that it belonged to me. He took possession of the medallion and informed the lady that it did not belong to the young diplomat. Then he went at once to find the latter and, without any preamble, demanded from him the casket and the watch which the banker at The Hague had confided to him with the portrait. The young man was much embarrassed and ended by restoring all of these articles, which Monsieur de Talleyrand sent to us at the farm.

CHAPTER FIVE

1796

DEPARTURE FOR EUROPE

News from France.— Return Decided Upon.— Regrets of Mme. de La Tour du Pin.— The Slaves Receive Their Liberty.— Departure for Europe.— The Wait at New York.— Arrival at Cadiz.— The Quarantine.— Visit of the Customs Officers.— Mode of Travel in Spain at This Epoch.— A Bull Fight.— Departure from Cadiz.— The Inns.— Cathedral of Cordova.— In the Sierra Morena.— At Madrid.

TOWARDS the end of the winter of 1795 and 1796, I had the measles and was quite ill. We were afraid that Humbert also would take them, but he did not, although he slept in my room. I soon found myself in good health, and it was at this moment that we received letters from Bonie in France which informed us that, joining his efforts to those of Monsieur de Brouquens, he had succeeded in having the sequestration raised at Le Bouilh.

The property of the persons who had been condemned had been restored. My mother-in-law in concert with her son-in-law, the Marquis de Lameth, acting in the name of his children, again entered into possession of the estates of Tesson and Ambleville and of the house at Saintes which the Department of the Charente-Inférieure had occupied. But when they repuested that the seals should be taken off at

Le Bouilh, the authorities objected on account of the absence of the proprietor. Our family represented that the owner was living in America with a passport, and that neither my husband nor myself, who personally owned a house at Paris, had been inscribed upon the list of émigrés. After numerous discussions they allowed us a delay of a year in which to put in a personal appearance, in default of which Le Bouilh would be placed on sale as national property. Our friends, therefore, urged us to return as soon as possible. Nevertheless, as the stability of the French Government inspired, even at this time, very little confidence, they recommended us at the same time not to take our passage for a French port, but rather to return by way of Spain, with which the Republic had just concluded a peace which seemed likely to be durable.

These dispatches fell in the midst of our tranquil occupations like a fire-brand which quickly lighted in the hearts of all around me the thought of a return to their native land. As for myself, I had an entirely different feeling. France had left in my mind only a recollection of horror. There I had lost my youth, which had been broken by terrors the remembrance of which I could not forget. I had not then, and I never have had since in my mind but two feelings which entirely and exclusively mastered me: the love of my husband and of my children. Religion, the only motive now for all my actions, commanded me not to oppose the least obstacle to a departure which frightened me and cost me dear. A sort of presentiment caused me to foresee that I was going to encounter a new life of trouble and anxieties. My husband did not dream of the intensity of my regret when I saw the moment of our departure arrive. I imposed only one condition, that of giving our slaves their liberty. My husband consented and reserved for me alone this happiness.

These poor people, on seeing the letters arrive from Europe, had feared some change in our life. They were disturbed and alarmed. Therefore, all four of them were trembling when they entered my room to which I had called them. They found me alone. I said to them with emotion: "My friends, we are going to return to Europe. What shall I do with you?" The poor creatures were overcome. Judith dropped into a chair, in tears, while the three men covered their faces with their hands, and all remained silent. I continued: "We have been so satisfied with you that it is just that you should be recompensed. My husband has charged me to tell you that he will give you your liberty." On hearing this word our good servants were so stupified that they remained for several seconds without speech. Then all four threw themselves at my feet crying: "Is it possible? Do you mean that we are free?" I replied: "Yes, upon my honor, from this moment, as free as I am myself."

Who can describe the poignant emotion of such a moment! Never in my life had I experienced anything so sweet. Those whom I had just promised their liberty surrounded me in tears. They kissed my hands, my feet, my dress, and then suddenly their joy ceased and they said: "We would prefer to remain slaves all our lives, if you would stay here."

The following day my husband took them to Albany before a judge, for the ceremony of the *manumission*, an act which had to be public. All the negroes of the city were present. The Justice of the Peace, who was at the same time the steward of Mr. Van Rensselaer, was in very bad humor. He attempted to assert that Prime, being fifty years of age, could not under the terms of the law be given his liberty unless he was assured a pension of a hundred dollars. But Prime had foreseen this case, and he produced his certificate of baptism which attested that he was only forty-nine. They made the slaves kneel before my husband, and he placed his hand upon the head of each to sanction his liberation, exactly in the manner of ancient Rome.

We let our dwelling, with the land which surrounded it, to the same individual from whom we had purchased it, and we sold the greater part of our equipment. The horses brought quite a high price. I distributed by way of souvenirs several little articles in porcelain which I had brought from Europe. As for my poor Judith, I left her some old silk dresses which have, without doubt, been handed down to her descendants.

Towards the middle of April, 1796, we embarked from Albany to descend to New York, after having paid tender and thankful adieux to all those who for two years had overwhelmed us with tender thoughts, friendship and kindness of every kind. How many times, two years later, when enduring another exile, have I not regretted my farm and my good neighbors.

DEPARTURE FOR EUROPE

At New York we stayed with Mr. and Mrs. Olive who received us in their pretty little country house. Here, we found Monsieur de Talleyrand, who had decided, like us, to return to Europe. Mme. de Staël was back at Paris, where she was living with Benjamin Constant. She urged him to return and enter the service of the Directory which demanded the aid of his ability. For a moment he had thought that he would take his passage upon the same vessel with us, but when he learned our intention to land at a Spanish port, whence we expected to gain Bordeaux, he changed his plans and resolved to take passage on a vessel bound for Hamburg. There was no ship leaving for Coruna or for Bilbao in the north of Spain, as we would have wished. Only one boat, a superb English vessel of four hundred tons, was going to Cadiz at an early date. For lack of anything better, and in spite of the long journey which we would have to make in Spain, we decided to engage our passage on this vessel. It sailed under the Spanish flag, although it as well as the cargo belonged to an Englishman. The proprietor, who was named Mr. Ensdel, was to go as a passenger. He was an old ship-owner who had been interested in whaling. He did not know a word of French. The captain who was originally from Jamaica also spoke only English, but he soon found a very intelligent interpreter in my son who although only six years of age was of great use to him. While occupying our time with our outfit and our arrangements for the voyage, we passed the three remaining weeks with Mrs. Olive, in company with Monsieur de Talleyrand.

In the harbor there was a French sloop of war, commanded by Captain Barré, whose father my husband had known in the household of the old Duc d'Orléans, the father of Philippe Égalité. Although a regular sea-dog, he was a very pleasant man. He came for us every day in his boat and conducted us to every part of the harbor, taking good care never to approach Sandy Hook where Captain, later Admiral, Cochrane had waited for two months to capture him if he attempted to come out. We visited his sloop, which was armed with fifteen guns. It was a jewel of order, neatness and care. How I should have loved to have returned to Europe in this fine boat.

But the "Maria-Josepha" awaited us. We went on board, my husband, myself, our young son, Humbert, and Monsieur de Chambeau, the sixth of May, 1796, and the same day we set sail. There were several other passengers on board. Among them was Monsieur de Lavaur, an émigré, a former officer of the Constitutional Guard of Louis XVI, who had escaped from a thousand dangers at the time of the massacres of the tenth of August. As he was from Bordeaux, a kind of attachment was formed between him and my husband. Then there was a French merchant, Monsieur Tisserandot, and his wife. He had been unfortunate in business at New York and was going to make another attempt at Madrid. His wife was young, sweet, quite well brought up, but lazy. The persons whom I have just named, with Mr. Ensdel and the captain, made up the table in the large salon.

I did not suffer from sea-sickness, and, the weather

being superb, I was occupied all day long. As I soon finished the work which I had brought for my husband and myself, I then set up for a general seamstress and announced that any one could give me work to do. Every one brought me something. I had shirts to make, cravats to hem and linen to mark. The voyage lasted forty days, because the captain, against the advice of Mr. Ensdel, had taken a southerly course, and had been carried away by the currents. This time was sufficient for me to put the wardrobe of everybody on the boat in order.

Finally about the tenth of June, we saw Cape Saint-Vincent and the next day we entered the harbor of Cadiz. The captain by his stupidity and ignorance had prolonged our voyage by at least fifteen days by allowing himself to be carried towards the coast of Africa, whence he had a great deal of trouble in returning to the north. He believed that he was so far from land that he had not even thought of sending a sailor as a look-out to the top of the mast. When he discovered, at daybreak, Cape Saint-Vincent, which is very high, he was entirely disconcerted.

We were moored alongside a French vessel with three decks, the "Jupiter." It was there with a French fleet which had been prevented from going out by the English men-of-war, superior in number, which were cruising every day almost in sight of the port.

We were visited at once by the boat of the health officer who notified us that we would be kept a week on board in quarantine. We preferred this to being sent to the lazarette where we would have been devoured by all the numerous insects which are so abundant in Spain. If we had been able to find a boat which was going to Bilbao or Barcelona, we should have taken passage. The voyage thus would have been shorter, less tiresome and less expensive.

The name of Monsieur de Chambeau had not been erased from the list of émigrés, and he was not able to return to France. He wished to go to Madrid where he knew several persons, but, nevertheless, he would have willingly accompanied us as far as Barcelona, which would have brought him quite near to Auch, a city in which he owned some property.

The uncertainty of our plans formed the subject of our conversation during the quarantine which lasted ten days and which might have been prolonged even more on account of the desertion of one of our sailors. This man, of French nationality, had been captured in a combat upon a sloop of war. He recognized a sailor on board the "Jupiter" which was moored alongside us and spoke to him through a megaphone. The same night he swam to the "Jupiter" and when the health officer proceeded to call the roll the following morning, no trace of him could be found, except his shirt and trousers. This was his whole wardrobe. This incident prolonged our quarantine until the day that it was ascertained that the fugitive was on the French vessel.

The quarantine was nearly fatal to me. Every day sellers of fruit came alongside the boat, and I passed my time with Mme. Tisserandot in lowering a basket by means of a cord in order to obtain figs, oranges and strawberries. Eating this fruit made me very ill.

Finally permission was received to give us our liberty. The captain put us on land, and never in my life have I been so much embarrassed as at this moment. On landing they ordered Mme. Tisserandot and myself to enter a little room looking out on the street, while they examined our effects with the most exaggerated minuteness. Our colored dresses and our straw hats soon attracted a large crowd of individuals of every age and of every condition: sailors and monks, porters and gentlemen — all anxious to see what they doubtless considered to be two curious animals. As for our husbands, they had been detained in the room where our baggage was examined. We were therefore alone with my son.

This indiscreet curiosity decided us, my companion and myself, immediately to dress like the Spanish women. Even before proceeding to the inn, we went to purchase black skirts and mantillas so as to be able to go out without scandalizing the whole population. We stopped at the hotel which was reputed to be the best at Cadiz, but which was so dirty as to cause me the greatest discomfort, accustomed as I was to the exquisite neatness of America, and I would willingly have returned on board our boat.

I happened to remember that one of the sisters of poor Théobald Dillon, massacred at Lille in 1792, had married an English merchant established at Cadiz, by the name of Langton. Having written him a polite note, he came at once and was very attentive to us. At that time his wife with his younger daughter was at Madrid visiting a married daughter, the Baronne d'Andilla. Nevertheless, Mr. Langton invited us to dinner and even wished to have us stay at his house. But we did not accept, as I was too ill to take the trouble to be polite. It was arranged that the dinner should be put off until the first day that I felt better.

The day after our arrival my husband took our passport to be viséd by the French Consul-General. He was a Monsieur de Roquesante, a former Comte or Marquis, now changed into a hot Republican, if not a Terrorist. He asked my husband a hundred questions and made a note of his replies. All this was very much like an examination. Then he suddenly exclaimed, "Citizen, we have received to-day excellent news from France. That rascal Charette has finally been taken and shot." "So much the worse," replied Monsieur de La Tour du Pin, "he was at least a worthy man." The Consul then kept silent and signed the passport, which he reminded my husband it would be necessary to present again to the French Ambassador at Madrid. Later we learned the manner in which he had recommended us at Bayonne.

At this time Spain, having concluded peace with the French Republic, had disbanded the greater part of her army, probably without paying them. The roads were infested with brigands, especially the mountains of the Sierra Morena which we had to cross. We travelled in a convoy composed of several carriages only. We did not take any military escort, which would have probably been in league with the brigands, the former soldiers, but the mounted travellers who joined the convoy had taken the precaution to be armed to the teeth. A convoy was usually composed of from fifteen to eighteen covered chariots drawn by mules.

It is thus that we set out from Cadiz. We occupied, my husband, my son and myself, one of these chariots, in which we were stretched out at full length upon our mattresses. Below, in the bottom of the chariot, was placed our baggage, covered with a bed of straw which filled the spaces between the trunks. A hood of cane artistically sewn and covered by a tarpaulin protected us from the sun during the day and from the humidity during the night, for it happened several times that we preferred the chariot to an inn.

But in speaking so soon of our departure, I have anticipated, because we remained a week at Cadiz. Every evening we walked upon the beautiful prome-nade of L'Alameda, which looks out on the sea, where you can breathe a little air after having endured during the day a heat of 95 degrees.

A spectacle which I have never forgotten was the magnificent bull-fight the day of Saint-Jean. This national fête of Spain has been described so often that I will not attempt to write of it here. The amphitheatre was immense and held at least four or five thousand persons who were seated upon the steps and were protected from the sun by a canvas awning similar to the *vélum* of the Roman amphi-theatres. This awning was kept constantly wet by a spray like fine rain which did not go through the cloth. Thus, although the performance began after the mid-day mass and lasted until sunset, I do not recall having suffered a moment from the heat.

RECOLLECTIONS OF THE REVOLUTION

They killed ten bulls, who were so beautiful and so well-bred that they would have made the fortune of an American farmer. The matador was the first of his kind at this epoch. He was a handsome young man of twenty-five years. In spite of the terrible danger which he ran, on account of his remarkable agility, you did not feel any anxiety. Certainly, at the moment when the two adversaries, alone face to face, looked steadily at each other, before the bull rushed upon the matador, the most poignant emotion which could possibly be felt gripped all of the spectators. You could have heard a pin drop. But you must understand that the matador does not give the coup d'épée. He only directs the point of the sword upon which the bull rushes to empale himself. This spectacle was an epoch in my life and no other has left upon me so powerful an impression. I have never forgotten the slightest detail and the recollection is as fresh in my memory after so many years, as if I had seen it yesterday.

The day fixed for our departure we let the convoy set out and remained, my husband, my son and myself, to dine with Mr. Langton. A bark which had been prepared by his thoughtfulness was to take us to the other side of the bay to rejoin our caravan at Port-Sainte-Marie where we were to pass the night. During this long journey we did not travel faster than a man can walk on foot.

I was feeling so ill that my husband hesitated to let me set out, and yet there was no means of drawing back. Our baggage had been sent forward. We had paid half of the cost of our trip as far as Madrid.

DEPARTURE FOR EUROPE

Our passport had been viséd and Monsieur de Roquesante, a Republican Consul, would have regarded any delay with suspicion. He would have attributed it to some pretext, and as I have always believed that one can surmount any evil, except perhaps a broken leg, the thought never occurred to me to remain at Cadiz. We therefore dined with Mr. Langton, after having been present at the departure of our travelling companions who were to sleep at Port-Sainte-Marie.

Nothing could be more delightful in point of neatness and care than this place of Mr. Langton, which was kept in the English fashion. He had adopted none of the Spanish practices except those customary to avoid the inconvenience of the very hot climate. The house was built around a square court filled with flowers. On the ground floor there was a line of arcades and an open gallery at the first floor. An awning stretched at the height of the roof covered the whole surface of the court. In the middle a jet of water reached the canvas, which being thus constantly wet communicated a delightful freshness to the whole house. I admit that I experienced a very painful feeling in thinking that instead of remaining in this agreeable place it was necessary for me to begin a long journey in a heat of 95 degrees. But the die was cast, and it was necessary to depart. After this farewell dinner, towards evening, we entered the bark, and in an hour and a half, the wind being favorable, we arrived at Port-Sainte-Marie. There we found our caravan, composed of fourteen carriages and six or seven *hidalgos*, armed from head to foot.

The aim of our second day's journey was Xérès, situated at a distance of only five leagues. As I had need of rest, we made up our minds once more to let the caravan go ahead and to rejoin it in the evening. We therefore took dinner at an early hour at Port-Sainte-Marie, a very pretty locality. Then we took a cabriolet similar to those which I see here at Pisa where I am writing these Recollections. Our vehicle was attached to a large mule which had no bridle, which seemed to me curious. Upon the head of the mule was balanced a high plume to which bells were attached. A young boy, with whip in hand, sprang lightly upon the shafts, uttered some cabalistic words, and the mule set out at a trot as rapid as a good hunting gallop. The route was superb and we went like the wind, the mule obeying docilely the voice of his little driver, avoiding obstacles, and winding through the streets of the villages which we traversed, with a wonderful sagacity. At first I was afraid, but reflecting that it was the custom of the country to drive this way, I became resigned.

Arrived at Xérès, I was curious to know the value of a mule like the one which had conducted us and was told that it was worth from fifty to sixty louis, which seemed to me quite dear.

The following day began our real travels. I was still indisposed, but, stretched out as I was upon a good mattress, and the road being very fine, I did not suffer more than I would have if I had remained quiet. At two o'clock we stopped for dinner in some wretched inn, and it happened two or three times that we preferred to pass the night in our chariot, rather than to sleep in beds so filthy as to be disgusting.

It was night when we arrived at Cordova. As we were travelling a certain distance behind, all the other members of the party had already found their lodgings when we reached the inn. As there were only beds to be had at the inn, it was necessary to look for a place to eat. We finally succeeded, with some difficulty, on account of the advanced hour, in finding a kind of cabaret, where we could only obtain some bread and a few slices of fried bacon.

The following morning there was a delay in the departure of the convoy, which gave me an opportunity to see the magnificent Cathedral of Cordova of which so many descriptions have been written. You can readily believe that travelling in so uncomfortable a manner and also feeling quite ill, in the heat which reigned in Andalusia from mid-day to three o'clock, the period of the day that we ordinarily stopped, I did not feel like visiting the monuments. This time we passed an hour in walking through the forest of columns of this cathedral. The muleteers came to urge us to set out. They were carrying sufficient provisions for two meals which we were to take in the open that day, as there was no dwelling in existence in the part of the country which we were going to traverse.

On leaving Cordova, we rode for a whole hour in the midst of groves of lemon trees, and of Moorish olive trees, which were abundantly watered, before arriving at the wall of the ancient city of which vestiges are still being uncovered. This will give an idea of the immense surface which was covered by this large Moorish city of other days, as in Italy you obtain an idea in the same way of the limits of ancient Rome.

We had our dinner, as had been arranged, near a well in the midst of a pasture covered with sheep. The eye could not measure the extent of this plain, which was several leagues long, and covered in part with fine grass, and in part with dwarf myrtle trees. Several pomegranates covered with blossoms arose around the well. This halt had something oriental about it which singularly pleased me. I preferred it very much to the stops of three hours in the dirty inns which were always so hot.

The next day and the days following we crossed the Sierra Morena and saw the two pretty little cities of La Carlota and La Carolina. These had been built by German Colonists, and we observed that certain characteristics of the German physiognomy had not yet been entirely effaced. We encountered children with blond hair whose complexion, as dark as that of the Spaniards, was in marked contrast with their blue eyes. These little cities are picturesque, and are constructed with regularity on fine sites. This route which is very beautiful is bordered on all the hills by a parapet of marble. At the time this was the only road between the south of Spain and Castile.

To my great regret we did not pass by Toledo. We arrived at Aranjuez for dinner the fifteenth day of our journey, I think. Here we remained for the rest of the day. We admired the fresh shade, the handsome weeping willows and the green prairies.

After having come from Andalusia which was baked by the sun of July, it seemed to us like a green oasis in the midst of a desert. The River Tagus, although very small, is conducted with such art through this charming valley as to produce everywhere a delightful freshness. The Court was not then at Aranjuez; nevertheless, for some reason which I have forgotten, we did not visit the Château.

The following day we reached Madrid, after a halt of two hours at Puerta del Sol, while our baggage was being examined, ransacked and inspected. It would have been useless to show any impatience for the *sang-froid* of the Castilians is not put out by anything. Finally the signal for our departure was given and they took us to the hotel, a mediocre inn located in a small street.

Here we were assigned quite a good room. My husband immediately dispatched the letters and packages with which Mr. Langton had charged us for his wife and his two daughters. Then I made a more careful toilette than that of my chariot, with the intention of going to see these ladies after our dinner. But they called on us first. A half-hour had hardly elapsed when we received a visit from two of the most beautiful ladies I have ever seen, Baronne d'Andilla and Mlle. Carmen Langton. The mother who was ill had not been able to go out. Their brother-in-law, Monsieur Broun, accompanied them. His wife who was dead had been the third Mlle. Langton, who was said to have been more beautiful even than her sisters. These ladies showed us great kindness and attention and their brother-in-law proposed that we should take a little furnished lodging in the quarter where these ladies lived. He took charge of all the necessary arrangements and placed himself at our disposal for all the time that we remained at Madrid. Our sojourn could not be shorter than a month or six weeks at least, because we were awaiting replies from Bordeaux to the letters which we had written from Cadiz.

However, on account of the delicate state of my health, I wished to be at Le Bouilh before the tenth of November. My husband went the following day to see the ambassador of the Directory to have his passport put in order. As he still preserved a very vivid recollection of the reception of the citizen, the former Comte or Marquis, de Roquesante, he was very agreeably surprised by the kind reception of the ambassador. He was the General, later the Maréchal, Pérignon. Formerly under the command of my father, he had received from him assistance which advanced his career. Not having forgotten this, he was full of politeness for my husband. Nevertheless, his gratitude did not go so far as to honor me with his visit. The *seigneurs* of other days were not yet in fashion, as they became later on.

We remained six weeks at Madrid, during which time we were overwhelmed with the thoughtfulness, the attentions and the kindness of the Langton and Andilla families. The son-in-law of Mme. Langton, Monsieur Broun, whose wife had died the preceding year, conducted us to all the most interesting parts of the city, and every evening Mme. d'Andilla took us to the Corso, then to take an ice in a fashionable café at the end of the Rue d'Alcala. Monsieur Broun showed us the portrait of his wife. She had been as beautiful as, if not more beautiful than, her sisters, and he could not be consoled for her loss, at the age of twenty-two years.

CHAPTER SIX
1796–1797

VISIT TO PARIS

Departure from Madrid.— The Escurial.— Arrival on Saint-Sébastien.— Bonie Rejoins Us.— Apprehensions on Returning to France.— Arrival at Bayonne.— Monsieur de Brouquens Again.— Arrival at Le Bouilh.— Devastation of the Château.— The Library Saved.— Return of Marguerite.— Birth of Charlotte.— Absence of Monsieur de La Tour du Pin.— Fortune Compromised.— Dispersion of the Family Souvenirs.— Trip to Paris.— Devastation of the Château of Tesson.— Talleyrand Minister of Foreign Affairs.— Jealousy of Tallien.

FINALLY we received a letter from Bonie stating the day that he would await us at Bayonne, and this time we engaged a little *collieras* to transport ourselves and our baggage. Monsieur de Lavaur, who had received word that his name had been erased from the list of émigrés, proposed to accompany us, and we consented, although this was not at all agreeable to us. Monsieur de Chambeau was obliged to remain at Madrid. The tender friendship which he bore us, and of which he had given us many proofs, rendered this separation very painful for him and for us. For a period of three years, he had shared all of our vicissitudes, our interests and our troubles. My husband considered him as a brother. During the long years of exile,

[256]

our thoughts had been the same. Thus our departure was a sad blow to our poor friend. He had no money, as no one had thought to send him any. We were happy to be in a position to leave him fifty louis, and he was fortunate enough to be welcomed in the house of the Comtesse de Galvez, where he remained until 1800.

We left Madrid at two o'clock in the afternoon to spend the night at the Escurial. The *collieras* was a fine old berline, drawn by seven mules, which were conducted, or rather counseled and exhorted, by a coachman seated upon the box and by an assistant-postillion armed with a long whip. The latter sprang alternately from one to the other of the mules, who had no bridles and obeyed only his voice. However, I think that the mules at the pole had reins, but the five others certainly not. One of them, the seventh, marched alone in front. She was named the "Generala" and guided all the others.

At a quarter of a league from Madrid, the coachman perceived that he had forgotten his mantle. In spite of the stifling heat, he was not willing to go another step before the postillion had gone back to look for it mounted on one of the mules. This delayed us much, and we reached the Escurial only late in the evening.

Nearly all of the following day was consecrated to a visit to this admirable monastery, of which so many descriptions have been written. Among all those which I have read since, none has seemed to me perfectly exact. They do not picture the kind of sad religious calm with which this place, this *chef-*

d'œuvre of all the arts, in the midst of a desert, imbues the soul. So many marvellous things seem to have been brought together in this solitude, only to recall to the mind the futility and the inutility of the works of man. Since then, when the events which have distracted Spain have been unrolled before me, I have been struck by the prophecy of the father who showed us the subterranean chapel in which are buried the Kings of Spain since Philip II. After having walked through the midst of these tombs, all of which are similar, he called our attention to one which remained empty: that destined for the reigning King, Charles IV, and at the same time placing his hand on the sarcophagus, which was kept open by a wedge of marble, he said to us in Italian: "Who knows whether he will ever occupy it?" At the moment, this remark did not arrest my attention, but long afterwards, when I saw this unfortunate Prince chased from his throne, this prophetic speech returned to my mind.

Since the discovery of America and of the gold and silver mines of Peru, the Kings of Spain have made every year, to the Church of the Escurial, a magnificent present of these two metals. It thus happens that the Treasury of the Church has become the richest in all Europe. All of the articles provided by this luxurious custom, arranged in order by years, testified, to an observing eye, to the successive deterioration in taste, from the first signed by Benvenuto Cellini, to the last of very recent date.

The top of the high altar, a *bas-relief* in solid silver, representing the apotheosis of Saint Laurent,

Patron of the Escurial, although of an unequalled magnificence, was not satisfactory as a work of art. I say "was" not, for there is reason to suppose that the misfortunes of Spain have led to the destruction of all these masterpieces. The different objects used for the religious worship were arranged in *armoires à glaces* made of the finest wood of the East Indies. I have preserved a clear recollection of a sacred ciborium (*ciboire*), in the form of a map of the world surmounted by a cross, the middle of which was ornamented by an enormous diamond and the arms with four large pearls. There were also monstrances (*ostensoirs*) entirely covered with precious stones. They showed us the *ornament du jour de Pâques*, made of red velvet embroidered entirely with fine pearls of different sizes, according to the design. Many persons would not perhaps have appreciated this magnificence, for the smallest piece of stuff embossed with silver produced more effect. Nevertheless, there were many million pearls upon these plain pieces of velvet.

We ascended to the rood-loft (*jubé*), where we saw some admirable books of the Church, formed of leaves of vellum, the margins of which were painted by the pupils of Raphael from his designs. These volumes in *grand in-folio*, ornamented with corners of silver, bound in a brown skin showing the reverse side, were placed in a kind of open case separated from one another by slender pieces of wood. On account of their weight, it would have been difficult to take them out of their case. To obviate this inconvenience, there was arranged at the bottom of each of these cases little ivory wheels traversed by iron pins around which they turned. In this manner, the slightest effort was enough to draw one of these books to you. I have never seen this method employed in any other library.

In this high gallery of the Escurial we found the magnificent Christ in silver, of life size, made by Benvenuto Cellini. After having visited and admired this magnificent Church, I was left alone while my husband and Monsieur de Lavaur went to visit the Monastery and the Library where they saw the beautiful picture of Raphael named *La Vierge à la Perle*. I had not been informed at Madrid that a woman was not able to visit the Library, which was situated in the interior of the Monastery, without a special permit. I regretted this greatly.

During the long time that I awaited my travelling companions, I had time for my mind to become lost in many meditations. I thought of the beauty of this edifice, then of the battle of Saint-Quentin, lost by the French, on the tenth of August, 1557, the fête day of Saint Laurent, in commemoration of which the Escurial was built by Philip II, the savage father of Don Carlos. So when my husband returned and tapped me on the shoulder, saying, "Let us go to see the house of the Prince," I was almost vexed to have my thoughts disturbed. My son, being only a boy, had accompanied his father and was very proud to be able to relate to me what he had seen.

We then proceeded to this house of the Prince, erected by Charles IV while he was Prince of the Asturias and where he retired when the Court was at the Escurial, to escape from the rigorous Spanish etiquette. It resembled a very elegant little house, which a modest broker would hardly be contented with in our day. Pretty furniture, little tables, ornaments of doubtful taste, a quantity of draperies of the most shabby effect, gave it the appearance of a *petit logis de fille*. What a contrast with the admirable Church which we had just left! It gave me a very disagreeable impression.

Having returned to the inn, we at once set out to go to pass the night at La Granja, where the Court was in residence at the Royal Château. Here we were to find dispatches from the American Minister, Mr. Rutledge, for his Consul at Bayonne. He invited us to supper, and the following day we set out for Ségovie, a very picturesque little city with a château, of which we saw only the court surrounded by arcades in the Moorish style. The remainder of our journey was very uneventful. We remained a day at Vittoria to care for the "Generala," without whom we could not proceed. Then a day at Burgos, where I went to see the Cathedral, and finally we arrived at Saint-Sébastien, where Bonie awaited us.

I felt no pleasure in returning to France. On the contrary, the sufferings which I had endured during the last six months of my sojourn had left in my mind a sentiment of terror and horror which I could not overcome. I thought that my husband was coming back with his fortune lost, and that difficult affairs would occupy him disagreeably and that we were condemned to live in a large devastated château, for everything had been sold at Le Bouilh. My mother-in-law was still living. She had again entered into possession of Tesson and Ambleville. Without any intelligence, very suspicious, very obstinate, in business she had confidence in no one. How much I regretted my farm, my tranquillity! It was with a very heavy heart that I crossed the bridge of the Bidassoa and realized that I was upon the territory of the Republic "one and indivisible."

We arrived at Bayonne in the evening. Hardly had we entered the inn when two members of the National Guard came to look for Monsieur de La Tour du Pin to take him before the authorities, represented then, it seems to me, by the President of the Department. This début caused me great terror. Accompanied by Bonie, he was conducted before the assembled members of the Tribunal. He was questioned as to his opinions, his plans, his actions, the causes and the reasons of his absence and those of his return. He at once perceived that he had been denounced by Monsieur de Roquesante and declared so frankly, while stating at the same time, how much, on the other hand, he had to praise in the attitude of the Ambassador at Madrid. After a discussion which lasted at least two hours, my husband returned. They had authorized him to continue his route as far as Bordeaux, but armed with a kind of official itinerary in which the stops were indicated and with the injunction to have this paper viséd at each place.

Bonie left us and returned to Bordeaux by the mail-coach. We engaged a wretched driver, who conducted us by short journeys. One event only marked our trip. At Mont-de-Marsan where I called a *perruquier* to dress my hair, he proposed to me, to my great surprise, to purchase my hair for 200 francs. He said that blond wigs were so much the fashion at Paris that he would certainly make a profit of at least 100 francs, if I would consent to sell him my hair. I refused this proposition, you may well believe, but I conceived a great respect for my hair, which was, modesty apart, very handsome and very fine at that time.

At Bordeaux we found again the excellent Brouquens. He had prospered during the war against Spain and was now engaged in providing provisions for our armies in Italy. He received us with the tender friendship which had never for a moment changed. But I was impatient to be at home, and I made arrangements at once with my good Doctor Dupouy who was to take care of me. Then, the affair of raising the sequestration terminated, we went to Le Bouilh to have the seals removed.

The first moment, I admit, sorely tried my philosophy. I had left the house very well furnished, and if nothing very elegant was to be found there, at least everything was convenient and in sufficient quantity. I found it absolutely vacant. Not a chair to sit down on, not a table, not a bed. I was on the point of giving way to discouragement, but to complain would have been useless. At the farm we set about unpacking our boxes which had long since arrived at Bordeaux, and the sight of these simple little pieces of furniture, transported to this vast château, gave rise to many philosophical reflections.

The next day many of the inhabitants of Saint-André, ashamed of having purchased our furniture at auction, came to propose to us to re-sell it for the price which it had cost them. Under these reasonable conditions, we again came into possession of those articles which we needed most. One of the things which had the most value was the equipment of our kitchen, which was very fine. It had been transported to a district of Bourg with the intention of sending it to the mint. This was re-sold to us, as well as the library which had also been deposited in the district. We passed several days very agreeably in placing the books on the shelves, and before the arrival of Doctor Dupouy all of our interior arrangements had been finished, and we were as well installed as if we had been at Le Bouilh for a year.

At this moment I experienced a great pleasure; this was the arrival of my dear maid Marguerite. Mme. de Valence, when she was released from prison at Paris, had engaged her to take care of her two daughters, but as soon as this excellent maid heard of my return, nothing could prevent her from coming to rejoin me. In spite of the aristocracy of her white apron, she had escaped from all the dangers of the Terror. She arrived at Le Bouilh in time to be present at the birth of my dear daughter Charlotte, who was born the fourth of November, 1796. I gave her the name of Charlotte, because she was the god-daughter of Monsieur de Chambeau. Nevertheless, upon the Registry of the Commune, she was inscribed under the name of Alix, which consequently was the only name she was able to use legally.

When I was up again, in the month of December, my husband started to make a circular trip to Tesson, Ambleville and La Roche-Chalais, where there remained to us only some old ruined towers, from the 20,000 francs of quit-rent and rents which this land was worth. I remained alone in the large Château of Le Bouilh with Marguerite, two servants, and old Biquet who got drunk every night. The peasants in the farm-yard were far away. Only some wretched planks closed the part of the ground floor which was not yet finished. This was the time when troops of brigands, called *chauffeurs*, spread terror in all the southern part of France. Every day new horrors were recounted regarding them. I admit to my shame that I was cold with terror. It seems to me that I never in my life passed a time more painful. How much I regretted my farm, my good negroes and my tranquillity of other days!

Our affairs, which were far from taking a favorable turn, also constantly preoccupied me. My husband had been advised not to accept the inheritance of his father except *sous bénéfice d'inventaire*, that is to say, in reserving the right to verify the charges or costs. Would to God that he had done so! But the sad manner in which we had lost my father-in-law and the profound respect which my husband had for his memory deterred him from adopting this course. This inheritance comprised the estate of Le Bouilh, several pieces of property in La Roche-Chalais, and our rights to the fortune of my mother-in-law which had formed a part of our marriage contract. I will not enter into the details of our ruin, the recollection of which escapes me now and which besides I have never clearly understood. I only know that at the time of our marriage, my father-in-law was supposed to have an income of 80,000 francs. Without going into further details, it may be said that our loss in all amounted to nearly 60,000 francs of income. To this can be added the house at Saintes, a fine dwelling in a perfect state of repair, and which could have been rented for 3,000 francs. The authorities of the Department had occupied it and when at the end of several years it was returned to us, it was in such a state of dilapidation that it had lost its entire value. We also lost the furniture of the Château of Tesson which Monsieur de Monconseil had left to my father-in-law. This furniture was sold at the same time as that of Le Bouilh, that is to say during the months which elapsed between the epoch of the condemnation, followed by the execution of my father-in-law, and the date of the decree which restored the property of the persons condemned to their children. It can be said that it was during this period of several months that nearly all the furniture of the châteaux of France had been sold. It is necessary, however, to except the libraries which, after having been transported to the chief places of the district, were subsequently restored to their owners. These sales struck the most disastrous blow to family souvenirs, and it is incontestable that the sudden dispersion of all these souvenirs of the paternal roof contributed strongly to the demoralization of the young noblesse.

We remained at Le Bouilh the whole winter and a part of the spring. About the month of July, 1797, my husband recognized the necessity of going to Paris to terminate his arrangements with Monsieur de Lameth. As if inspired by presentiment, I requested to accompany him. Mme. de Montesson, who was still full of kindness for me, arranged with Mme. de Valence that I should live in her house at Paris. She herself was established for the summer in the country in a house which she had just purchased near Saint-Denis. The six weeks which we expected to pass at Paris before returning to Le Bouilh for the harvest of the grapes did not require any great quantity of baggage. We therefore transported only what was strictly necessary for us and our children. A large number of émigrés had returned under borrowed names. Mme. d'Hénin, who had come back under the name of a milliner of Geneva, Mlle. Vauthier, was situated with Mme. de Poix at Saint-Ouen. Mme. de Staël, protected by Barras, the Director, and many others were at Paris.

Monsieur de Talleyrand had summoned us to come to Paris and had particularly urged my husband to come there. People had commenced to speak of a counter-Revolution, in which everybody believed. The Government had been formed, and two Assemblies, the Council of the Five Hundred and that of the Ancients, comprised many Royalists. The salon of Barras, the influential Director, of which the Duchesse de Brancas did the honors, was full of them, and although the other Directors did not seem disposed to follow the example of their colleague, it is certain that never had the Bourbon cause had so much chance of success as at this epoch.

We set out in a sort of little carriage, my husband, myself, my maid Marguerite and our two children: Humbert, seven and a half years of age and Charlotte who was only eight months old.

We passed several days at Tesson, where we found the Château in a terrible state of dilapidation. They had not only carried off the furniture but had destroyed the papers, taken away the locks of many of the doors, the blinds of several windows, the irons of the kitchen and the bars of the furnaces. It was a regular devastation. Fortunately Grégoire had piled upon his bed and those of his wife and daughter as many mattresses as he had been able to save, and these served as beds for us during our sojourn at Tesson.

My emotion was vivid in finding again this good family of Grégoire who had concealed my husband with so much care and devotion. Before this, in passing by Mirambeau, I had seen the locksmith, Potier, and his wife, with whom my husband had remained three months, shut up in a hole where there was not enough light to read by. How I again rendered thanks to God that He had permitted him to escape from all the frightful times of the Terror!

We finally arrived at the end of our journey. Mme. de Valence received me with pleasure, and Mme. de Montesson, who was not yet in the country, greeted me with a thousand acts of kindness. At Paris any little thing out of the ordinary always attracts attention. Accordingly, I made a hit, immediately on our arrival. As my husband and I were taking supper in the room of Mme. de Valence, Monsieur de Talleyrand was announced. He was very glad to see us, and at the end of a moment he said:

"Eh bien! Gouvernet, qu'est-ce que vous comptez faire?"

"Moi?" replied Monsieur de La Tour du Pin with surprise, "mais je viens pour arranger mes affaires."

"Ah!" said Monsieur de Talleyrand, "je croyais ..."

Then he changed the conversation and spoke of indifferent matters. Several moments later, addressing Mme. de Valence, he began to say with that air of nonchalance which it is necessary to have seen to understand:

"A propos, vous savez que le ministère est changé; les nouveaux ministres sont nommés."

"Ah," said she, "et quels sont-ils?"

Then after a moment of hesitation, as if he had forgotten the names and was trying to recall them, he said:

"Ah! oui, voici: un tel à la guerre, un tel à la marine, un tel aux finances ..."

"Et aux affaires étrangères," said I. ...

"Ah! aux affaires étrangères? Eh! mais ... moi, sans doute!"

Then taking his hat, he went away.

We looked at each other, my husband and myself, without surprise, for nothing could be surprising in the case of Monsieur de Talleyrand except an act on his part of bad taste. He remained eminently the *grand seigneur*, while serving a government composed of the refuse of the rabble. The next day found him established at the office of Foreign Affairs as if he had occupied this post for the past ten years. The intervention of Mme. de Staël, all powerful at this moment with Benjamin Constant, had made him Minister. He had gone to her house and throwing upon the table his purse which contained only a few louis had said: "Voilà le reste de ma fortune! Demain ministre ou je me brûle la cervelle!" None of these words were true, but it was dramatic, and Mme. de Staël loved that. Besides, the nomination was not difficult to arrange. The Directors, and above all, Barras, were very much honored to have such a Minister.

I will not relate here the history of the 18 Fructidor. You can read it in all the memoirs of the time. The Royalists had a great deal of hope and the different intrigues were mixed up in every sense of the word. Many of the émigrés had returned. They wore the rallying signs, all of which were perfectly known to the police: the collar of the coat of black velvet, a knot, in I know not what form, in the corner of the handkerchief and so on. It was by absurdities of this kind that they thought to save France. Mme. de Montesson returned from the country expressly to give a dinner to the Deputies who were well disposed. Monsieur de Brouquens, our excellent friend, was also one of the hosts of these dinners where they talked with an unbelievable imprudence. We met again every day, my husband and I, some people of our acquaintance, and the originality of the life which I had led in America and the desire which I evinced of returning there rendered me for a month very much in vogue.

CHAPTER SEVEN
1797–1798
EXILE IN ENGLAND

The 18 Fructidor.— A Promenade in Paris.— Mme. de Staël
and Benjamin Constant.— Expulsion of the Returned
Emigrés.— Situation of Monsieur and Mme. de La Tour
du Pin.— Conduct of Talleyrand and Tallien.— New
Exile.— A Friend from America.— Cordial Reception by
Lady Jerningham.— Visit of Mme. Dillon.— Mme. de
Rothe and the Archbishop of Narbonne.— Lord Dillon.—
His Apostasy and Marriage with an Actress.— Lord Kenmare and His Daughter.— Dominating Character of Mme.
d'Hénin.— Society of the Emigrés.— Departure for Cossey.
— The Races at Newmarket.— Kindness of Lady Jerningham.— Life at Cossey.— The Family Table.— Residence
at Richmond with Mme. d'Hénin.— An Inheritance Difficult to Realize.— Money Troubles of Mme. de La Tour
du Pin.

MY husband was busy with his affairs and
had undertaken negotiations to repurchase
a part of the estate of Hautefontaine
which had been sold, when one morning at daybreak,
the 18 Fructidor, the fourth of September, 1797, I
thought I heard upon the boulevard a noise of
artillery carriages. As my room looked out on the
court, I told Marguerite to go to the window of the
salle à manger to see what was going on. On her
return she told me that the boulevard was filled with
a number of generals, with troops and cannon. I
arose as soon as possible and sent to awaken my

husband who was sleeping in the room above mine. We both went to the window, where a short time later we were joined by Mme. de Valence. Augereau was there giving orders. The Rue des Capucines and the Rue Neuve-du-Luxembourg were barricaded.

Towards mid-day, as nobody had brought us any news, Mme. de Valence and I, inspired by curiosity, went out, quietly dressed in order not to be remarked, with the intention of going to see Mme. de Staël. As the streets above mentioned were barricaded by pieces of cannon, and the Rue de la Paix was not in existence at that period, we were obliged to ascend as far as the Rue de Richelieu to find a free passage. All the shops were closed. There were a good many people out but no one was talking. Finally we arrived at the residence of Mme. de Staël. She was with Benjamin Constant and very much incensed with him because he maintained that the Directory in arresting the Deputies had only performed an indispensable coup d'etat.

From M. Constant we learned that all of the émigrés who had returned had received an order once more to leave France under pain of being judged by military commissions. This news filled me with consternation, and I hastened to return home to inform my husband. On arriving I found my husband very much perplexed as to the means of notifying my aunt of these events. She was living at Saint-Ouen and the gates of Paris were closed. No one was able to pass the barriers without a special permission.

By a singular piece of good fortune, I met Mme. de Pontécoulant, whom I knew, as I had often seen her with Mme. de Valence. I will tell later on who she was. As she had a permit of the Section for herself and her maid, she was able to go to Saint-Denis, where her country house was located. I begged her to let me take the place of the maid and with her usual kindness she consented.

You can easily imagine with what exclamations I was received by Mme. de Poix and my aunt. The latter decided to leave at once for England. With these ladies were several former émigrés, who were in despair over the necessity of once more leaving France.

By the terms of the decree, all the émigrés who had returned upon French territory were ordered to leave Paris within twenty-four hours and France within a week. My idea was to return at once to Le Bouilh. Having left France with a proper passport and having returned with this same passport duly viséd by the French authorities in the United States and in Spain, I thought that the decree could not apply to us as we had not returned secretly. To assure himself on this point my husband went to find Monsieur de Talleyrand. The latter, very much occupied with his own future, was not giving much thought to that of others. He at once replied without hesitation that it was not his affair and told us to submit the case to Sottin, the Minister of Police.

I accordingly went to see Tallien who received me very cordially. He promised to go at once to see Sottin, to have him annotate the paper without which we could not have viséd the passport of the municipality of Saint-André-de-Cubzac, with which we had come to Paris and which we must have in our possession in order to pass the barriers.

I came home quite disturbed and commenced to pack my trunks. A police decree had just been posted ordering all proprietors to send in a report as to the persons living in their houses who were at Paris without papers in regular order. We were unwilling to cause any trouble to Mme. de Montesson with whom we were lodging.

Finally after a trying delay of several hours Tallien sent me back the request which he had submitted to the inspection of Sottin. The Minister had added with his own hand and signed the following annotation: "This private individual is within the law." Tallien, in the note which he wrote me at the same time in the third person excused himself politely for not having been able to obtain anything, but the end of his note could be translated by the words: "I wish you a *bon voyage*."

There were two alternatives from which to choose. We could ask for a passport for Spain and proceed to Le Bouilh, where I could remain some time while my husband went to Saint-Sébastien. This would have been the wisest course. We could also go to England and from there, according to circumstances, return to America. My aunt, Mme. d'Hénin, had much influence with my husband and she induced him to adopt the latter course. We had very little money, but were assured of finding at London my step-mother, Mme. Dillon, and many other very close relations, who without doubt would be disposed to come to our aid. We therefore decided to leave for England.

Having come to Paris with the intention of remaining only five or six weeks, we had brought with us only the most necessary baggage. I had in addition several dresses which I had had made at Paris. Two very small trunks contained all of our baggage, including that of my maid, Marguerite, who had decided this time not to leave us. This departure was destined to have the most unfortunate consequences for us. We were in negotiations with the new owners of Hautefontaine to repurchase the property, but this new emigration put an end to all of our arrangements.

The two or three days which preceded our departure were passed in a state of sadness and disquietude. Perhaps it would have been better for us to have returned to Le Bouilh. The report was current that Barras, who had yielded for the moment to the demands of his colleagues, would soon regain his authority and at the same time resume his favorable disposition regarding the émigrés.

Everywhere you met people who were in despair over this new emigration. We reserved three places in a carriage which was to take us in three days to Calais. Two other places were occupied by Monsieur de Beauvau and by a cousin of Mme. de Valence, the young César Ducrest, an amiable young man who was destined to perish so miserably several years later.

The French are naturally light-hearted. So in spite

of the fact that we were all in despair, ruined, furious, we found, nevertheless, the means of being in good humor and of laughing. Monsieur de Beauvau, our cousin, was going to rejoin his wife, who had been a Mlle. de Mortemart, and his three or four children. She was living in a country house at Staines, near Windsor, with her grandfather, the Duc d'Harcourt, formerly Governor of the first Dauphin who died at Meudon in 1789. Mme. de Beauvau was the youngest of the three grand-daughters of the Duc d'Harcourt. Their mother had married the Duc de Mortemart and had died long before the Revolution. Monsieur de Mortemart had then married a Mlle. de Brissac, the mother of the present Duc.

We appeared before all the municipalities in the localities situated on the route, including those of Calais, where we embarked on the packet one evening at eleven o'clock.

I was seated upon the deck holding my daughter in my arms while Marguerite was occupied in putting my son to bed, and my husband was suffering as usual from sea-sickness, although there was little wind and the night was superb. Beside me was a gentleman who, seeing me embarrassed with my child, proposed to me, with an English accent, that I should lean against him. As I turned to thank him, he saw my face in the moonlight and cried: "Bon Dieu, est-ce possible!" It was young Jeffreys, son of the editor of the "Edinburgh Review." I had seen him every day at Boston at his uncle's at the time of our sojourn in that hospitable city three years before. We talked much of America and of the regret which I had felt in leaving it. I gave him to understand that in spite of the presence of all my family in England, I was going there inspired only by the desire and the plan of returning to my farm, if all hope of a return to France vanished or at least became indefinite.

The night passed in talking of England with my companion, and the first rays of the sun revealed to us the white cliffs of England to which a strong southeast wind had brought us near. We landed to find ourselves handed over to the brutality of the English Customs officers who seemed to me worse even than those of Spain. At the sight of my passport which I presented at the alien office, I was asked if I was a subject of the King of England, and upon my affirmative reply, they told me that I should give as reference some person who was known in England. Having named without hesitation my three uncles, Lord Dillon, Lord Kenmare and Sir William Jerningham, the tone and manner of these employés changed very quickly. These details took up the morning. After an English luncheon, or rather dinner, we left Dover for London. We spent the night at Canterbury, or at Rochester, my recollections are not very precise as to the locality, and the following morning we arrived at London and went to one of the inns in Piccadilly. As I had written my aunt, Lady Jerningham, from Dover to announce our arrival, she had sent her son Edward to bring us to her house in Bolton Row. Her reception was entirely maternal. She immediately informed us of her departure for her country place at Cossey, where she said she expected to stay at least six months. She invited us to come and pass this time with her. My good aunt was particularly amiable towards my husband, and, being very fond of children, she conceived at once a great affection for Humbert.

We therefore took up our residence in Bolton Row like children of the family. Here I found again my excellent old friend, the Chevalier Jerningham, brother of Sir William, the husband of my aunt. The faithful friendship which he had shown me since my childhood was as sweet as it was useful during my sojourn in England.

I was arranging to go to see my step-mother, Mme. Dillon, who had been living in England for two years, when she came to see my aunt.

My arrival in London was an event in the family. Here I met again Betsy de La Touche, the daughter of my step-mother. She had been confided to my care in 1789 and 1790 when she was at the Convent of the Assumption where I often went to see her and whence I alone had permission to take her out from time to time. She had married Edward de Fitz-James. She was a sweet and amiable young woman, worthy of all good fortune. She was passionately fond of her husband, who did not return her affection, and his cruel and public infidelities had broken her heart.

Alexandre de La Touche, her brother, was three years younger than herself. He was a handsome young man, light headed, gay, but with little mind and still less education. He had all the whims of the young émigrés who had nothing to do, was destitute of any talent, loved horses, society and small intrigues, but never opened a book. My step-mother, who as long as I knew her never had a book on the table, could not have given him any taste for reading. She herself was not lacking in natural intelligence and had good manners and was well bred. Nevertheless, I have often asked myself why my father, who was endowed with a superior mind and was a man of fine education, had married a woman older than himself. It is true that she was rich, but, nevertheless, she could not pass for being what was called an heiress. Although he desired a son above all things, they had only three daughters. Two died as small children and only the eldest, Fanny, survived.

My uncle the Archbishop and my grandmother were living in London. I had not seen them since my departure from their house in 1788, nine years before. My aunt, Lady Jerningham, thought that I would do well to pay them my respects, and the good Chevalier, her brother-in-law, undertook to ask them if they would consent to receive me. My grandmother, seeing that the Archbishop desired it, dared not offer any opposition. At the same time she made a condition that my husband should not accompany me. I could have made this condition a pretext for not going to see them but I feigned ignorance. My husband besides was very happy to be relieved of this visit, for even at this time, he confessed to me later, he knew that my grandmother had spoken very unkindly of me since she had been in London. If I had known this at the time, I should certainly have refrained from going to see her.

One morning, therefore, I turned my steps towards Thayer Street with my little Humbert. It was not without an emotion mingled with many different feelings, that I knocked at the door of this modest mansion inhabited by my uncle and my grandmother. This house seemed to me to take the place, without transition, of the fine hôtel of the Faubourg Saint-Germain, where I had passed my childhood surrounded by the luxury and the splendor which can be obtained in life with an income of 400,000 francs, which the Archbishop of Narbonne enjoyed at that time.

An old domestic opened the door for me. On seeing me he burst into tears. He was one of the servants of Hautefontaine, where he had been present at my marriage. He preceded me and I heard him announce me in a voice full of emotion, saying: "Here is Mme. de Gouvernet." My grandmother arose and came to meet me. I kissed her hand. Her reception was very cold and she called me "Madame." At the same moment the Archbishop entered and throwing his arms around my neck he kissed me tenderly, and then seeing my son, he embraced him several times. He addressed several questions in English and in French to the boy, who replied with an intelligence which charmed my uncle.

My uncle invited me to come to dinner the following day, with six old Bishops from Languedoc whom he had taken *en pension* at his table. They were all former acquaintances of mine. As for my husband he was not mentioned. I announced my plan to go and visit my aunt at Cossey during the period of her sojourn there. The Archbishop expressed his satisfaction but my grandmother was certainly much put out.

Lady Jerningham, who had been very anxious as to the result of my visit, was happy that everything had gone so well. The following day my aunt took me to see two other uncles. One was Lord Dillon, elder brother of my father. He lived in a handsome mansion in Portman Square, with his second wife, two of her daughters, and a young son eight or nine years of age, who was a beautiful boy. Lady Dillon had been a Mlle. Rogier of Belgian origin. She had all the appearance of what she was in reality, a former actress. She had been the mistress of my uncle before his marriage to Miss Phipps, daughter of Lord Mulgrave. From this liaison had been born a son who, according to the custom allowed in England among the Protestants, had been authorized to bear the name of his father. As I have already stated at the commencement of these Recollections, Lord Dillon, at the time that he bore only the title of the Honorable Charles Dillon, was a gambler and a spendthrift and was loaded with debt. He abjured the religion of his fathers to become a Protestant at the instigation of his grand-uncle, Robert Lee, fourth and last Earl of Lichfield, who had demanded this as the price of his inheritance, an income of 15,000 pounds sterling and the beautiful castle of Ditchley. Assured of this handsome fortune and wishing to have an heir, he married a Protestant, Miss Phipps, and made her so unhappy that she died at the age of twenty-five years, leaving him a son, Henry

Augustus, who later became Viscount Dillon, and a daughter who married Sir Thomas Webb.

My uncle then lived openly with Mlle. Rogier, by whom he had had two daughters during the life of his wife. After his wife's death he publicly married her. His sister, Lady Jerningham, was extremely dissatisfied, and to appease her, he confided to her his legitimate son to bring up, and only kept with him the two bastards. These used his name, with this difference, that they did not put upon their visiting cards "Honorable Miss Dillon," but "Miss Dillon" only. They were both charming girls, pretty and well brought up. One died at the age of eighteen and the other married Lord Frederick Beauclerk, brother of the Duke of Saint-Albans.

As my aunt was not particularly anxious to see Lady Dillon, I went to her house with her daughter, Lady Bedingfeld, my cousin, who was at that time in London for several days. Lord Dillon received us very politely, but as a man of the world, without showing the least interest. He offered us his box for the Opera for the same evening, and we accepted. This was the only benefit that I received from him. He gave a pension of 1,000 pounds sterling to his uncle the Archbishop, who was eighty years of age. As far as I was concerned, although I was the daughter of his brother, he never came to my aid during the two years and a half I passed in England.

The second uncle whom I visited, this time with Lady Jerningham, was Lord Kenmare who had formerly borne the name of Valentine Browne. He received me in a very different manner, although I was his niece only by his first wife, a sister of my father, who had been dead for many years. He was then remarried. By his first wife he had a daughter, Lady Charlotte Browne, who was accordingly my cousin. She later became by marriage Lady Charlotte Goold.

Lord Kenmare, his daughter and all his family received me with the greatest kindness and goodness, and the friendship of Lady Charlotte in particular has never become cold. She was then eighteen years of age and had many aspirants for her hand as she had a fortune of 20,000 pounds sterling.

I went to see my aunt Mme. d'Hénin at Richmond. She was much displeased over our plan of passing some time at Cossey with Lady Jerningham. Mme. d'Hénin was exceedingly domineering, even to the point of tyranny, and everything which brought the slightest umbrage to her empire put her out to a most unreasonable degree. Her authority was exercised principally upon Monsieur de Lally, although it must be admitted that she was very useful to him through the firmness and decision of her character. But she did not suffer any rival and Monsieur de Lally had committed the imprudence, during the two or three months that Mme. d'Hénin had passed in France, of going to Cossey where he had enjoyed himself like a school-boy on his vacation. Mme. d'Hénin had accordingly conceived a great aversion for Lady Jerningham. Accordingly on learning that her nephew, Monsieur de La Tour du Pin, and I had formed the project of passing six months in the country with Lady Jerningham, she had a feeling of vexation which she did not try to dissimulate. In spite of her character, Mme. d'Hénin nevertheless did not lack a spirit of justice. She was forced to admit that, having arrived in England without resources, it was very natural for us to accept with pleasure an invitation from a relative so near and so highly considered in the world as my aunt Jerningham. Mme. d'Hénin and Monsieur de Lally had an establishment in common. The age of the two should have prevented the public from finding any scandalous motive in this association. Nevertheless, people turned the matter into ridicule. Mme. d'Hénin in spite of her real and great qualities was not generally liked.

After a residence of three days at London, I realized that I would not have any pleasure in staying there longer. The society of the émigrés, their gossip, their little intrigues and slander had rendered my sojourn disagreeable.

Finally to my great joy the time came for our departure for Cossey. Lady Jerningham had preceded us to the country. It was therefore arranged that I should stay with my step-mother, Mme. Dillon, for several days. There I learned with great satisfaction that Edward de Fitz-James had some saddle-horses. As I had the reputation of being an excellent horsewoman, he procured for me a side-saddle. My step-mother gave me a fine equestrian habit and every day we took long rides.

We set out from London like a caravan: my step-mother, myself, my daughter, my son, my maid Marguerite and Flora, the colored maid of Mme.

Dillon, in one berline; Mme. de Fitz-James, Alexandre de La Touche and my husband in another. Then followed the aged governess of Betsy and finally Monsieur de Fitz-James, his horses, grooms and so on.

We stopped for the night at Newmarket where are held the famous horse-races, which I was very curious to see. We remained here all the next day. It was the last day of the races and the one on which was run the Royal Cup. We passed the whole day upon the turf and by a good chance, quite rare in England, the weather was very fine. I have guarded the memory of this day as one of those in my life when I was the most amused and interested. The following day we set out to arrive for the night at Cossey. It was, I think, during the first days of October, 1797.

My aunt, who was very fond of children, took possession of Humbert. Every morning after breakfast she took him to her room and kept him all the morning, occupied in giving him lessons and making him read and write in English and in French. His toilette also was the object of her care. She furnished him with suits, overcoats, linen and a complete child's wardrobe. She was also extremely kind to me. Having observed that I was able to make my dresses myself, under the pretext of inspiring in Fanny Dillon a love of work, she brought to my room and placed at my disposal pieces of muslin and material of every kind, an attention which was all the more agreeable as I had arrived from France very lightly dressed for the climate of England.

My aunt had learned that my children had not

been inoculated (vaccination having then only recently been discovered) and she took charge of supplying this omission and had her own surgeon come from Norwich to perform the operation. In fine, she surrounded us with care of every kind, and the time which I passed at Cossey was as agreeable as we could have possibly wished.

Sir William possessed an income estimated at 18,000 pounds sterling, which does not constitute a large fortune in England, but was sufficient to enable him to live handsomely. His house was old but convenient. The chapel in which the chaplain officiated was installed in the garret, following the usage of the Catholics prior to the Emancipation.

The winter passed very agreeably. Towards the month of March, Mme. Dillon, my sister Fanny, and Monsieur and Mme. de Fitz-James returned to London. But we remained at Cossey until the month of May. As my aunt was to pass the summer at London, Sir William proposed to us to take possession, during the period of his absence, of a pretty cottage which he had built in the park. I preferred, however, not to remain there alone, and furthermore Mme. d'Hénin was very much enraged at the idea of the prolongation of our sojourn in the country and insisted on having us with her at Richmond where she could give us lodging. We therefore agreed to go there and rejoin her, although it was much against my desire; but my husband did not wish to disoblige his aunt and besides this, we had some business in London about which I am going to speak.

PRINCE DE TALLEYRAND-PÉRIGORD

1754 - 1838

As I have not re-read the first part of these Recollections, I am not certain that I stated that at the time of my arrival at Boston I had written my excellent instructor, Monsieur Combes, who was then living with my step-mother at Martinique. My father had given him a good position, that of Recorder of the Island. He had exercised this function at Saint-Christophe and Tabago and, living in the house, he had been able to accumulate his salary until it amounted to the sum of 60,000 francs. Mme. Dillon had borrowed this capital from him, agreeing to pay him interest. When Monsieur Combes learned at Martinique of our arrival at Boston, and also of our intention to buy property, the excellent man, who loved me like a father, had the thought of joining this sum, his entire fortune, to the funds which we possessed, in order to permit us to acquire a more considerable establishment, where he would come to be with us and pass the rest of his days. He therefore asked Mme. Dillon to repay the capital which he had loaned her. She not only refused his demand, but she also would not set the time when she would repay his money. He was in despair over the failure of his plans and prayed and menaced Mme. Dillon, but all without effect. Every vessel which came from Martinique to the United States brought me a letter from him. He wrote that he did not dare to leave Mme. Dillon, hoping that by his presence he would finally succeed in obtaining his money. In the midst of all this, Mme. Dillon left for England. Before her departure, poor Monsieur Combes who remained at Martinique succeeded in obtaining a paper, in due form, acknowledging the debt of 60,000 francs of capital and the interest which then amounted to nearly 10,000 francs, in addition.

Upon my arrival at Richmond, I received the sad news of the death of my old friend. A short time before, in his last letter, he had told me that the climate of the Islands, and still more the chagrin at knowing that I was again in France without resources, was killing him. He added that he was writing to Mme. Dillon requesting her to pay me the interest of the capital of 70,000 francs which she owed him.

By will, in legal form, he left me his credit of 70,000 francs on Mme. Dillon, as well as the running income which amounted to 1500 or 1800 francs. From the very day that she knew of this legacy the attitude of Mme. Dillon towards us completely changed. She kept a fine house at London and spent freely in dinners and evening entertainments, but if we had need of money she referred us to a Creole émigré who was charged with the care of her affairs. To all our demands with the object of having her fix a date when she would pay the interest of our credit, she replied evasively. One time there was no sale for her sugar, another time her funds had not been received. In short, every day some new excuse was offered. Having addressed myself directly to her, I was very badly received. We spoke of the matter to her son, Alexandre de La Touche. My husband also took the matter up with her man-of-affairs, but all of our attempts remained without success.

The money which we received was given us like

alms, although it came from our own property. Nevertheless, it was necessary for us to pay our part of the expenses with Mme. d'Hénin, and this constituted for us a new cause of embarrassment. How many times I regretted that I had not remained at Cossey!

Our participation in the household of Mme. d'Hénin was to me insupportable. She had given us such bad quarters that we were not able to receive any one. Our lodging comprised only two small bedrooms on the ground floor, and in England it is not customary to receive visitors in your bed-rooms. I occupied one of these rooms with my daughter, and my husband the other with our son. In the evening only, we found our aunt in a handsome salon which she had on the first floor. It was very inconvenient certainly, but, if our life had been pleasant, I would not have been disturbed. While admitting the great and fine qualities of Mme. d'Hénin, and never failing to show her the respect which I owed her, I was forced nevertheless to recognize that our characters were not sympathetic. Perhaps it was my fault and I should have remained insensible to the thousand pin pricks which she gave me. Monsieur de Lally, the most timid of men, would not have dared to venture the least drollery which might have amused me. I was still young and gay. At twenty-eight years of age how could I have had the severity of mien imposed by the fifty years of my aunt? Absorbed in politics, the only thing which interested her was the Constitution which it was necessary to give to France. This bored me to death. And then came the writings of Monsieur de Lally which it was necessary to read and re-read, word by word, phrase by phrase. In fine, I aspired to have a household of my own, no matter how small it might be. As I could not see any opportunity, I was resigned.

CHAPTER EIGHT

1798–1799

LIFE AT RICHMOND

The Princesse de Bouillon in England.— Birth and Death of
Edward.— Change of Residence at Richmond.— Facilities
of Life in England.— Narrow Circumstances of Monsieur
and Mme. de La Tour du Pin.— Distress of Monsieur de
Chambeau.— He is Aided by Monsieur de La Tour du
Pin.— The One Hundred Pounds of Edward Jerningham.—
A Week at London.— An Eight Days' Excursion.— Plans
for Return to France Abandoned.— The Circulating
Library.

IT was at the beginning of the summer of 1798
that the Princesse de Bouillon, of whom I have
spoken at the commencement of these Recollections, came to England to arrange the affairs of an
inheritance which had been left her by her friend,
the Duchesse de Biron. If I am not mistaken, the
sum involved was 600,000 francs in English funds.
Mme. de Bouillon was a German, Princesse de Hesse-
Rothenbourg, although she had passed her life in
France where she had married the cripple who had
never been her husband except in name. Joined by
a long and faithful attachment to Prince Emmanuel
de Salm, she had had a daughter who was brought
up under the name of Thérésia. During the emigration this daughter had married a young counsellor
of the Parlement of Aix who has since become well
known, M. de Vitrolles.

One morning after my aunt had gone to make a call on Mme. de Bouillon, I saw these two ladies return together. Several moments later, Mme. d'Hénin entered my room accompanied by my husband. "We have arranged for you," she said. "Monsieur de Vitrolles is going away, and Mme. de Bouillon does not wish to remain alone in her lodging, although she has it at her disposal for three months still. She wishes to give it up to you in exchange for your own. You will be much more comfortable there." A sign from my husband gave me to understand that I ought to accept this proposition.

I therefore moved to the dwelling of Mme. de Bouillon, and here was born a boy to whom we gave the name of Edward, as he was the god-son of Lady Jerningham and her son Edward. The good Chevalier Jerningham came to see me and said that my aunt, his sister-in-law, thought that with three children, I could not, when I left my present residence, return to the two little rooms of the modest lodging which I had occupied with Mme. d'Hénin. He had therefore undertaken to find a small house at Richmond where we would be at home. His search had succeeded beyond anything we could have hoped for.

The house belonged to a former actress of Drury Lane who had been at one time very beautiful and very popular. She never occupied it, but the dwelling was so neat and well kept that she was not anxious to lease it. However, the eloquence of the Chevalier and the forty-five pounds sterling offered as rent by Lady Jerningham decided her. This little house which was a real jewel was only fifteen feet wide.

On the ground floor was a hall, a pretty salon with two windows and then a stairway which was hardly visible. The first floor comprised two charming bedrooms, and the floor above, two other rooms for servants. At the end of the hall, on the ground floor, was a nice kitchen which looked out on a miniature garden, with only a path and two flower-beds. There were rugs everywhere and fine English oilcloth in the passage-ways and upon the staircase. Nothing could have been more attractive, cleaner and more gracefully furnished than this little house which could have all been put in a room of medium size.

However, I was very unhappy in taking possession, for that very day I lost my little boy, aged three months. He was carried off in a moment by an attack of pleurisy which I attributed to the neglect of the English maid who cared for him. I was very ill and almost dying when I took possession of the little house with my two surviving children, Humbert and Charlotte. Having only these two children to look after, we discharged our English servant. My maid, Marguerite, had learned a little cooking during my absence in the United States and she very willingly placed her experience and above all her zeal at our disposal.

England, where there are fortunes so immense, existences so luxurious, is at the same time the country in the world where poor people can live in the most comfortable manner. For instance, there is no necessity for going to market. The butcher never fails a single day to come at a fixed hour crying, "Butcher," at your door. You open the door and tell him what you want. Is it a leg of lamb? He brings it all arranged ready to put upon the spit. Is it lamb chops? They are arranged on a little wooden platter which he calls for the following day. On a slip of paper are written the weight and the price.

About this time, as Mme. Dillon refused to pay our income, we found ourselves much embarrassed. All the money which we had on hand was five or six hundred francs, and when this sum was spent we did not know what we could do, not for a lodging, for our little house cost us nothing, but literally for our food. My friend, Chevalier Jerningham, had informed me that my uncle, Lord Dillon, had refused with the greatest severity to come to our aid. In addition to this, all communications had ceased with France.

At this moment we received from Monsieur de Chambeau, who was still living in Spain, a despondent letter in which he said that he had no news from France and that nobody had sent him a sou. His uncle, a former Fermier Général, of whom he was the sole heir, had just died after having made a will in his favor, but the government had confiscated the inheritance on the ground that he was an émigré. The day that he wrote us, a last louis composed his entire fortune, and he could no longer count upon his friends in Spain, whose good will he had already exhausted. Upon receiving this letter, my husband did not hesitate a moment to share with his friend the last of his funds. He rushed to a banker where he purchased a draft for ten pounds sterling, payable to bearer. The same day he sent it to Madrid. This was nearly a half of our own resources. There remained with us only twelve pounds sterling on hand, without any other resources to pay our bills when this sum was spent. We were not willing to ask the aid accorded by the English government to the émigrés, on account of my family, and above all, on account of Lady Jerningham. So far as Lord Dillon was concerned, I had no scruples of any kind. Out of respect for the memory of my father, I did not wish to declare publicly that his widow, Mme. Dillon, my step-mother, who was proprietor of a house at London where she gave dinners and evening entertainments, had refused to come to my succor.

A last five pound note was all we had left, when one morning my good cousin, Edward Jerningham, came to see me. He was a charming young man who had just passed his twenty-first birthday. He well justified the passionate love which his mother felt for him. As he arose to leave, I went to the door to see him mount his horse. He remained a moment behind and I saw him slip something into my work-basket. I made a pretense of not noticing anything, on account of his extreme embarrassment. After his departure I found in my basket a sealed letter addressed to me. It contained only these words: "Offered to my dear cousin by her friend, Ned," and a note for one hundred pounds sterling.

My husband returned a moment afterwards, and I said to him: "See, here is the reward for what you have done for Monsieur de Chambeau." The next day, as you may well suppose, he went to London to thank Edward but found that he had already left for Cossey. Several days later, I also went to London with two English ladies whom I knew and whom I frequently saw at Richmond. They were two sisters, of whom the elder, Miss Lydia White, has been celebrated as a famous "Blue Stocking." She had conceived for me a kind of romantic passion, on account of my adventures in America. One of these ladies sang well, and we enjoyed our music together. Their books were at my disposal. When I went to visit them in the morning they kept me with them the whole day, and, when the evening arrived, I was only able to tear myself away by promising to return before the end of the week. Having formed the plan of passing a week at London, they implored Monsieur de La Tour du Pin to permit me to accompany them. This little trip to London with Miss Lydia White and her sister put me somewhat in touch with society. We went to the Opera and they also took me to a large assembly at the house of a lady whom I hardly saw. There were people on the stairway, and no one was able to sit down. We had great difficulty in leaving the house, the crowd of guests was so numerous. At the end of the week, which appeared to me long and tiresome, I returned with pleasure to Richmond.

Monsieur de Poix, who was living at Richmond, had an excellent horse and a tilbury. Frequently I went on foot to Teddington, a village about two miles from Richmond, and he brought me back to Richmond in his carriage.

In this way passed the summer of 1798.

We made an excursion of a week of which I retain

the pleasantest recollections. My children were so safe with my excellent maid, that this little absence did not cause me any disquietude. We set out, Monsieur de Poix and I in his tilbury, my husband on horseback, and, having passed Windsor, we went to spend the night at Maidenhead. From there we went to Oxford, to Blenheim, to Stowe, and returned by Aylesbury and Uxbridge. The beautiful country estates which we visited charmed me. It is in the country only that the English are really *grands seigneurs*. We were favored by very fine weather during the whole week which we employed for this excursion. In this connection, I must say that the climate of England, outside of London, is very much calumniated. I have not found it worse than that of Holland, and incomparably better and less uncertain than that of Belgium. Our little trip left with me the most agreeable impression.

Returned to Richmond, I resumed my household occupations. The news from France appeared somewhat better. My husband even formed the plan of sending me over for several days, armed with an English passport, which would not have been entirely false, since I should have signed it by my maiden name, Lucy Dillon. At this moment unfavorable news was received, and this determined me to renounce my trip to France. The news came the very day that I was to set out. Personally I was much pleased not to undertake this trip which was very disagreeable to me, not because I was afraid, but because the thought of leaving my husband and children caused me a real chagrin. At this time, I made the resolution never to return to France without them.

My life at Richmond was very monotonous. I no longer saw anything of Mme. Dillon, since we had succeeded in getting some money from her at the end of a very lively correspondence between my husband and her man-of-affairs. When I went to London, which happened only once or twice, I saw no one except Lady Jerningham or Lord Kenmare, who for a year past had given me six louis a month. Once a week I paid a visit to Mme. de Duras at Teddington where I went sometimes alone on foot and sometimes with Monsieur de Poix in his carriage.

Towards the end of the winter, Miss White left Richmond. This was a real grief to me, not because we had formed a durable friendship, but because she had been so kind to me that I had found her sojourn in our neighborhood very agreeable.

For some time past my health had not been good. I felt very languid, without knowing exactly what was the matter with me. I was not able to have a carriage, and our house was situated in a remote quarter called "The Green." I had therefore given up going out after supper and devoted my evenings to reading the books which Miss White, who had a fine library, had sent me in large numbers. A subscription to the Circulating Library is very dear in England and I was not able to take one. Therefore, you can imagine my joy when one day I received a box addressed in my name, of which the messenger

gave me the key. I opened it and found ten volumes
from Ookam's Circulating Library at London, with
a catalogue of twenty thousand volumes of all kinds,
English and French, which were contained in this
library. Joined to this consignment was a receipt
in my name for a year's subscription, with a notice
that by putting the box on the stage at seven o'clock
in the morning, I would receive the same evening the
new books which I had ordered. Nothing could have
been more agreeable to me than this attention. I
attributed it to Miss White. Having written to
thank her, she made no reply, from which I inferred
that she did not wish to admit that she had sent the
books.

The summer of 1799 my health was somewhat
better. Our house on "The Green" had a party wall
with that of a rich alderman of London. A little
fence, eight or ten feet from our windows, formed a
barrier between the two properties, as is usual in
England. The house of the alderman had a pretty
yard covered with turf, surrounded like our own by
a fence. My son had arranged a small flower-bed in
the little space which he called his garden. He entered
this by the window of our sitting room where I always sat with my work. His sister, Charlotte, often
accompanied him to the garden. As we were living
in an out of the way place, hardly any one ever
passed our house.

CHAPTER NINE

1799–1800

RETURN TO PARIS

Again at Cossey.— News of the 18 Brumaire.— Plans for Return to France.— The Wait at Yarmouth.— The Crossing. — The Debarkment at Cuxhaven.— In the North of Germany.— The Ball at Wildeshausen.— Birth of Cécile.— En Route for Holland.— At Utrecht.— Unexpected Meeting with Mme. d'Hénin.— Arrival at Paris.— Residence in the Rue de Miromesnil.— Mme. Bonaparte.— Monsieur de Beauharnais the Best Dancer in Paris.— The Morality of Talleyrand.— A Visit to Mme. Bonaparte.— Certificates of Residence.— At Malmaison.— The Gallery of Mme. Bonaparte.— Mme. de Staël and Bonaparte

THE summer of 1799 passed without anything unusual. Lady Jerningham was again settled at Cossey, where she had invited me to rejoin her and pass the six months of her sojourn in the country. The lease of our house at Richmond, which she had taken for us, was on the point of expiring, and it would have been hardly considerate on our part to ask her to renew it, with the view of not accepting the hospitality which she offered us. My aunt was alone at Cossey. Her niece, Fanny Dillon, my cousin, whom she had brought up, had just married Sir Thomas Webb, a Catholic Baronet who was quite an ordinary man although very well born. Her eldest son, George Jerningham, had also married a Miss Sulyard, a very beautiful young lady belonging to an old and noble Catholic family. William Jerningham was in Germany. Her favorite son, Edward, had not left her, and that was all that was necessary. Under these circumstances, it would have been a real disgrace for us not to go to Cossey. We were making our preparations accordingly to set out, when there arrived the news of the unexpected return from Egypt of General Bonaparte who had landed at Fréjus.

On learning of this event we left at once for Cossey with the hope of being able soon to go over to the Continent and perhaps to return to France. It was during our sojourn there that we received the happy news of the fall of the Directory and of the Revolution of the 18 Brumaire. Some time later we received letters from Monsieur de Brouquens and our brother-in-law, the Marquis de Lameth, urging us to return to France by way of Holland with German passports.

Lady Jerningham proposed that my husband should leave alone. This would perhaps have been better on account of the state of my health, but no consideration could determine me to be separated from my husband for an indefinite time. The communications between England and France, in time of war, might be entirely interrupted. The news which we received from Hamburg was often a month old; so we rejected all the propositions of Lady Jerningham.

A Danish passport was sent from London for my husband, my children and myself. We set out for Yarmouth with the idea of taking passage on a packet of the Royal Marine. At this time there were no steamboats. Our wait at Yarmouth was prolonged during the whole month of December. We did not dare to return to Cossey, although the distance was only eighteen miles, as the Captain had declared that as soon as the wind became favorable, that is to say, from the southeast, he would sail immediately. He would hardly consent to let us remain on land, as he was in such haste to leave as soon as possible. Every courier brought dispatches from the government.

Never had I passed such tedious days as during the month we were at Yarmouth. We were living in a very poor lodging with two rooms, and we were not able to go out for the weather was frightful. The contrary winds blew with fury. Every day there were reports of vessels which had been lost. You can imagine how such news was of a nature to discourage persons who might be called upon to embark at any moment.

Finally one morning they came to inform us that it was necessary to go on board, where our baggage had been already for a long time. Hardly had we set foot on deck when the anchor was lifted. The sea was very rough and we had a very disagreeable passage which lasted forty-eight hours. About the middle of the second night we were for some hours uncertain as to whether or not we might be left on Heligoland, a little island off the mouth of the Elbe, in case the current did not loosen the ice. The Captain subsequently declared that on account of the violent weather, if the wind had veered a single point to the north, he would have been forced to return to Eng-

CHÂTEAU DU BOUILH

PRÈS DE St ANDRÉ-DE-CUBZAC, GIRONDE

From this moment he placed himself at our disposal with the greatest zeal.

In two weeks I was up again, and at the end of another week we set out after having taken tea with the bailiff, the burgomaster and the curate. As there was a Catholic Church at Wildeshausen, my little daughter was baptized there. She was held at the font by the old perruquier, and his wife, who during the forty years of their marriage had never learned a word of French.

We took the route of Lingen to enter Holland. For several leagues we were accompanied by a number of young men. Before leaving they insisted that I should drink a cup of a German mixture of which they had prepared the ingredients. I thought it would be detestable but nevertheless, after having tasted it, I found the beverage delicious. It was composed of warm Bordeaux wine in which they had put yolks of eggs and spices. The Doctor was among those who had accompanied me and it was by his advice that I swallowed this mixture which somewhat inebriated me. The worthy fellows of our escort then left us and wished us with fervor a *bon voyage*. Their wish brought us good fortune for nothing troublesome happened, and my little girl endured the trip in an astonishing manner for a baby who was not a month old.

We finally arrived at Utrecht, and my husband went at once to The Hague to obtain a passport *en règle*, from the Ambassador of the French Republic, Monsieur de Semonville. The latter, who turned with each wind which blew, had already succeeded in pleasing the new government of which Bonaparte was the head. My husband had known Monsieur de Semonville very intimately for a long time, so he was received with open arms, and they fabricated for him a superb passport, attesting that he had not left Utrecht since the 18 Fructidor.

During the short absence of Monsieur de La Tour du Pin, Mme. d'Hénin, by the merest chance, passed through Utrecht, and my husband was very much surprised to find his aunt on his return from his trip to The Hague. I think that Mme. d'Hénin was on her way to see Monsieur de La Fayette who had been living at Vianen near Utrecht, since his release from prison after the Peace of Campo Formio. I do not recall whether she had come from France or England. She always had two or three passports and changed her name and her route at every moment.

We remained two days with her, and then taking advantage of a carriage which was being sent to Paris, and which we were charged to deliver at its destination, we set out.

On arriving at Paris we stopped at the Hôtel Grange-Batelière. My brother-in-law Lameth and our friend Brouquens were at Paris. Monsieur de Lameth installed us in a charming little house entirely furnished, Rue de Miromesnil, which had been occupied prior to that by two or three friends who had just left to go and pass the whole summer in the country. We were predestined to live in the houses of courtesans. That at Richmond belonged to an actress; this one had been arranged for Mlle. Michelot, former mistress of the Duc de Bourbon. All the walls were ornamented with mirrors, with such prodigality that I was obliged to hang pieces of muslin to conceal the greater part of them, as I was much annoyed at not being able to move without encountering my form reflected from head to foot.

At Paris I found many persons of my acquaintance who had already returned from the emigration. All the young people from this moment turned their eyes towards the rising sun, Mme. Bonaparte, who was installed at the Tuileries, where the apartments had been entirely refurnished as if by enchantment. She already put on the airs of a queen, but of a queen the most gracious, the most amiable, the most kind hearted. Although she had very little intelligence, she had nevertheless well penetrated the projects of her husband. The First Consul had given his wife the mission of bringing to him *la haute société*, having been persuaded by Josephine that she belonged to it, which is not strictly true. I do not know whether she had ever been presented at Court or visited at Versailles, but thanks to the name of her first husband, Monsieur de Beauharnais, the thing was certainly possible.

During the years 1787 to 1791, I met Monsieur de Beauharnais constantly in society. As he had seen my husband frequently when he was aide de camp of Monsieur de Bouillé, during the war in America, Monsieur de Beauharnais said to him one day: "Come and see me, so that I may present you to my wife." My husband went there once but never went again. The society which met in their salon was not ours. Monsieur de Beauharnais nevertheless went everywhere, for during the war he had formed ties with a number of leaders of high society. He had a charming figure and had the reputation, justly, of being the finest dancer in Paris. I had often danced with him and I therefore experienced a very painful feeling when I heard of his death on the scaffold.

I again saw Monsieur de Talleyrand, who was always animated by the same sentiments towards me: amiable without being really useful. During the past two years he had worked so successfully at increasing his fortune that I found him settled in a beautiful house, his personal property, in the Rue d'Anjou. He laughed in his sleeve at the disposition on the part of all those who had returned to France to rally to the government. He said to me:

"Que fait Gouvernet? Veut-il quelque chose?"

"Non," I replied, "nous comptons aller nous installer au Bouilh."

"Tant pis," he exclaimed, "c'est une bêtise."

"Mais," I replied, "nous ne sommes pas en état de rester à Paris."

"Bah!" he said, "on a toujours de l'argent quand on veut." Voilà l'homme!

As soon as Mme. Bonaparte learned through Mme. de Valence and Mme. de Montesson of my presence in Paris she wished me to come and see her. To draw to her a woman still young, a former Lady of Honor very much in vogue, would be a conquest, if I dare say so, of which she was very impatient to boast to the First Consul. In order to give value to my con-

descension, I allowed myself to be implored a little,
then one morning, I went with Mme. de Valence to
call on Mme. Bonaparte. I found in the salon a
number of ladies and a group of young men, all of
whom I knew. Mme. Bonaparte came to me crying:
"Ah! la voilà!" She seated me beside her and said
a thousand pleasant things, repeating all the time:
"Comme elle a l'air anglais!" which ceased to be a
praiseworthy trait a short time later. She examined
me from head to foot and her attention was particularly drawn to a tress of blond hair which surrounded
my head and from which her eyes could not be drawn.
As we rose to leave she could not refrain from demanding in a low tone of Mme. de Valence if this
tress was indeed my own hair.

Mme. Bonaparte spoke to me with much kindness
of Mme. Dillon, my step-mother, and expressed a
warm desire to make the acquaintance of my sister
Fanny, who was at the same time her cousin (the
mother of Mme. Dillon and of Josephine having been
sisters). Then she continued by saying that all the
émigrés were going to return and that she was
charmed, that they had suffered enough and that
General Bonaparte wished above everything else to
bring to an end the evils of the Revolution and so on,
in short a lot of reassuring statements. She also asked
for news of Monsieur de La Tour du Pin and evinced
a desire of seeing him. She was leaving for Malmaison and invited me to come there. She was very
pleasant in every way and I saw clearly that the
First Consul had intrusted to her the department of
the ladies of the Court and the task of their conquest

when she met them. The task was not very difficult, for all were rushing towards the rising power, and I do not know any one, except myself, who refused to be Lady of Honor to the Empress Josephine.

Monsieur de La Tour du Pin and I had never been inscribed, I cannot explain why, upon the list of émigrés. It was necessary however for us to obtain a certificate of residence in France, signed by nine witnesses, an indispensable formality of which, nevertheless, no one was dupe. With this end we went to the Municipality of the quarter with our squad of witnesses. When the certificate was signed and clothed with all the necessary *mensonges*, the Mayor said to me in a low tone: "That does not prevent you from bringing from London all your effects." Then he began to laugh. What a comedy!

The place in Paris, during this summer, where the most distinguished company was brought together, was under the arch of a house in the Place de Vendôme: that which forms the angle of the Place on the right in going towards the Rue Saint-Honoré and on the side of that street. It was there that the Commission of the émigrés held its sessions, a tribunal very easy to conciliate if you did not come with empty hands. In the crowds which assembled at this point you met the greatest personages mingled with brokers of every kind.

The French find amusement in everything. The Commission of émigrés had become a place of re-unions; people made appointments there; they went there to meet former acquaintances; to talk over their plans, their choice of residence. Many of those who came back considered the place as an employment bureau. We had no business with this Commission as we did not figure on the list of émigrés. It was necessary, however, to have erased from this list the name of my mother-in-law. Although she had resided for thirty years in the Convent of the *Dames Anglaises*, of the Rue des Fossés-Saint-Victor, which she had never left, they had, nevertheless, inscribed her name. The sale of all the furniture of the Château of Tesson and of two farm houses had been the consequence of this unjustifiable inscription.

One morning I went to Malmaison. It was after the battle of Marengo. Mme. Bonaparte gave me a wonderful reception, and after luncheon, which was served in a charming *salle à manger*, she invited me to see her picture gallery. We were alone and she took advantage of the occasion to tell me the story of the origin of the masterpieces which the gallery contained. This fine picture had been presented to her by the Pope; two others had been given her by Canova; the city of Milan had offered her this picture and that. Having a great admiration for the conqueror of Marengo, I should have esteemed Mme. Bonaparte more highly if she had told me that all these masterpieces had been conquered at the point of his sword. The good woman was naturally a liar. Even when the simple truth would have been more interesting and more piquant than a lie, she would have preferred to lie.

Mme. de Staël had given up her house. Her husband had returned to Sweden, where he died two years later. After having settled in a small apartment, she was preparing to go to join her father at Coppet. Bonaparte could not endure her, although she tried in every way to please him. I think that she never went to see Mme. Bonaparte. One day, however, I met Josephine Bonaparte in her salon. She received people of all the régimes. The émigrés, returned to France, mingled at her house with the former partisans of the Directory.

CHAPTER TEN
1800–1808

LIFE AT LE BOUILH

Sale of the Paris House.— Departure for Le Bouilh.— Life There.— Education of Mlle. de Lally.— Establishment of the Empire.— Birth of Aymar.— Marriage of Mlle. de Lally and Henri d'Aux.

FINALLY about the month of September, we decided to leave for Le Bouilh. About three years before we had sold our house in Paris at a very low price. It was situated in a bad quarter, the Rue du Bac. I no longer remember the disposition which my husband made of the proceeds of this sale. On his return he found the affairs of his father, as well as his own, in such great disorder, and he was so unfortunate in everything he undertook, that in spite of his intelligence and his capacity, he did not seem to succeed in anything. My husband set out alone for Tesson, and I engaged a driver who took me home by short journeys in a large carriage which held besides myself, my son, my two daughters, the instructor, Monsieur de Calonne, and my maid, Marguerite.

We finally arrived at Le Bouilh where I was happy to be once more. I had great need of repose. An excellent girl whom I had left there had taken care of everything in good shape. My husband arrived a few days later, and we finally found ourselves all reunited in our home.

My husband devoted himself to agriculture and the education of his son, in which I assisted in order that he should not forget his English. Humbert was then ten and a half years of age, while Charlotte was four and Cécile six months. My excellent maid, Marguerite, devoted herself with as much attention and tenderness to the dear children as I did myself.

A short time after our arrival at Le Bouilh, a cousin of my husband, Mme. de Maurville, came to stay with us. She had lost all the property which she possessed in France and her principal resource was a pension of forty pounds sterling, paid to her by the English government. This had been given her as the widow of a general officer of the French Marine, who had taken service with England, a thing which I may say in passing was very villainous. Mme. de Maurville was very fond of Monsieur de La Tour du Pin. She was four years older than he and had known him since his childhood. She was very happy to be with us.

Mme. d'Hénin came to Le Bouilh on several occasions during the eight years we resided there. At the time of her first visit, which lasted several months, she brought Elisa, the daughter of Monsieur de Lally, who had just left the school of Mme. Campan. I was asked to undertake finishing her education. Mlle. de Lally at that time was fifteen years of age, and I received her with pleasure. She was a sweet,

L'impératrice JOSÉPHINE

1763 - 1814

the reins of government. When he proclaimed himself Consul for Life, this gratitude was shown by the almost unanimous approbation of those who were called upon to vote upon this proposition.

A little later there appeared in the communes the lists upon which it was necessary for the voters to inscribe their names and respond by "yes" or "no" to the question as to whether the Consul for Life should be proclaimed Emperor.

Monsieur de La Tour du Pin was in a state of great indecision before he decided to write "yes" upon the list at Saint-André-de-Cubzac. I saw him walk up and down alone in the garden, but I did not try to penetrate his thoughts. Finally one evening he entered and I learned with pleasure that he had just written "yes" as a result of his reflections.

In 1805, I went with Elisa de Lally to pass some time at Bordeaux. One day at mass Elisa was observed by a young man, the most distinguished in Bordeaux, by birth, face and fortune: Monsieur Henri d'Aux. Elisa was very small, but she had a superb head of black hair, very brilliant color, the freshness of a rose and the handsomest eyes in the world. Our friend Brouquens, after the loss of his fortune caused by the failure of his company which furnished provisions for the army, had returned to take up his residence at Bordeaux for an indefinite time. He learned through friends that Monsieur Henri d'Aux had spoken in terms of eulogy to certain of his comrades of the young lady who was being brought up by Mme. de La Tour du Pin, and had declared that none of the young ladies of Bordeaux had so pleasant and agreeable a manner. He asked for information regarding us, our manner of life and so on.

My husband who had been named President of the Canton, without having solicited the office, had gone to Paris for the coronation. I wrote him of the gossip which had been reported to me and he spoke of it to Monsieur de Lally. The latter was then taken up with the endeavor to secure the repayment of quite a large sum of money which the State owed him since the rehabilitation of his father and the cancellation of his death penalty, that is to say, since three years before the Revolution. This indebtedness of the State had been recognized as valid by the Council of State, but the sum having been reduced two thirds, like all the Funds, did not amount to more than 100,000 francs. Napoleon, who desired to rally Monsieur de Lally to his government, wished that the reclamation should be entirely successful. When my husband spoke to Monsieur de Lally of the contents of my letter, he declared without hesitation that if he received this sum he would give it to his daughter the day of her marriage. You will see how he kept his word. We arranged to go to Bordeaux for the Carnival season in order to give Monsieur d'Aux the chance of seeing Elisa at the balls which were given in the salons of the former *Intendance*.

About this time I had the great sorrow of losing our dear maid, Marguerite, whom I loved as a mother. This caused me very sincere grief.

LIFE AT LE BOUILH

My husband had seen at Paris several persons of his acquaintance, all of whom had entered the service of the government, among them, Monsieur Maret, afterwards Duc de Bassano. They urged him to attempt to obtain some employment. Without exactly refusing, he replied that if the Emperor wished to have his services, he well knew where he could find him and that the rôle of solicitor did not please him. Monsieur de Talleyrand could not comprehend reluctance of this kind, but he felt, nevertheless, in his mind rather than his heart, that there was a sort of distinction in not mingling with the crowd of solicitors. He only said, shrugging his shoulders: "Cela viendra," and then he thought no more about it.

My husband returned to Le Bouilh. He had seen Monsieur Malouet who had just been named Préfet Maritime at Antwerp, in charge of the large shipyards there to which he gave so tremendous an impetus. These gentlemen had come to an understanding that when Humbert was seventeen years of age he should receive a position in the office of Monsieur Malouet. The *Institution des Auditeurs* of the Council of State was not then in existence. They had commenced, however, to talk of it, and we were of the opinion that it would be useful for a young man who was destined for business to work for a time under the eyes of a man as keen and as competent as Monsieur Malouet. As he had much friendship for us, we could intrust our son to him with entire confidence. The thought of this separation, nevertheless, weighed heavily on my heart.

RECOLLECTIONS OF THE REVOLUTION

The eighteenth of October, 1806, as I was dressing in the morning, I saw passing on the terrace our good doctor Dupouy, who had been at Le Bouilh for several days. I asked him laughingly where he had come from so early in the morning. He replied that he had just been to report the death of one of our neighbors who had passed away suddenly in getting up that morning. I knew this person very well and had had a long talk with her only the evening before. This event upset me to such a degree that that very morning I gave birth to my youngest son, Aymar, the only one of my children who is living at this writing.

In the meantime, we had not lost sight of the important affair of the marriage of Elisa. Under pretext of having our baby vaccinated, we went, about Christmas time, to pass six weeks at Bordeaux with our excellent friend Brouquens. He had succeeded in winning to our side Monsieur de Marbotin de Couteneuil, former Counsellor of Parlement, the uncle of Monsieur d'Aux. His wife having been the sister of the mother of Monsieur d'Aux, this young man, after the death of his mother, which happened a long time before, felt towards his aunt a real filial affection. Monsieur de Couteneuil desired to reënter the *Judicature*, and Monsieur de Lally was understood to have good standing with the government. This was another reason which led Monsieur de Couteneuil to favor the marriage of his nephew. Besides this, pride apart, we enjoyed such consideration at Bordeaux that a person admitted into our family life would have a certain standing.

The young people met at several balls. They also

met on the street and at church, where we were always sure to see Monsieur d'Aux. Finally, one day, Mme. de Couteneuil presented herself officially at my house to ask for the hand of the young lady for her nephew. As a good old diplomatist, I replied that I was ignorant of the plans of Monsieur de Lally for his daughter, but that Monsieur de La Tour du Pin would go to see him at Le Bouilh where he was at the moment and present the proposition to him.

My husband went there as arranged and returned the following day with Monsieur de Lally. All was soon arranged. Then followed the congratulations, the dinners, the evening entertainments. We received a call from the aged father of Monsieur d'Aux. He was a gentleman of the olden days, without the least vestige of intelligence or instruction. It was said that he had bored his wife to death. This did not prevent him, however, from possessing more than 60,000 francs of income.

The day of the signature of the contract, Monsieur de Lally counted out for Monsieur d'Aux, as he had agreed, 100 bags of 1000 francs, representing the dot of his daughter. It was the only time in my life that I ever saw so much money at one time.

The marriage took place at Le Bouilh the first of April, 1807. At this season there were no flowers except little pink and white marguerites. Mme. de Maurville, Charlotte and I constructed a charming *épergne* for the dinner, the bottom of which was of moss with the names of Henri and Elisa written in flowers.

All these preliminaries and the marriage itself had very much upset me and taken me out of my tranquil and regular habits. I was, therefore, very glad to return home to enjoy the last months which my son was to pass with us. My aunt and Monsieur de Lally returned to Paris, and I remained alone with Mme. de Maurville.

CHAPTER ELEVEN

1808

THE EMPEROR AT BORDEAUX

Humbert Leaves for Antwerp.— Grief over the Separation.—
Visit of the Emperor to Bordeaux.— His Passage of the
River at Cubzac.— Mme. de La Tour du Pin Summoned to
Bordeaux.— The Court Assembly.— Presentation to the
Emperor.— The Salon of the Empress.— Her Entourage.—
Strict Rules for Her Days Dictated by the Emperor.—
Anxiety of Josephine over the Rumors of her Divorce.—
A Note from the Emperor.— Departure of the Empress.—
Return to Le Bouilh.— Monsieur de La Tour du Pin Ap-
pointed Préfet at Brussels.— Mme. de La Tour du Pin
Dame d'Honneur of the Queen of Spain.— Presentation to
the Queen.— The Prince de La Paix.— Departure of the
Spanish Sovereigns.

TOWARDS the end of the summer, or to
speak in agricultural terms immediately
after the harvest of the grapes (*vendanges*),
it was necessary for me to be separated for the first
time from my dear son Humbert. He set out with
his father who accompanied him as far as Paris.

Bordeaux was very much taken up with the affairs
of Spain, and several refugees from that country had
already arrived there. My aunt wrote us from Paris
that the Emperor was to go to Spain, accompanied
perhaps by the Empress Josephine, and that Monsieur de Bassano would form part of his suite. She

advised her nephew to pay his court to the Emperor and to see Monsieur de Bassano, who was interested in him. My husband received this letter at the moment when he was setting out on horseback for Tesson. A matter of business absolutely claimed his presence there. In leaving he said that he would be gone only two days and that he had plenty of time to go and return. The very next day the order was received at the posting station to prepare horses for the Emperor. This news filled me with despair, but I was none the less anxious to see this extraordinary man.

Mme. de Maurville, my daughter Charlotte and I went to Cubzac resolved not to return before we had seen Napoleon. We demanded hospitality from Ribet, the *Grand Commissionnaire de Transport* who knew us and who installed us in a room looking out on the port. The brigantine destined for the passage of the Dordogne was already there with the sailors at their posts. The whole population of the country lined the road; the peasants, while cursing the man who took their children to send them away to war, wished to see him nevertheless. A first courier arrived. People tried to question him. General Drouet d'Erlon, the Commander of the Department, asked him when the Emperor would arrive. The man was so fatigued that the only response they could get from him was the word: "Passons." His horse was saddled, he accompanied it on the boat, then fell at the bottom of the boat like a dead man and it was necessary to rouse him and put him on his horse at the other side of the river. After the passage of the courier, our impatience was very great. As for myself, I was taken up with the fatality which kept my husband far from the place where his functions demanded his presence. The municipality of Cubzac was present, and he, the President of the Canton, whose place was there, was absent. It was an occasion lost which might not return. I felt very much put out. Finally, after a wait which lasted the entire day, towards evening, a first carriage arrived and a little later a berline with eight horses escorted by a picket of cavalry stopped under the window where we were. The Emperor descended, dressed in the uniform of *chasseur de la garde*. Two chamberlains, one of whom was Monsieur de Barral, and an aide de camp accompanied him. The Mayor paid his compliments. The Emperor listened with an air of great boredom, then entered the brigantine which immediately set out. This was all we saw of the great man. We returned to Le Bouilh, all three of us, tired out and in bad humor.

The next day my husband arrived. I gave him only time to eat his breakfast and then forced him to set out for Bordeaux, where the Empress was expected the next day. Immediately on his arrival, he went to see Monsieur Maret, who professed for him much friendship and interest. He found him kind and obliging, but what was his astonishment when Monsieur de Maret said to him:

"You have felt much annoyance over the necessity of going to Tesson, exactly at the time that the Emperor was passing your home, and you have shown great diligence in returning."

"You have then seen Brouquens," replied Monsieur de La Tour du Pin.

"No."

"But, then how do you know all that?"

"The Emperor told me."

You can imagine how much my husband was surprised.

"Mme. de La Tour du Pin should come to Bordeaux," added Monsieur Maret. "She should remain here during the time of the sojourn of the Empress. There will be an Assembly tomorrow and the Emperor wishes that she should be present."

My husband immediately sent a carriage for me, for it was not a time to hesitate. I had several dresses at Bordeaux, made at the time that I was taking Elisa to the balls and evening entertainments given at the time of her marriage, but among these there was no black dress, and the Court was in mourning. The Assembly was for eight o'clock, and it was already five. Fortunately, I had a pretty robe of gray satin. I added several dark ornaments, the good coiffeur arranged some black ribbons in my hair, and this seemed to me very appropriate for a woman of thirty-eight, who can say, without vanity, that she did not have the air of being more than thirty. The reunion was in the large *salle à manger* of the palace. I knew very few persons at Bordeaux. Sixty or eighty ladies were present. We were arranged according to a list read aloud by the chamberlain, Monsieur de Béarn. He enjoined us that no one was to leave her place under any pretext, as otherwise it would be impossible for him to find the name to give to each person. This sort of military manœuvre had hardly been arranged when a loud voice announced: "L'Empereur!" which caused my heart to beat. He began at the end of the line and addressed a word to each lady. As he approached the place where I was standing, the chamberlain said a word in his ear. He fixed his eyes on me, smiling graciously, and when my turn came he said to me laughing, in a familiar tone, while he regarded me from head to foot:

"Why, you are not then afflicted over the death of the King of Denmark?"

"Not sufficiently, Sire," I replied, "to sacrifice the pleasure of being presented to your Majesty. I had no black dress."

"Oh, that is an excellent reason." And then he added: "You were in the country!"

Speaking then to the lady beside me, he said: "Your name, Madame?" She stammered and he did not comprehend.

"Montesquieu," I said.

"Ah, really, that is a fine name to have. I went this morning to La Brède to see the cabinet of Montesquieu."

The poor woman replied, thinking that she had found a fine inspiration:

"C'est un bon citoyen."

This word "citoyen" displeased the Emperor. He gave Mme. de Montesquieu, with his eagle eyes, a look which would have terrified her if she had understood, and replied very brusquely:

"Mais non, c'était un grand homme," and then

shrugging his shoulders he looked at me, as if to say: "Que cette femme est bête!"

The Empress followed at some distance behind the Emperor and the ladies were named to her in the same order. But before she arrived at my place, a valet de chambre came to request me to go to the salon to await Her Majesty. When the Empress entered the salon, she showed herself very amiable for me and for my husband, whom she had also summoned. She expressed the desire to see me every evening during her sojourn at Bordeaux, and then began to play backgammon with Monsieur de La Tour du Pin. They served tea and ices. I was still in hopes of seeing the Emperor again, and my disappointment was great when I learned that upon the arrival of a courier from Bayonne, he had immediately left Bordeaux to go there.

The Emperor, having all Spain and all Europe on his hands, to use the common expression, had nevertheless the time to dictate the order of the day of the Empress, in the most minute detail, even to the toilettes which she was to wear. She would neither have wished nor dared to change this in the slightest particular, unless she was sick in bed. I learned from Mme. Maret that the Emperor had ordered that we should come, my husband and I, every day to pass the evening, which we did.

However, the poor Empress was beginning to be cruelly disturbed over the rumors of divorce which were already being circulated. She spoke of it to Monsieur de La Tour du Pin, who reassured her as well as possible. He endeavored to stop the confidences which the imprudent and light-headed Josephine seemed disposed to make to him, and which it seemed to him indiscreet to hear. She was much turned against Monsieur de Talleyrand, whom she accused of urging the Emperor to obtain a divorce. No one was better aware of this fact than my husband, for he had talked the matter over with him during the trip he made to Paris, but he took care not to let Josephine know this. Accustomed to the adulation of some, the deception of others, she found great relief in talking with my husband and opened her heart to him on a subject which she had not dared to broach to any persons of her entourage. She was very desirous of leaving for Bayonne and demanded every day of Ordener: "When do we go?" to which he replied with his German accent: "Indeed, I do not yet know."

One evening I was seated beside the Empress at the tea table when she received a note of several lines from the Emperor. Leaning towards me she said very low: "He writes like a cat. I cannot read this last phrase." At the same time she handed me the note, while putting her finger upon her lips as a sign of mystery. I had only the time to read several "thous" and "thees"; then the last phrase thus worded: "I have here the father and the son. This gives me much embarrassment." Since then this note has been quoted in a dispatch, but much amplified. There were only five or six lines written across a sheet of paper which had been torn and folded in two. If it were shown to me I should recognize it.

After tea, General Ordener approached the Empress and said to her: "Your Majesty will leave tomorrow at mid-day." At this decision, every one rejoiced. The sojourn at Bordeaux had been a cause of expense for me, as it had been necessary, during the ten days, to be in full-dress every evening. I was crazy to return to my children. Elisa, on account of her baby, was not able to come to see the Empress, to her great regret. She had been present only at the Assembly where she received a very flattering reception. Her husband had entered the mounted Guard of Honor which was composed of all the most distinguished young men of Bordeaux.

We returned accordingly to Le Bouilh, and notwithstanding the fine reception from the distinguished personages whom we had seen at Bordeaux, we entertained only small hopes for the future. How could I believe indeed that a man averse to all intrigue, unknown, so to speak, to those in power, since he had not mingled in any of the events for the past few years, living retired at his château, in a retreat all the more profound, because he was almost without fortune, how could I suppose, I say, that he should have attracted the eye of the eagle who was the master of the destinies of France! My husband had remained at Bordeaux to finish some business, and I was seated beside my lamp, talking with my poor cousin, Mme. Joseph de La Tour du Pin, whom we had received at our house through kindness. At this moment, as nine o'clock was striking, a peasant sent expressly from Bordeaux arrived with a note from my husband in which were written only these words: "I am Prefect of Brussels, of Brussels only ten leagues from Antwerp!"

I admit that I experienced a great joy in which the thought of again seeing my son touched me above all.

Monsieur Maret was ignorant of the vacancy in this prefecture. The papers of the Minister of the Interior arrived at Bayonne, exactly as if he had been present at the Tuileries or at Saint-Cloud, for nothing was allowed to change the habits of the Emperor. He was upsetting the Spanish monarchy and sending to prison or into exile the two Kings, father and son. This gave him "much embarrassment," as I had read written in his own hand, but in spite of that, when the work of the Minister arrived, he read, rectified and changed the nominations. *Préfecture de La Dyle:* a name is proposed for this post. He takes his pen, erases it, and writes above it *La Tour du Pin.* That is what we learned later from Monsieur Maret, who never raised any objection, but who also never made any proposition. He was a very useful machine.

My son was at Antwerp, seated at his desk as secretary to Monsieur Malouet, when he saw the latter running across the court. Never had any one seen Monsieur Malouet, the most dignified of men, hasten his pace for any reason whatsoever. On entering he cried: "Your father is Préfet of Brussels!" Dear Humbert, how great was his joy!

Several days before the departure of my husband from Le Bouilh to go to Brussels, I received a courier, in great haste, from our friend Brouquens, who announced that he had sent a carriage to Cubzac. He informed me at the same time that King Charles IV of Spain and his unworthy wife were to arrive at

Bordeaux at the Palace and that the Emperor had given orders that I should serve as Lady of Honor to the Queen during her sojourn at Bordeaux, which would be for two or three days. Fortunately, all my ceremonial costumes were still with Monsieur de Brouquens. My packing was therefore soon finished. My husband accompanied me and we set out. Arrived at Bordeaux, I dressed hastily and went to the Palace where Their Spanish Majesties had just arrived. On entering the salon I found some gentlemen of my acquaintance who cried: "Come at once, we are awaiting you for dinner!" This was very agreeable to me for I had taken only a cup of tea before leaving.

The King and Queen had retired to their own apartment with the Prince de la Paix. I met Monsieur d'Audenarde and Monsieur Dumanoir, the one *écuyer*, the other chamberlain of the Emperor, a few others, and two or three Spaniards whose names I did not know and who did not speak French. We immediately sat down to dinner. These gentlemen told me that two other Ladies of Honor had been named, one of whom was Elisa d'Aux, and I was charged to notify them to be at the Palace the next day at mid-day. The next day at eleven o'clock, I went to the Palace, and Monsieur Dumanoir requested to enter the Queen's apartment to present me. Turning to me before opening the door, he said: "Don't laugh!" This of course gave me a desire to, and, in truth, there was sufficient reason. There I saw the most surprising and unexpected spectacle.

La reine d'Espagne se tenait au milieu de la chambre devant une grande psyché. On la laçait. Elle avait pour tout vêtement une petite jupe de percale très étroite et très courte, et sur la poitrine (la plus sèche, la plus décharnée, la plus noire que l'on pût voir) un mouchoir de gaze. Sur ses cheveux gris était disposée, en guise de coiffure, une guirlande de roses rouges et jaunes. Le reine s'avança vers moi, la femme de chambre la laçant toujours, en opérant ces mouvements de corps que l'on fait quand on veut, en termes de toilette, se retirer de son corset.

Near her was the King, and several other men whom I did not know. The Queen demanded of Monsieur Dumanoir:

"Who is that lady?"

He told her.

"What is her name?" she said.

He repeated it, and the Queen addressed several words in Spanish to the King who replied by saying that I was, or that my name was, very noble. Then the Queen finished her toilette while relating that the Empress had given her several of her dresses, as she had brought none from Madrid. This degree of degradation gave me a very painful impression. The Sovereign indeed was wearing a gown of yellow crêpe, lined with satin of the same shade, which I remembered having seen the Empress wear. All desire to laugh had left me; I was more inclined to weep.

When the Queen was dressed, she dismissed me. I went to the salon where I found Elisa and together we awaited the arrival of the authorities, whom I was to present to Her Majesty. At this moment a fat man with a black plaster upon his forehead passed through the salon. I recognized him for the famous

Prince de la Paix. He passed impolitely before us without saluting and we both agreed that neither his face nor his figure justified the favors which the scandalous chronicles attributed to him.

The salons were then filled and the Queen was notified. I presented to her, one by one, the chiefs of the Administration, commencing with the Archbishop, to whom alone she addressed a word. Monsieur Dumanoir did the same for the King who showed himself more gracious.

The following day I made a visit of a quarter of an hour in the morning, and there was the usual entertainment in the evening. The day after, to my great joy, I learned of the early departure of the members of the Royal Family of Spain. The Préfet and the Archbishop came to bid them adieu. Then we entered a carriage to go to the passage of the river, for at this time there was no bridge. We found there the brigantine all ready, and, the crossing effectuated, I took leave of these unhappy sovereigns. The unfortunate King did not have the air for a single instant of comprehending the sadness of his situation. His attitude was completely lacking in dignity and seriousness. During the passage of the river he had talked all the time with my servant, who was on the deck. He was a good German, who could hardly believe that he had talked with the King. He said to me afterwards: "Mais, Madame, il n'a donc pas de chagrin!"

Such is the history of my brief functions at the Court of King Charles IV and of the Queen, his horrible wife.

CHAPTER TWELVE

1808–1810

THE PREFECTURE AT BRUSSELS

Commencement of a New Life.— Judicious Choice of Monsieur de La Tour du Pin for the Prefecture.— Departure from Le Bouilh.— Mlle. Fanny Dillon and the Prince Pignatelli. — Project of her Marriage with General Bertrand.— A Delicate Mission to the Empress Josephine.— Wives of the Officers at Brussels.— The Dowager Duchesse d'Arenberg.— Her Suppers.— Her Reception of Monsieur and Mme. de La Tour du Pin.— A Study of Brussels Society.— Organization of the House.— Napoleon Obtains Consent of Mlle. Fanny Dillon to Marry General Bertrand.— Eight Days for the Marriage.— Meeting with General Bertrand. — Details of the Marriage Arranged by the Emperor.— Mme. de La Tour du Pin Received by the Emperor at Saint-Cloud.— Signature of the Contract.— Marriage at Saint-Leu.— The Emeralds of Queen Hortense.

THIS was the commencement of a new life. I was to leave my garden, my chickens, my cows, my flowers, my regular and tranquil occupations which suited my taste, to lead an entirely different existence. But Providence had given me the desire to endeavor always to make the best of any situation in which I found myself. It was about nine o'clock in the evening, as I have said, when I received, by messenger, the note from my husband announcing his nomination as Prefect at Brussels. When he arrived the following morning for breakfast he found me already prepared to discuss the change in our existence and the arrangements and plans which I thought we should make in consequence.

Charlotte was then over eleven years of age. Very advanced for her age, she had a great desire to be informed on all subjects. She had immediately begun to study all the geographical dictionaries regarding Belgium, to examine the maps of the country, and when her father, who knew her well, arrived and questioned her regarding the department of the Dyle, she already knew all the statistics. As for little Cécile, who was already a good musician, at eight years of age, and also a good Italian scholar, her first question was whether she would have a music teacher at Brussels.

My husband immediately made all the necessary arrangements at Le Bouilh, but unfortunately confided his affairs to a man in whom he believed he could have entire confidence. To me he left the care of closing the house and the packing.

Monsieur de La Tour du Pin had received an order to report at Paris without delay, as Monsieur de Chaban, his predecessor, had already left Brussels to go to organize the department of Tuscany, which had just been united to the Empire. Our friend, Brouquens, happier even than my husband himself over his good fortune, came to pass several days with us, and they left for Paris together.

The news of this nomination had surprised all those who for a long time had solicited favors without obtaining them. Nobody was willing to believe that the Government had come to look for Monsieur de La Tour du Pin at his plow, like Cincinnatus, in order to give him the finest préfecture in France.

This choice was, however, the most judicious that the wonderful foresight of Napoleon could have made, and for the following reason: Brussels was a conquered capital and no effort had yet been made to attach it to France. The seat of the Court and of high society, it had been governed up to the present time only by obscure and worthless representatives.

Monsieur de Pontécoulant, the first Préfet, was assuredly a man of birth and aristocratic leanings, a former officer of the French Guards. His youth had been passed at Versailles and at Paris and he would perhaps have succeeded at Brussels except for his wife, of whom I have already spoken. It was understood that she had saved his life during the Terror. Formerly she had been the mistress of Mirabeau, of whom Lejai, her first husband, was the librarian. It was said that she had been pretty, but if so she did not retain the slightest vestige of beauty. After her marriage with Monsieur de Pontécoulant, she had been frequently seen in the salon of Barras and this did not exactly constitute a recommendation. Taken to Brussels by her husband, her antecedents had not been very attractive to the high and aristocratic society which formerly constituted the Court of the Archduchess.

Surrounded by French intriguers who had fallen upon Belgium as upon a prey, Monsieur de Pontécoulant did not give much time to the cares of the administration. The Emperor had recalled him, at the same time nominating him for the Senate, and had sent Monsieur de Chaban to replace him. The latter, who was an honest and enlightened man, a firm and excellent administrator, had reformed many abuses, punished breaches of trust and dismissed the culpable parties. All his acts had been just and enlightened. It was only necessary for him to follow out this course to administer the country well, but he had not succeeded in overcoming the aloofness which the upper classes felt for the French government. This task was encumbent upon my husband, and I dare say upon me, also, as the source of all influence is found in the salon.

It is true that Monsieur de Chaban was married, but his wife who was sickly, insignificant and of obscure origin, never received, and consequently nobody had ever seen her.

I had been preceded at Brussels by a kind of romantic reputation which I owed to my adventures in America.

After having made all my arrangements at Le Bouilh and sent off by the wagon everything which we thought would be useful to us at Brussels, to diminish the very great expense of our establishment in a large mansion, I set out by post with Mme. de Maurville, my daughters and my little son. A friend at Bordeaux, Monsieur Meyer, lent me a carriage which I sold for him at Brussels. En route I passed three or four weeks at Paris with my aunt, who was then living with Monsieur de Lally in a fine house, in the Rue de Miromesnil which she has since sold.

Mme. Dillon had returned from England some

time before. I went to see her, for she had received my husband very cordially when he visited Paris with Humbert the preceding year. My sister Fanny had grown up. She was then twenty-three years of age and without being pretty had a very distinguished air. Several suitors had already presented themselves for her hand, but the one whom she would have preferred among them all and would have married was no longer living. This was Prince Alphonse Pignatelli who had died of a malady of the chest. Before his death he had wished to marry Fanny so as to be able to leave her his fortune, but she had refused. As the days of the unfortunate man were numbered, she thought that it would have shown a lack of consideration on her part towards the family of Monsieur Pignatelli, if she had married him at the last moment, although she loved him dearly and would have been happy, even in losing him, to bear his name. I also was grieved, for I should have preferred to have my sister called Pignatelli rather than Bertrand.

Since this common name has come from my pen, this is the place to relate what had passed at the time of the last trip of my husband to Paris.

The Emperor had repeatedly informed the Empress and Fanny herself of his wish that she should marry General Bertrand, his aide de camp, who was later Grand Maréchal of the Palace, who had been in love with her for a long time. My sister was not willing to consent, and the Emperor was much put out. When he learned of her preference for Alphonse Pignatelli, however, he dropped the matter, but after the death of the Prince he took the affair up again. My husband was at Paris just at the moment when Mme. Dillon had promised a definite answer, and she requested him to see the Empress and notify her of the formal refusal of my sister. The commission was quite a delicate one, nevertheless he undertook it. The Empress received him in her bed-room where the deep alcove was closed during the day by a thick drapery of heavy material which formed a kind of wall of embroidered damask with a deep border of golden fringe. She asked him to sit down beside her on a couch which was placed against the curtain. As they were *en tête à tête*, Monsieur de La Tour du Pin without any circumlocution acquitted himself to the Empress of the commission with which he had been charged, while at the same time excusing himself for having brought a decision contrary to the wishes of the Emperor. As the Empress continued to insist, in the course of the conversation, which was quite long, he gave expression to very aristocratic sentiments which were not unpleasant. Finally, after having spoken to him of himself, of me, of our children, of his fortune, of his plans, the Empress dismissed him. My husband then went to make his report to Mme. Dillon regarding the interview which he had just had. That same evening he called on Monsieur de Talleyrand, who took him by the arm, as he was in the habit of doing when he wished to talk informally with him in a corner.

"What possessed you," he said, "to refuse General Bertrand for your sister-in-law. Was that any of your affair?"

"Why, Fanny wished it," replied Monsieur de La Tour du Pin, "and my age allows me to act for her as a father."

"Well," said the cunning old fox, "fortunately you have not hurt your affair with all your aristocracy. They love that at the Tuileries now."

"Who then told you that?" demanded my husband. "Have you seen the Empress?"

"Not at all," replied Talleyrand, "but I have seen the Emperor who was listening to you!"

It was perhaps this conversation overheard behind the curtain which made Monsieur de La Tour du Pin Préfet at Brussels.

It would be difficult for me to tell, with exactitude, the story of my sojourn at Brussels. They were very fond of society there and they were much pleased to have at last a *salon de Préfet* held by a woman who belonged to the aristocratic class. There were two ladies residing at Brussels who were my superiors on account of the positions occupied by their husbands: the wife of the General, Commander of the Division which had its headquarters at Brussels, and the wife of the First President of the Imperial Court seated also at Brussels.

The first, Mme. de Chambarlhac, had been a beautiful Savoyarde, Mlle. de Coucy. She was the aunt of Monsieur de Coucy whom we have known since. It was said that she had been a *religieuse* or *novice* when her husband, during one of the campaigns in Italy, carried her off and married her. Although forty years of age, she was still quite pretty. Ac-

[345]

customed to live with military men of every kind, she had acquired very common manners which, however, were relieved by a certain aristocratic gloss. You can understand that I was neither able nor willing to associate with such a person. Her antecedents repelled me. I always pictured her to myself, attired in the costume of a hussar which she had worn, it was said, in order to follow her husband during several campaigns. As for General de Chambarlhac, he was an imbecile who, from the very first day, took a hostile position regarding my husband on account of jealousy.

The second woman was the wife of the First President, Monsieur Betz, a learned German with much intelligence and capacity. She belonged to the lowest class in the social scale. Although she was quite homely at the age of fifty years, she might nevertheless have been pretty in her youth. She was always *coiffée, parée, décolletée* like a young person. I received her at my house on State occasions, but I do not remember ever having entered her home, although I did not neglect to leave my card from time to time.

The great jealousy of these two ladies was due to the fact that they were never invited to supper with the "Dowager." To be invited to these suppers was considered a mark of great distinction and formed the line of demarcation in the society of Brussels.

The "Dowager" was the Duchesse d'Arenberg, née Comtesse de La Marck and the last descendant of the "Boar of the Ardennes," Guillaume de La Marck, born about 1436, who was decapitated in

1485. She represented, according to the words of the Archbishop of Malines, the ideal of the *reine-mère*. Living in retirement in the mansion assigned to the widows of the House of Arenberg, she maintained there a simple but noble style and invited every day to supper a certain number of persons of every age, both men and women. She always dined alone, went out in an open carriage in all kinds of weather, and saw, during the course of the day, her children, especially her blind son whom she tenderly loved. Every time that a slight indisposition, caused by the gout, prevented the latter from going out, she did not fail to go to see him. From seven to nine in the evening she received visits. After that hour, if any one called, the Swiss demanded if he had been invited to supper. If the response was negative, he was not admitted. At this hour the guests arrived, and such was the respect in which the Duchesse was held that no one in Brussels would have ventured to arrive at half past nine. At ten o'clock the Duchesse rang and ordered the supper served.

After supper we played at lotto until midnight. When her son was present he had a game of whist or by preference a game of backgammon with Monsieur de La Tour du Pin, if he was there. These reunions never comprised more than fifteen or eighteen guests chosen from the most distinguished persons of the city or from strangers of distinction. But the presence of strangers was rare, since France, at war with all Europe, could not be visited then as it has been since.

I had often met the Duchesse d'Arenberg at Paris

before the Revolution, at the Hôtel de Beauvau, where I was received with great kindness. Besides this, I knew that Mme. de Poix and Mme. de Beauvau had written letters regarding me prior to my arrival at Brussels. The day following our arrival I went, therefore, accompanied by my husband, to see this distinguished lady. We were received with the greatest possible kindness and invited for supper on the following day. The Duchesse also expressed the wish that I should present to her my son, Humbert, who had come to Brussels to meet us. This was a token of the consideration with which we were to be treated. All the members of high society hastened to inscribe their names at our house or came to see us in person. I took very particular care to return all these visits without forgetting any one. I prepared a methodical list of all the persons who had come to call. After each name I made a note of all the particulars which I had been able to gather as to the family, either in conversation or from the nobiliary records which I procured at the Burgundy Library which was, and is still, very rich in information of this kind. As assistants in this work, for the present time, I had Monsieur de Verseyden, Secretary General of the Préfecture of Wareck, and, for times past, an old Commander of Malta, who came to see me every evening. At the end of a month I was as familiar with the world of Brussels as if I had lived there all my life. I knew the liaisons of every kind, the animosities, the *tracasseries* and so on.

Our establishment cost us a great deal of money. It seems to me that my husband received a certain sum to maintain the house, but I am not sure of this: The personnel of the service comprised two domestics and an employé of the Bureau, dressed in livery, a porter, a valet de chambre maître d'hôtel, the usher of the cabinet, who also waited the days of receptions, and two men in the stable. We occupied the Palace where the King of Holland has lived since.

The Palace at that time comprised only the east wing of the present Royal Palace. The west wing was then occupied by the Hôtel Bellevue. Between the two wings was the Rue Héraldique, which was closed in 1826 when the two wings were joined by the central colonnade. My private rooms, on the same floor with the State apartments, were pleasant and commodious. They comprised, in particular, a fine salon and a billiard room. From the very first I announced that I would never receive in the morning under any pretext whatsoever. The morning hours I devoted to the education of my daughters, helping them in their lessons and going out with them for promenades, either on foot or in a carriage.

We soon became intimate with a number of persons. My husband met again with pleasure the Comte de Liedekerke, one of his old companions in arms before the Revolution in the Regiment of Royal-Comtois, of which Monsieur de La Tour du Pin had been the Colonel en Second. The Comte de Liedekerke had married Mlle. Desandrouin, who was heiress to an immense fortune of which she already possessed a considerable part. They had only one son, Florent-Charles-Auguste, and two daughters. The young man, then twenty-two years of age, was *auditeur* of the Council of State. As there was talk of attaching one of these *auditeurs* to the person of each préfet, in order to give these young men an acquaintance with the administration, and with the idea of employing them as secretaries in the private cabinet of the préfet, Monsieur de Liedekerke requested Monsieur de La Tour du Pin, his former Colonel, to give his son such a post.

Our son Humbert had left Antwerp, where Monsieur Malouet had been to him a second father, and returned to Brussels to take up the preparatory studies which were necessary for his examination for the Council of State which was to take place in several months.

During the month of September, 1808, I received a letter from my step-mother, Mme. Dillon. She informed me that my sister had finally decided, after much hesitation and uncertainty, to marry General Bertrand. She had been overcome, in part by his constancy, and in part by the persistency of the Emperor to whom you could refuse nothing, as he used so much charm and fascination in obtaining what he desired. My sister at that time was extremely frivolous, with the frivolity of a Creole like her mother. Napoleon had desired that she should accompany the Empress Josephine to Fontainebleau, and in order to enable her to appear to advantage, he had sent her 30,000 francs to cover the expenses of her wardrobe during the week that the Court was to be there. At this time he finally succeeded in obtaining her assent to the proposed union which she had refused so obstinately.

L'Impératrice MARIE-LOUISE

1791 - 1847

Château of Queen Hortense, who was very careful to carry out in all particulars the orders given by the Emperor for the ceremony. Thus at the moment when he was going to assemble around him all the potentates who were then at his feet, the great man had found the time to regulate the minutest details of the celebration of the marriage of his favorite aide de camp.

I was presented to the Emperor by Mme. de Bassano at Saint-Cloud. Towards eight o'clock in the morning, it was necessary for me to go to her house in Court costume, with a plumed toque. The Emperor received me in the most gracious manner, asked me many questions regarding Brussels, the society, *la haute société*, with a smile which seemed to say: "Vous n'aimez que celle-là." Then he laughed at having made me get up so early in the morning and made a little fun of Mme. de Bassano on this subject, a mockery which she took with a little sulky air which was very becoming to her. She has since told me that the Emperor at that time was quite smitten with her.

The great ones of the earth arrived with their wives. The clauses of the marriage contract were read, but I do not remember the details, although I think they were favorable to my sister. Fanny, that day, appeared to very great advantage.

The evening which preceded the day of the marriage passed in a very tiresome manner. The déjeuner the next day was not more amusing. The marriage was to take place at half past three. All the *"archi"* arrived:

[353]

the Marshals, the Generals and so on. We marched in a procession to the chapel. The Abbé d'Osmond, Bishop of Nancy, later Archbishop of Florence, gave the nuptial benediction. Then the dinner was served, and after dinner we danced. Many young people came from Paris. Queen Hortense, who loved to dance, nevertheless was in bad humor, on account of a little incident which was quite amusing. The Emperor had not appeared, but he had intimated to Queen Hortense that, after having examined the set of emeralds surrounded by diamonds which the Empress had given Fanny, he did not think it was sufficient. As he knew that Hortense had a similar set, he requested her to add hers to that given by her mother, in order to complete the gift. She did not expect anything of this kind and was very much displeased, but it was necessary to submit.

CHAPTER THIRTEEN

1810–1811

VISIT OF THE EMPEROR

The Winter Season at Brussels.— The Ennui of Queen Hortense. — Arrival of Marie-Louise at Compiègne.— High Society at Brussels and the Imperial Government.— The Guard of Honor.— Napoleon and Marie-Louise at Brussels.— Dinner with the Emperor.— Ball at the Hôtel de Ville.— Departure of the Emperor.— The Summer at Brussels.— Examination of Humbert at the Conseil d'Etat.— Humbert Appointed Sous-Préfet at Florence.— Birth of the King of Rome.— The Private Baptism.— The Old Guard.

I RETURNED to Brussels after several grand dinners given in honor of the marriage, which were very boring. I set out with joy to be again with my husband and my children. The autumn and the winter passed quite agreeably at Brussels. I gave two or three handsome balls. Mme. de Duras came with her daughters to pass two weeks with us. I gave them dances and took them to the theatre in the excellent box of the Prefecture. They had a very good time.

Queen Hortense had passed through Brussels in the course of the last journey which she made to rejoin her husband for a period of several days at Amsterdam. I saw her when she went through and she expressed a great boredom over the necessity of going to resume her duties as Queen.

[355]

As I have no pretension of writing history, I will not speak of the marriage of the Emperor Napoleon with the Archiduchesse Marie-Louise. I will only report what my sister told me regarding the arrival of this Princess at Compiègne.

The Emperor was then at Compiègne with the new Ladies of Honor of the Empress and was in a state of boundless impatience to see his new wife. A little calèche was waiting all hitched up in the court of the Château to take him to meet her. When the advance courier came, Napoleon rushed to the calèche and set out to meet the berline which was bringing the spouse so much desired. The carriage stopped. The door was opened and Marie-Louise prepared to descend, but her husband did not give her the time. He entered the berline, embraced his wife, and then having pushed her sister, the Queen of Naples, without ceremony onto the front seat of the carriage, he seated himself beside Marie-Louise.

Arriving at the Château he descended first, offered her his arm and conducted her to the salon de service, where all the invited guests were assembled. It was already evening. The Emperor presented, one after another, all the ladies of the mansion, and then the men. This presentation over, he took the Empress by the hand and conducted her to her apartment. All of us thought that the Empress was proceeding with her toilette. We waited for an hour and then commenced to be very anxious to have our supper. At this moment, the grand chamberlain came to announce that Their Majesties had retired. The surprise was great, but no one ventured to let it be seen, and we went to supper.

This marriage with an Archiduchesse was celebrated at Brussels with great rejoicing. The recollections of the Austrian domination were far from being effaced. The nobility of Brussels, which until then had kept aloof from the new government, attracted now by the good administration of a Préfet of the aristocratic class, found the moment favorable to lay aside its former antipathy, which had commenced to be irksome.

When Monsieur de La Tour du Pin learned that the Emperor was going to bring the young Empress to the capital of the ancient possessions of her father in Belgium, he created a Guard of Honor to form the service at the Château of Laeken. This Guard was composed entirely of Belgians, to the exclusion of all French. The uniform was very simple: a green coat with amaranthine breeches. It was a cavalry corps and very well mounted. My sister came to Brussels and stayed with us at the Prefecture. She was present at the grand dinner which we gave in honor of this Guard, at which the ladies were adorned with ribbons of the same colors as the uniform.

The Emperor arrived at Laeken for dinner. The next day he received the Guard of Honor and all the officials. The Mayor, the Duc d'Ursel, presented the municipal authorities to him. In the evening there was an Assembly at which I presented the ladies, nearly all of whom I knew. Marie-Louise did not address a personal word to any of them. The name of the most illustrious lady present, for example the Duchesse d'Arenberg, or the Comtesse de Mérode, meant no more to her ear than that of Mme. P——, wife of the Receiver General.

[357]

After the Assembly. I had the honor of playing a game of whist with Her Majesty. The Duc d'Ursel named the cards which I must throw upon the table and warned me when it was my turn to deal. This kind of comedy lasted half an hour. After this, the Emperor having retired, we separated, and I was charmed to return home.

The following day there was to be a grand ball at the Hôtel de Ville. I was therefore somewhat put out when I was invited to dinner at Laeken, as I did not well see how I could find a moment to change my toilette, or at least my gown, between the dinner and the ball. However, the pleasure of seeing and listening to the Emperor during a period of two hours was so great that I could not but appreciate the value of such an invitation. The Duc d'Ursel accompanied me, and as we were to go afterwards to the Hôtel de Ville to receive the Emperor, I ordered my femme de chambre to be there with another toilette all ready.

This dinner was one of the events of my life of which I have preserved the most agreeable recollection. Here is the way in which the guests, to the number of eight, were placed at the table: The Emperor; at his right, the Queen of Westphalia, then Maréchal Berthier, the King of Westphalia, the Empress, the Duc d'Ursel, Mme. de Bouillé, finally myself, at the left of the Emperor. He talked to me nearly all the time, regarding the manufactures, the laces, the daily wages, the life of the lace-makers; then of the monuments, the antiquities, the establishments of charity, the manners of the people, the *béguines.* Fortunately I was well posted regarding all of these subjects. The Emperor demanded of the Duc d'Ursel: "What are the wages of a lace-maker?" The poor man was embarrassed in the endeavor to express the sum in centimes. The Emperor saw his hesitation, and turning to me asked: "What is the name of the money of the country?" I replied: "An *escalin,* or sixty-three centimes." "Ah! c'est bien," said he.

We did not remain more than three-quarters of an hour at table. On returning to the salon, the Emperor took a large cup of coffee and began again to talk. First he spoke of the toilette of the Empress which he admired. Then, changing the topic, he asked me if I found my lodging satisfactory.

"Pas mal," I replied, "dans l'appartement de Votre Majesté."

"Ah! vraiment," said he, "il a coûté assez cher pour cela. C'est ce coquin de . . . (le nom m'échappe) le secré-taire de Monsieur Pontécoulant, qui l'a fait arranger."

The Emperor then turned to an entirely different subject of conversation. He spoke of Charles the Bold, Duc de Bourgogne, and of Louis XI, from whom he descended quite abruptly to Louis XIV, saying that he had never been really great except in his latter years. Observing with what interest I listened to him, and that I understood him, he returned to Louis XI and expressed himself thus: "J'ai mon avis sur celui-là, et je sais bien que ce n'est pas l'avis de tout le monde." After several words regarding the shame of the reign of Louis XV, he pronounced the name of Louis XVI, upon which, stopping with

an air at once respectful and sad, he said: "Ce
malheureux prince!"

At this moment someone announced that it was
necessary to set out for the ball. Monsieur d'Ursel
and I rushed to the carriage, and the horses, at a
gallop, brought us to the Hôtel de Ville. I went up
four steps at a time. A toilette which was all ready,
awaited me. I changed my costume and was able to
be in the ball-room when the Emperor arrived. He
paid me a compliment on my promptitude and asked
me if I intended to dance. I replied: "No, because I
am forty years old." At this he began to laugh, saying:
"There are many others who dance who do not reveal
their age like that." The ball was very fine and was
prolonged after the supper where everyone drank to
the health of the Empress.

The Emperor and his wife left the following morning. A yacht highly decorated took them to the end
of the Canal of Brussels where they found the
carriages which conveyed them to Antwerp. On
boarding the yacht, my husband noticed the Marquis
de Trazegnies, the Commander of the Guard of
Honor. Fearing that the Emperor would not invite
him to take a place on the yacht, where there was
only room for a few persons, he named him, at the
same time adding: "His ancestor was Constable under
Saint Louis." These words produced a magic effect
on the Emperor, who immediately summoned the
Marquis de Trazegnies and had a long talk with him.
A short time later, his wife was named Dame du
Palais. She pretended to be displeased over this
nomination, although secretly she was delighted.

VISIT OF THE EMPEROR

After this trip of the Emperor, we resumed the ordinary train of our life at Brussels. The summer passed in visiting different country houses where we were invited to dine. We went to Antwerp to be present at the launching of a large vessel of Seventy-four, one of the new ones at that moment on the ways. Our excellent friend, Monsieur Malouet, was at the head of this work through his position as Préfet Maritime. All the details of these constructions interested me in the highest degree.

Our son Humbert went to Paris to pass his examination. It was a very trying thing for a young man of twenty years to reply to a whole series of questions which were asked him. But it was even more so, when the Emperor, seated in an armchair, with the candidates standing before him, took up the examination and asked you a lot of unexpected things. Humbert heard the examiner say in the ear of Napoleon in pointing him out: "This is one of the most distinguished," and this good word comforted him. The Emperor asked him if he knew any foreign language, to which he replied: "English and Italian, as well as French." It was the facility with which he spoke Italian that decided his nomination as Sous-Préfet at Florence.

Towards the end of the winter of 1810 and 1811, we went, my husband and I, to pass two months at Paris, to accompany our son Humbert, who was setting out for Florence. My sister Fanny was at Paris with her two children, of whom the younger, little Hortense, was only three months old.

We had left at Brussels, Mme. d'Hénin, my two daughters and Monsieur de Lally, who passed for an English prisoner. He was very anxious not to lose this position, in order to preserve the pension of 300 pounds sterling which was paid him on that account by the English government.

My dear Humbert left for Florence. This departure, the beginning of a long absence, was very painful to me. I was his friend, as well as his mother. I was therefore desirous of returning at once to Brussels, but my husband did not think it advisable to leave Paris before the birth of the Imperial child which was expected at any moment.

One evening I was invited to an entertainment given at the Tuileries, in a little gallery where a theatre had been improvised. We assembled in the salon of the Empress. The Emperor came directly to me. With an extreme kindness he spoke to me first of my son, then he exclaimed regarding the simplicity of my dress, my good taste and my distinguished air, to the great surprise of several ladies covered with diamonds, who were asking each other who this new-comer could possibly be. When we entered the gallery, I was placed upon a bench very near that of the Emperor. The play, "L'Avocat Patelin," was performed by some admirable actors. The piece which was very comical amused Napoleon very much and he laughed heartily. The presence of the great man did not prevent me from doing the same. This pleased him very much, as he said afterwards in mocking the ladies who thought it necessary to maintain their gravity. It was considered a great favor to be invited to this spectacle, and only about fifty ladies were present.

The morning of the twentieth of March, 1811, we heard the first discharge of the guns of the Invalides. Every one rushed into the street. All the carriages stopped; the merchants, upon the thresholds of their shops, the people at their windows, counted the strokes. We heard everyone say: "Three, four, five," and so on. There was an interval of about a minute between each discharge. After the twenty-first, there was a profound silence, but at the twenty-second, there were spontaneous cries of: "Vive l'Empereur!"

That evening I dined with my sister, Mme. Bertrand, and there we were notified that the child would be privately baptized at nine o'clock and that the ladies who had been presented at Court could attend the ceremony.

Mme. Dillon, my sister and I went. We had to enter by the Pavillon de Flore and pass through all the apartments, as far as the Salle des Maréchaux. The salons were full of the dignitaries of the Empire, men and women. Every one endeavored to be at the edge of the passage-way, kept open by the ushers, where the procession was to pass to descend to the chapel. We managed to manœuvre so as to find ourselves on the landing of the stairway. From this point we enjoyed a very rare sight, that of the old *grognards* of the Vieille Garde, arranged in order upon each step, every one wearing the cross upon his breast. They were forbidden to make a movement, but a very vivid emotion was depicted upon their stern faces, and I saw tears of joy in their eyes. The Emperor appeared at the side of Mme. de Montesquiou, who bore the child with his face uncovered, upon a cushion of white satin covered with lace. I had the opportunity to obtain a good look at him.

CHAPTER FOURTEEN

1811–1813

AN AUDIENCE WITH NAPOLEON

Marie-Louise at Laeken.— Opening of the Russian Campaign.—
Movements of Troops.— Monsieur de Liedekerke Demands
the Hand of Charlotte de La Tour du Pin.— Humbert is
Appointed Sous-Préfet at Sens.— Dismissal of the Préfet
of Brussels.— Mme. de La Tour du Pin Leaves for Paris.—
Request for an Audience.— Conversation with the Emperor.— Surprise of Monsieur de Montalivet.— Monsieur
de La Tour du Pin Appointed Préfet at Amiens.— The Assembly at the Tuileries.— Amiability of Napoleon.— The
Last Days at Brussels.— Regrets of the Population.—
Marriage of Charlotte.

A FEW days later we returned to Brussels
where the Emperor was expected during
the spring. His brother Louis had deserted
the throne of Holland where the iron hand of Napoleon had prevented him from carrying out his policy
for the good of the country. He had left in Holland
a very honorable record, as I know from King
William himself. The people felt very differently
about the administration of Monsieur de Celles, the
son-in-law of Mme. de Valence, whose memory there
has been held in horror. The Emperor appointed him
Préfet at Amsterdam where he did all the evil of
which a man is capable who is absolutely devoid of
principle.

It was towards the spring of this year 1811, as nearly as I can remember, that we received the visit, always dreaded by the Préfets, of a Councillor of State, *en mission*, a kind of spy of high rank, determined to find fault even with those whom he could not help esteeming. Monsieur Réal fell to the lot of Monsieur de La Tour du Pin, who realized, at the time of the first visit, that he would endeavor to do him all the harm possible. Nevertheless, during his sojourn, we gave him a dinner followed by a reception. I had said to the ladies who had shown kindness to me that they would do me a favor in coming to pass the evening with us. After dinner, on returning to the grand salon, we found united there all the most distinguished persons of the society of Brussels, both men and women. Monsieur Réal was stupified by the names, the manners, and the jewels. He could not refrain from saying to Monsieur de La Tour du Pin: "Monsieur, voilà un salon qui m'offusque terriblement." To which my husband replied: "I am very sorry, but fortunately, it does not have the same effect on the Emperor."

The nineteenth of September, 1811, the Emperor set out from Paris to visit the camp at Boulogne, the French Fleet and the north of the Empire. The Empress went to Laeken near Brussels, where she arrived the night of the twenty-first or twenty-second of September. We were invited to come to Laeken every day to pass the evening and play at lotto. This lasted for a week and was very boring. The Empress on every occasion showed the greatest insipidness. Every day she said the same thing to me in giving me her pulse to count: "Do you think that I have any fever?" to which I invariably replied: "Madame, I do not know anything about it." The Duc d'Ursel was charged with the task of arranging the morning promenades, according to the weather. One day when Marie-Louise visited the Museum she seemed to be struck by a handsome portrait of her illustrious grandmother, Marie-Thérèse. The Duc d'Ursel proposed to her to place the portrait in a salon at Laeken. She replied: "Oh no, the frame is too old!" Another time he suggested as an interesting promenade that part of the Forest of Soignes known as the "pilgrimage of the Archiduchesse Isabelle," whose sanctity and goodness have remained in the hearts of the people. She replied that she did not like the woods. In fine, this insignificant woman, so unworthy of the great man whose destiny she shared, seemed to make it a point to be as disagreeable as possible to the Belgians whose hearts were so disposed to love her. I never saw her again until after she lost her throne, and then she was still as destitute of intelligence.

During the summer of 1811, Monsieur de Talleyrand came to preside over an electoral college, summoned I think to elect a senator and two deputies to the Corps Législatif. He arrived with a large household and gave several dinners in the fine apartments of the Hôtel d'Arenberg, placed at his disposal by the blind Duc. On this occasion he showed again all his great and charming manners, which contrasted in a comical fashion with those of the Archbishop of Malines who had the appearance of a Scapin in a violet cassock.

About the middle of the spring of 1812, we began to see the troops passing through on their way to Germany. Several regiments of the Young Guard came to Brussels and remained there. Other regiments only passed through the city. Instructions were received to bring together the farmers' wagons hitched to four horses. Sometimes the order was received only in the morning, and it was necessary the same evening to have eighty or one hundred wagons assembled, provided with forage for two days. The gendarmes had to gallop in every direction to notify the farmers. The latter, obliged to leave their plows, and their work, were in very bad humor. But who would have dared to resist? The thought never occurred to any one from Bayonne to Hamburg. We served several substantial meals to the corps of officers who came at ten o'clock in the evening and left at midnight. Doubtless very few of these brave fellows ever returned from this disastrous campaign.

No one had any idea that the French army would go as far as Moscow. Therefore, when my husband, upon his return from a trip of several days to Paris, brought back a very fine map of Poland and Russia, we were astonished that Lapie had added upon the margin a little square of paper on which was the name of Moscow. The map did not go as far as the meridian of that city, and when pinned to the draperies of the salon, every one thought that this precaution on the part of the map-maker was very unnecessary. It was a prognostic!

During the last months of this same year, young Auguste de Liedekerke-Beaufort paid very marked

COMTE HUMBERT DE LA TOUR DU PIN DE GOUVERNET

1790 - 1816

attentions to my elder daughter Charlotte, who at this time was sixteen years of age. She was very tall, and without being pretty had a very distinguished air. She was a *noble demoiselle* in every sense of the term. In this affair both the heart and mind of young Liedekerke were involved. He felt that Mlle. de La Tour du Pin, with her personal charms, her name and her connections, although without fortune, suited him better than some good Belgian girl who was very rich and very obscure. He declared to his parents that he would not marry any other woman than my daughter. His father raised some objections, but his mother in the hope that the political career of her son would be favored by a marriage which would take him out of his country, obtained the consent of her husband. The first day of the year 1813, at ten o'clock in the morning, Mme. de Liedekerke was announced. She demanded the hand of my daughter for her son. I was prepared for this request which I received and agreed to with pleasure. Mme. de Liedekerke wished to see my daughter whom she embraced and it was arranged that the marriage should take place within six weeks.

My daughter Cécile was at the Convent of the Dames de Berlaimont where she had been for six months preparing for her first communion. I promised to take her out the day of her sister's marriage. At the same time we received news that Humbert, then sous-préfet at Florence, had just been named as sous-préfet at Sens, Department of the Yonne. This news filled the measure of our contentment.

My husband had gone to Nivelles to be present at the drawing of the conscription necessitated by the continuation of the war which the Emperor had undertaken. I was alone at home before luncheon when I saw the secrétaire-général of the Prefecture enter with a dejected face. He informed me that the courier from Paris had just brought word of the dismissal of my husband and of his replacement by Monsieur d'Houdetot, Préfet of Ghent.

This news struck me like a thunder clap, and in it I saw at the first moment a cause of breaking off the marriage of my daughter. However, I made up my mind not to yield without a fight. Without awaiting the return of my husband to whom I sent a courier, I decided to leave at once for Paris. I owe it to Monsieur de Liedekerke, to state that he came to see me with an eagerness and a warmth which must surprise him now, if he recalls this circumstance, to beg me not to change our plans in any respect.

I left my aunt and Mme. de Maurville to pack everything which belonged to us in the Prefecture, and at four o'clock I set out for Paris. I had had so many things to do and to arrange in the space of two hours, that I was already fatigued when I set out. The night passed in a wretched *chaise de poste* and the anxiety caused by our new position gave me quite a high fever, with which I arrived at Paris at ten o'clock in the evening. I went to the house of Mme. de Duras whom I found out. Her daughters had just gone to bed. They arose and sent some one in search of their mother who on returning found me lying on her sofa worn out with fatigue. There was no room in the apartment to lodge me, but she had the key of the apartment of the Chevalier de Thuisy, our common friend. My femme de chambre and the servant who had followed me went and prepared a bed in which I took refuge at once, but without finding the repose of which I had great need. The next morning at an early hour, Mme. de Duras came with Doctor Auvity whom she had summoned. He found that I still had a good deal of fever. But I told him that it was necessary for him to get me on my feet at no matter what cost, and that I must be in a state to go to Versailles before night. He then gave me a calming draft which caused me to sleep until five o'clock. I do not know in what state of health I then found myself, but at any rate I did not pay any attention to it.

I had a carriage called and, dressed in a very elegant toilette, I went in search of Mme. de Duras. We set out at once for Versailles where the Emperor was staying at Trianon. We stopped at an inn, Rue de l'Orangerie, where they put us together in an apartment. I at once opened my ink-stand. Mme. de Duras, to whom I had confided only my desire to have an audience with His Majesty, saw me take a fine large sheet of paper and then copy a rough draft which I had drawn from my portfolio, and said to me: "To whom are you writing?" "To whom?" I replied, "apparently to the Emperor. I do not like small measures."

The letter written and sealed, we again got into a carriage to take it to Trianon. There I asked for the chamberlain on duty. I had taken the precaution to prepare a little note for him. By a fortunate chance he was Adrien de Mun who was one of my best friends. He approached the carriage and promised me that at ten o'clock, when the Emperor came from tea with the Empress, he would hand him my letter. He kept his promise and was as satisfied as he was surprised when, on looking at the address, Napoleon said, speaking to himself: "Mme. de La Tour du Pin writes very well. It is not the first time that I have seen her hand-writing." These words confirmed my suspicion that a certain letter written to Mme. d'Hénin had been seized before arriving at its destination.

After our trip to Trianon, we returned to our hotel. About ten o'clock in the evening, while Claire and I were debating as to whether I would have my audience, "yes" or "no," the hotel waiter who up to that moment had considered us as simple mortals, opened the door and cried: "De la part de l'Empereur!"

The same moment a man covered with gold lace entered and said: "His Majesty awaits Mme. de La Tour du Pin tomorrow at ten o'clock in the morning."

The good news did not trouble my slumber. On the following morning, after having drunk a large bowl of coffee, which Claire had prepared with her own hands to brace me up, as she said, I set out for Trianon. I had to wait ten minutes in the salon which preceded the one where Napoleon received. I was very glad to find no one there for I had need of this moment of solitude to arrange my thoughts. A conversation *en tête à tête* with this extraordinary man was an event of great importance in my life, and nevertheless I declare here in all the sincerity of my heart, perhaps with pride, that I did not feel in the least embarrassed. The door opened; the usher, by a gesture, made me a sign to enter and then closed the double door behind me. I found myself in the presence of Napoleon. He advanced to meet me and said with quite a pleasant air:

"Madame, I am afraid that you are very much displeased with me."

I inclined my head in sign of assent and the conversation began. Having lost the notes which I wrote of this long audience which lasted fifty-nine minutes by the clock, after the lapse of so many years I am not able to remember all the details of the interview. The Emperor endeavored, in short, to prove to me that he had been forced to act as he had done. Then I pictured to him in a few words the state of society at Brussels, the consideration which my husband had acquired there compared with all the preceding préfets, the visit of Réal, the stupidity of General Chambarlhac and of his wife, a *religieuse défroquée*, and so on. All this was recited rapidly, and, as I was encouraged by his air of approbation, I ended by announcing to the Emperor that my daughter was going to marry one of the greatest seigneurs of Brussels. Upon which, he interrupted me, placing his beautiful hand upon my arm, and said:

"J'espère que cela ne fera pas manquer le mariage, et, dans ce cas, vous ne devriez pas le regretter."

Then while promenading the length of the large salon, while I followed, walking at his side, he pronounced these words (and it is perhaps the only

time in his life that he ever said them and the privilege
was reserved for me to overhear him):

"I have made a mistake, but what can I do?"

I replied, "Your Majesty can repair the error."

Then he placed his hand on his forehead and said:
"Ah! they are at work upon the prefectures; the
Minister of the Interior is coming this evening."

Then he mentioned the names of four or five departments and added: "There is Amiens. Will that
suit you?"

I replied without hesitation: "Perfectly, Sire."

"In that case, it is arranged," said he. "You can
go and notify Montalivet."

And with that charming smile of which so much
has been said: "A présent, m'avez-vous pardonné?"

I replied to him in my best manner: "J'ai besoin
aussi que Votre Majesté me pardonne de lui avoir
parlé si librement."

"Oh! vous avez très bien fait."

I made a courtesy and he went to the door which
he opened for me himself.

On coming out I found Adrien de Mun and Juste
de Noailles, who asked me if I had arranged my
business. I only replied that the Emperor had been
very kind to me. Without losing time, I entered my
carriage and taking Mme. de Duras who, unable to
overcome her impatience, had come to await me in
an alley of Trianon, we returned to Paris.

After having left Mme. de Duras at her door, I
went to see Monsieur de Montalivet, where I arrived
at about two-thirty o'clock. He received me in a
friendly manner, but with a very sad air, saying:

"Ah! I could do nothing to prevent it. The Emperor is very displeased with your husband. They have told him a thousand tales. They pretend that people went to your house as to a Court."

With the idea of amusing myself a little with him, I replied: "But would it not be possible to find another place for my husband?"

"Oh! I would never dare to propose such a thing to the Emperor. When he is put out justly or unjustly with any one, it is very difficult to change him."

"Well," I replied, with a hypocritical air, "it is necessary to bow the head. However, as you are going to Trianon to present four nominations for préfets to be signed . . ."

"But, how do you know that?" he cried hastily.

Without having the appearance of understanding, I added: "You will propose Monsieur de La Tour du Pin for the préfecture of Amiens."

He looked at me with stupification and I continued very simply, "The Emperor has charged me to tell you that."

Monsieur de Montalivet gave an exclamation, took my hands with much friendship and interest and at the same time looking at me from head to foot:

"Indeed," he said, "I should have divined that that pretty toilette this morning was not intended for me."

The nomination of Monsieur de La Tour du Pin appeared the same evening in the "Moniteur," and I received the compliments of all the people of my acquaintance who had been afflicted by the news of his disgrace. In fact this dismissal was a fortunate event for my husband, as you will see later on.

I remained several days at Paris where I awaited my husband and the Comte de Liedekerke who came to rejoin me for the signature of the contract of marriage. At this time there was an Assembly at Court and I went with Mme. de Mun. I was dressed very simply, without a single gem, contrary to the custom of the ladies of the Empire who were covered with jewels. I found myself placed in the last row in the Throne Room where I was a head taller than two little women who had placed themselves unceremoniously before me. The Emperor entered. He glanced his eyes over the three rows of ladies, spoke to several with an inattentive air, and then having perceived me, he smiled in that manner which all the historians have endeavored to describe and which was truly remarkable, from the contrast it presented to the usual expression of his face which was always serious and often severe. But the surprise of my neighbors was great when Napoleon, still smiling, addressed to me these words: "Êtes-vous contente de moi, Madame?" The persons who surrounded me then withdrew to the right and left, and I found myself, without knowing how, in the front rank. I thanked the Emperor in an accent of very sincere gratitude. After several very amiable words, he passed on. This was the last time I saw this great man.

I set out for Brussels where I was very desirous of seeing my children, and where I had besides a thousand things to do. My husband went by way of Amiens to prepare for our installation. He then came to rejoin me with Humbert, who was back from Florence and who had received at Paris his nomination as sous-préfet at Sens. Who could have possibly foreseen at that moment that ten months later he would be chased from that city by the Würtembergers?

When Monsieur de La Tour du Pin arrived at Brussels, he found me settled with my children with the Marquis de Trazegnies, who had offered us a very cordial hospitality. Monsieur d'Houdetot had announced, without delicacy, that he would take possession of the Prefecture the second day after the date of my return to Brussels. I was desirous that he should find no vestige of our sojourn of five years in the house which he was to inhabit. Everything which belonged to us was packed and dispatched. As for the furniture of the Prefecture, every article had been put back in the place designated by the inventory. Nothing was lacking. Monsieur d'Houdetot was rather put out by this exactitude and was even more disturbed by the regrets which all classes loudly expressed over the recall of Monsieur de La Tour du Pin. He found a pretext to return to Ghent, and lived there until after our departure which was fixed for the second of April. My daughter was to be married the twentieth. My husband could say with Guzman:

"J'étais maître en ces lieux, seul j'y commande encore."

He therefore summoned the Chief of Police, Monsieur Malaise, and enjoined him to see that there was no manifestation, too pronounced, on the part of the people on the occasion of the marriage of our daughter. The Mayor, the Duc D'Ursel, to the same end, fixed an advanced hour of the evening, half past ten, for the marriage at the Municipality. This did not prevent the people from assembling in crowds in all the streets through which we were to pass in going to the Hôtel de Ville which was brilliantly illuminated. On all sides were heard only expressions of regret and kindness in connection with Monsieur de La Tour du Pin. When we returned, after the civil marriage at the Hôtel de Ville, to the house of Mme. de Trazegnies, we found all the salons of the ground floor lighted up and in the street under the windows was a large band composed of all the musicians of the city to give us a serenade. My husband was naturally very much pleased at this manifestation of the public good-will.

The following day my daughter was married in the private chapel of the Duc d'Ursel. After a fine déjeuner attended by relatives and friends, she left with her husband for the Château de Noisy, situated near Dinant in the Belgian Ardennes. There her father-in-law had preceded her by several hours. I accompanied them as far as Tirlemont.

Up to this moment, I have not spoken again of Monsieur de Chambeau, our friend and companion in misfortune during our emigration to America. He had fallen into possession of a small fortune and had passed at Brussels the greater part of his leisure time. His business, however, obliged him to make long sojourns in the south of France. For a year past he had occupied at Antwerp a position which was temporary, it is true, but which held out the assurance of advancement. When he learned of the catastrophe which forced our departure from Brussels so suddenly, he came at once, and, knowing the bad state of our affairs, he said to my husband: "You are about to marry your daughter and at the same time you are losing your position. I have 60,000 francs in securities which I have brought you. Use them as your own." He was present at the marriage of Charlotte who was his god-daughter.

At the moment I write these lines, at Pisa, at the beginning of the year 1845, I do not know anything more about this excellent man. I saw him again ten years ago at Paris. At this time he was living in a little country house at Épinay where he had fallen entirely under the influence of two young serving maids who had acquired an unfortunate control over his old age. They took care to prevent him from coming near us. Our poor friend is probably no longer living.

CHAPTER FIFTEEN

1813-1814

RETURN OF THE KING

Society at Amiens.— The Prefecture.— General Dupont.— Arrival of the Cossacks.— Conversation with Talleyrand.— His Hatred of Napoleon.— Flight of Humbert from Sens.— In the Ante-chamber of Talleyrand.— "Vive le Roi!"— Distribution of White Cockades.— Preparations for the Reception of the King.— The King Enjoys His Dinner.— Ill-nature of the Duchesse d'Angoulême.— Monsieur de La Tour du Pin Re-enters Diplomacy.— Humbert is Appointed Lieutenant of the Black Musketeers.

IT was in the month of April, 1813, that we arrived at Amiens where we were destined to see happen events which we were far from looking for. Here we found our brother-in-law, the Marquis de Lameth, whose friendship had already assured us a very favorable reception on the part of the nobility and of the people of importance in the city, who up to then had been very much dissatisfied with their Préfets.

The house set apart for the Prefecture was charming. It had just been entirely refurnished with elegance and luxury. The ground floor comprised a complete apartment where I lived with my husband. On one side was the cabinet of the Préfet, communicating with the bureaus. The house looked out on a magnificent garden of seven or eight acres, well cultivated. This gave us almost the pleasure of being in the country.

The first days of summer passed very agreeably. We often went to dinner in the neighborhood with friends who resided there during the fine season. My daughter Cécile, who was thirteen years of age at this time, already showed very great talent for music and also had a charming voice of great compass. During the five years that we had passed at Brussels I had given her an excellent teacher in Italian. Formerly from Rome and not knowing French, he had taught my daughter to use the fine Roman idiom. She expressed herself in this language with facility. Charlotte and she also read not only Italian, but also English. We were very well settled at Amiens when we commenced to hear the grumbling of the storm. Every one was so confident of the fortunes of Napoleon, that the idea did not occur to any one to admit that he could possibly have any other enemy to fear than the frosts that had been so fatal to him during the Russian campaign.

However, after the Battle of Leipsic, there began the requisitions, the enlisting of men and the organization of Guards of Honor. This last measure caused desolation among the families.

Under these circumstances, my husband had need of all his firmness. He served the Government in good faith and the thought of the Restoration had not yet occurred to his mind. He neither foresaw it nor desired it. All the faults and all the vices which had been the causes of the First Revolution were still too fresh in his memory for him to desire to see the exiled Royal Family return, bringing in its train the former weakness and abuses of all kinds. The expression, so well justified: "They have learned nothing and forgotten nothing," often came to his mind. However, he endeavored so far as possible to mitigate the application of the rules for the organization of the Guards of Honor. The greatest resistance to certain measures was found among the rich classes, and I often heard him say: "They give their children more willingly than their money." In a city devoted to the manufacture of woolens, like Amiens, the requisitions were very burdensome, and my husband suspected above all things the greediness and the rascality of the *réquisitionnaires*.

The cannon of Laon which we heard at Amiens gave us the first news of the invasion of French territory. Several days later, Monsieur d'Houdetot, the Préfet of Brussels, fleeing before the invasion, entered our salon one evening, at the very moment that the Receiver General, Monsieur d'Haubersaert, who saw everything in a rosy light, was saying to us that he had just received a letter from Brussels and that Belgium was in no danger of a *coup de main*.

Soon afterwards, we were informed of the appearance of a corps of Cossacks commanded by General Geismar, in the plains around the city. It was at this time that General Dupont passed through Amiens, under the escort of the gendarmes. He had previously been transferred from the Château of Joux, where Napoleon had had him confined after the capitulation of Baylen, to the citadel of Doullens. They were now conducting him to Tours, in order that he might not fall into the hands of the Allies. He did not go any further than Paris, however, and the severity with which he was treated made his fortune.

The Cossacks approached so near to Amiens that they could be seen from the tower of the Cathedral. The squadron of cavalry in garrison in the city, commanded by our worthy Major, presented such a formidable appearance that they did not appear again.

My aunt, Mme. d'Hénin, was settled for the autumn at the Château of Mouchy, near Beauvais with her friend the Princesse de Poix. Mme. de Duras was also there with her daughters, and they invited me to come and pass several days. My husband urged me to accept and asked me to return by way of Paris, to see Monsieur de Talleyrand and ascertain the news. Monsieur de Talleyrand had sent him a note by Merlin de Thionville, but this note was so nonsensical, and the reputation of the bearer was so bad, that my husband, averse to all intrigue, was afraid of being drawn, in spite of himself, into some adventure of Monsieur de Talleyrand, who hesitated at nothing and who willingly pushed other people forward while quite ready to abandon them later on to save himself.

I accordingly set out for Mouchy where I remained three days. I left in the morning after breakfast to return to Amiens by way of Paris. Not wishing to pass the night there, I stopped at the apartment of Monsieur de Lally who was at Mouchy.

After the time necessary to make a slight change in my toilette, I went to see Monsieur de Talleyrand whom I found alone in his room. He received me as always with that familiar grace which he has ever shown towards me. People have said many hard things of him, and perhaps he has merited even worse, so that the expression of Montesquieu regarding Cæsar could well be applied to him: "Mais cet homme extraordinaire avait tant de grandes qualités, sans pas un défaut, quoiqu'il eût bien des vices." Well, in spite of everything, he possessed a charm which I have never found in any other man. It was all very well to be armed at all points against his immorality, his conduct, his life, against everything with which he was reproached, nevertheless, he attracted you as a bird is fascinated by the eye of the serpent.

There was nothing particularly remarkable about our conversation that day. I noticed only that he repeated with a certain affectation that Monsieur de La Tour du Pin was "well, very well" to be at Amiens. I informed him of my intention to leave in the morning. He told me not to do so. The Emperor was expected in the course of the next day, he would see him and would come to find me after his interview and would let me know at what hour I could command my post horses, which would certainly not be before ten o'clock in the evening.

I returned home very much put out at being kept another twenty-four hours in Paris. After having written my husband to notify him of this delay, I endeavored to occupy the morning of the day following in going to breakfast with my good friend Mme. de Maurville and in making several calls.

At ten o'clock my horses were attached and waiting at the door. The postillion was beginning to get impatient, as well as I myself, when Monsieur de Talleyrand arrived.

"What folly to set out in this cold!" he said. "And above all things, in a calèche. But whose apartment is this?"

"That of Monsieur de Lally."

Then, taking a candle from the table, he began to look at the engravings which were hung in fine frames around the room.

"Ah! Charles II, James II, just so!" And he put the candle back on the table.

"Mon Dieu!" I cried "il est bien question de Charles II, de Jacques II! Vous avez vu l'Empereur. Comment est-il? que fait-il? que dit-il après une défaite?"

"Oh! laissez-moi donc tranquille avec votre Empereur. C'est un homme fini."

"Comment fini?" I said. "Que voulez-vous dire?"

"Je veux dire," he replied, "que c'est un homme qui se cachera sous son lit!"

This expression at the moment did not surprise me so much as at the end of our conversation. I indeed knew the hatred and rancor of Monsieur de Talleyrand towards Napoleon, but never had I heard him express himself with so much bitterness. I asked him a thousand questions to which he replied only by the words:

"Il a perdu tout son matériel . . . Il est à bout. Voilà tout."

Then, searching in his pocket, he brought out a paper printed in English, and, while putting two logs on the fire, he added:

"Let us burn a little more of the wood of poor Lally. Since you know English, read this passage for me."

At the same time he indicated quite a long article marked with a pencil on the margin. I took the paper and read:

"Dinner given by the Prince Regent to Mme. la Duchesse d'Angoulême."

I stopped and raised my eyes to his. He had his usual impassible countenance.

"Go on and read. Your postillion is getting impatient."

I resumed my reading. The article gave a description of the dining room hung in sky-blue satin with bouquets of lilies, the top of the table entirely decorated with this same royal flower, with the service of Sèvres showing views of Paris and so on. Arrived at the end, I stopped and looked at him like one stupefied. He took the paper back, folded it slowly, put it back in his vast pocket and said, with that sly and malicious smile which he alone possessed:

"Ah! que vous êtes bête! A présent partez, mais ne vous enrhumez pas."

Then ringing, he said to my valet de chambre: "Call the carriage for Madame."

He then left me, crying out as he put on his mantle:

"Give my best regards to Gouvernet. I send him that for his breakfast. You will arrive in time."

I reached Amiens at so early an hour that my

husband had not yet risen. Without losing a moment I related to him the above conversation which had worried me during the night to such a degree that I could not sleep. In it he saw the explanation of certain perplexing expressions of Merlin de Thionville, and enjoined me to guard as the most absolute secret what I had learned, for if it was by such means, he said, that the Bourbons thought they could mount the throne, they would not remain there long.

A little later, my husband ordered Humbert to leave for Paris to secure further news. My son had been at Amiens for two weeks. Driven from his sous-préfecture by the Würtembergers, he had taken refuge with us in order to care for his health which had been compromised by an attack of pleurisy which he contracted at Sens and of which he had been very ill when the enemy approached that city.

Humbert arrived at the residence of Monsieur de Talleyrand, at Paris, at the very moment that the latter was receiving as his guest the Emperor Alexander. He passed the night on a bench which Monsieur de Talleyrand had assigned to him, in enjoining him not to move, so that he could find him at hand when he thought that the time had come for him to return to Amiens. At six o'clock in the morning, Monsieur de Talleyrand tapped him on the shoulder. Humbert saw that he was fully dressed.

"Leave," he said, "with a white cockade, and cry 'Vive le Roi!'"

Humbert was not sure that he was entirely awake. Shaking himself, he set out nevertheless and arrived at Amiens, where the news of the events had already been received, and where Monsieur de La Tour du Pin was not entirely sure what position he was going to take. But the voice of the people was not long in making itself heard. The requisitions, the Guards of Honor and so on had exasperated all classes of society. In an instant, as by an electric movement, cries of "Vive le Roi!" issued from all mouths. People rushed to the court of the Prefecture to demand white cockades with which Humbert, on leaving Paris, had filled the coffers of his calèche. The supply was soon exhausted.

During the day, when the news of the arrival of Louis XVIII became known, people began to pay us marked attention. Several days after, when they learned that the Préfet had left for Boulogne to await the arrival of the King, and that His Majesty would stop at Amiens and that he would pass the night at the Prefecture, a large number of people came to offer me articles of every nature which could be used to ornament or embellish the house, such as clocks, vases, pictures, flowers and so on.

Monsieur de Duras, having been designated to take up his service with the King as Gentleman of the Chamber, had passed through the city to go and await the King at Boulogne. In spite of so many changes, he had preserved all the prejudices, all the hatred, all the littleness, all the rancors of other days, as if there had never been a Revolution.

Monsieur de Poix had also taken the road for Boulogne, but he stopped at Amiens, very much disturbed as to the reception which he might receive

from the King, on account of his son who was
Chamberlain of the Emperor, and of his daughter-
in-law who had been Lady of the Palace of the
Empress. But I had no time to raise his courage, and
I confided to my daughter, Charlotte, the task of
talking with him while I superintended the arrangement of the table of twenty-five covers, which the
King was to honor with his presence. I was in the
dining-room when a gentleman entered and said
several words to my servant in a tone which displeased me. Approaching him, I demanded unceremoniously why he was interfering. He endeavored to
make an impression on me by saying that he belonged to the suite of the King. His surprise was very
great when he learned that I was determined to
remain mistress of my house and that I was little
disposed to let him give orders there. He went away
grumbling. It was Monsieur de Blacas.

A word from my husband had told me that the
King had received him with much kindness, and that
he was quartered at the Prefecture with the Duchesse
d'Angoulême. All was ready at the appointed hour.
Twelve young ladies of the city, at the head of whom
was my daughter Cécile, were waiting to present
their bouquets to Madame.

The carriage in which were the King and Madame
was drawn by the company of millers of Amiens who
had demanded this ancient privilege. These worthy
fellows, to the number of fifty or sixty, all attired at
their own expense in new costumes of gray-white
cloth, with large hats of white felt, then drew the
Royal carriage to the Cathedral where the Bishop

entoned the Te Deum. The doors of the Church had been kept closed and were not opened until the moment when the King was seated in his armchair at the foot of the altar. Then, in less than a moment, this immense church was filled to such a point that there was not room for another person.

In thinking at this writing of the innumerable stupidities which later precipitated his brother, Charles X, from the throne, I have almost a feeling of shame at the recollection of the emotion which I felt on seeing this old man thanking God for having replaced him upon the throne of his fathers. Madame knelt at the foot of the altar, in tears, and my heart shared the sentiments which she felt. Alas! this illusion did not endure for twenty-four hours.

The flour-dealers then conducted the King to the Prefecture where he received the whole city, men and women, before dinner, with that grace, with that presence of mind, with that charm which eminently distinguished him. At seven o'clock we sat down at the table. The dinner was excellent, the wines perfect, which particularly pleased the King, and which brought me many kind compliments. It was then for the first time that this simple provincial gentleman, Monsieur de Blacas, who had thought that he could issue his commands, discovered that in the wife of the Préfet he had to deal with a former Lady of Honor. He was very much confused by his mistake and paid me a thousand compliments in the endeavor to make me forget his first attitude, but without success.

THE RETURN OF THE KING

My cousin, Edward Jerningham, and his charming wife, had accompanied the King from England to France, and His Majesty stated with much kindness that Edward had been of great service to his cause, in the English journals, by the articles which he had written, which had had a very great success. Both Edward and his wife suggested that the extremely English costume of Madame would displease the Court of Napoleon, which was united at Compiègne to await the new sovereign. Both of them represented the necessity of not alienating sympathy at the very beginning. At their suggestion I spoke of the matter to Mlle. de Choisy, Lady of Honor to Madame, and to Monsieur de Blacas who spoke about it to the King. But nothing could overcome the obstinacy of this Princesse.

My son-in-law had ceased to be a Frenchman and had now become a subject of the new King of the Low Countries, William the First, who was the same Prince d'Orange whom I had seen in England under very different circumstances. He returned with my daughter to Brussels to his family, and this separation was very grievous to me. I went back to Paris and we established ourselves, my husband and I, in a pretty apartment, 6 Rue de Varenne, where my son Humbert was also located.

The very evening of my arrival, I went with Mme. de Duras to a fête which was given by Prince Schwarzenberg, Generalissimo of the Austrian troops. There I saw all the conquerors and was witness of all the baseness with which they were surrounded and so to speak overwhelmed. What a curious spectacle for a philosophical mind! Everything recalled Napoleon: the furniture, the supper, the guests. The thought came to me that among all those who were united there, there were some who had trembled before the Emperor when he had vanquished them, and others who had formerly solicited his favor or even his smile, and that there was not one present who seemed worthy to be his conqueror. Certainly the situation was interesting, although profoundly sad. Mme. de Duras saw in it only the happiness of being the wife of the First Gentleman of the King's Chamber. The fall of the great man, the invasion of her country, the humiliation of being the host of the conquerors did not appear to trouble her. As for myself, I had a feeling of shame which was probably not shared by any one else.

Monsieur de La Tour du Pin foresaw that the administrative career, although suited to his taste, would fall into a class inferior to that in which he had a right to be placed. He therefore desired to resume his rank in the diplomatic service where he had been before the Revolution. Monsieur de Talleyrand, Minister of Foreign Affairs, proposed to him the Embassy to The Hague. The new King of Holland desired it, and my husband willingly accepted this post, although he could have aspired to a higher mission. But a word from Monsieur de Talleyrand, telling him to accept it, gave him to understand that he was destined for other employment.

My son Humbert was led away, alas, by the charm of entering the military household of the King. General Dupont, the Minister of War, was a former aide de camp of my father and professed for me a great attachment. Humbert, who was desirous of being married, preferred to remain at Paris rather than to go elsewhere to be Préfet in some little city at a distance. He was appointed Lieutenant of the Black Musketeers, a name which came from the color of their horses. This gave him the grade of Chef d'Escadron in the army.

CHAPTER SIXTEEN

1814–1815

THE FIRST RESTORATION

Monsieur de La Tour du Pin, Envoy to the Congress of Vienna.—
His Wife Accompanies Him to Brussels.— Alexandre de
Lameth, Préfet of Amiens.— Life at Paris.— Monsieur de
Liedekerke Decorated with the Legion of Honor.— Mme.
de Liedekerke Leaves for Vienna with Her Husband.— The
Court of Louis XVIII.— Two Balls at the Duc de Berry's.
— Lord Wellington.— News of the Debarkment of Na-
poleon at Cannes.— Madame de La Tour du Pin Decides
to Leave for Brussels.— She Visits the Minister of Finance.
— A Night of Anxiety.— At Brussels.— Visit to the King
of Holland.— Separation of the Congress of Vienna.—
Mission of Monsieur de La Tour du Pin to the Duc
d'Angoulême.

AT the time it was decided to hold the Congress of Vienna, I happened to be one
morning in the cabinet of Monsieur de
Talleyrand. My husband had gone to Brussels to be
present at the coronation of the new King, William
the First, and to deliver his credentials. He was to
return in a day or two.

I was preparing to leave the cabinet of the Minister
of Foreign Affairs and had already placed my hand
on the handle of the door to open it, when looking
at Monsieur de Talleyrand, I saw upon his face that
expression with which I was familiar when he wished
to do some one a good turn in his line.

"When is Gouvernet coming back?" he said.

"Why, tomorrow," I replied.

"Well!" said he, "hasten his return, because he must set out for Vienna."

"For Vienna!" I exclaimed. "And why?"

"You understand nothing. He is going as Minister to Vienna while waiting for the Congress to open, when he will be one of the Ambassadors."

I made another exclamation, and he continued:

"It is a secret. Do not speak of it to any one, and send your husband to me as soon as he arrives."

I waited impatiently, keeping the secret of the good news, except from my son Humbert.

This nomination aroused a great deal of envious feeling towards my husband. Mme. de Duras was wild. She would like to have seen Monsieur de Chateaubriand obtain the post. Adrien de Laval was not even able to console himself with the promise of the Embassy to Spain. Every one cried out that it was an abuse because my husband had also kept his place at The Hague.

We decided in the family, though with great regret on my part, that Monsieur de La Tour du Pin should leave alone for Vienna, and that I should remain at Paris to occupy myself with the marriage of Humbert. My husband wrote to Auguste, our son-in-law, who was desirous of entering the diplomatic career in his country, and invited him to come to Vienna, either as his private secretary or simply as a looker-on, since, having become a subject of the Low Countries, he was no longer French. We thought that if Monsieur de La Tour du Pin remained at

Vienna, after the Congress, we would have no difficulty in obtaining from the King of Holland a position for Auguste as attaché at the Vienna Legation. These projects, like many others, were upset by events both public and private. It was arranged that I should accompany my husband as far as Brussels. There he would be joined by his son-in-law and I would take my daughter and her child back to Paris with me. This plan was carried out.

Our trip to Brussels and back passed very agreeably, although I felt very sad and disappointed at not accompanying my husband to Vienna. There was no reason then to suppose that his absence would be prolonged as it was in reality. Besides, the assurance had been given me that two special couriers would set out every week from the Foreign Affairs which permitted me to hope that I would receive regularly news as fresh as possible from my husband.

On our return to Paris, we found news from our travellers. I settled in my apartment and Charlotte took possession of the rooms previously occupied by her father.

General Dupont, who was still very devoted to my interests, arranged to have the cross of the Legion of Honor given to Auguste, as a reward for his excellent services as Sous-Préfet at Amiens, at the moment of the Restoration. I sent it to him at Vienna, and it gave him great pleasure.

My poor Charlotte had the misfortune at this time to lose her little girl who was carried off in the short space of two days. The next day, Monsieur de Liedekerke arrived unexpectedly from Vienna charged with dispatches. It was necessary for him to set out on his return the following day. The despair of Charlotte over the loss of her child suggested to me the thought of sending her to Vienna with her husband. As her father loved her tenderly, her presence there would be a great pleasure for him also. I possessed an excellent travelling calèche. I took charge of the purchase and packing, in all details, of the elegant toilettes to be worn by my daughter at the fêtes of the coming Congress. Besides, I placed at her disposal my maid who was a very experienced person. Thanks to my usual activity, the resolution once made, the second day following my daughter was ready to set out. She left for Vienna with her husband, who was carrying dispatches from Monsieur de Talleyrand who had not yet left Paris.

I remained alone with Cécile, then fifteen years of age, and my two sons, Humbert and Aymar.

It may be interesting to state how I passed my time after this restoration of the Monarchy. I went to the Tuileries when the King received the ladies, about once or twice a week. As a former Dame du Palais of the Queen, I had the "honors," that is to say, instead of mingling with the crowd of ladies who were assembled in the first salon, called "Diane," while waiting for the King to be rolled into the Throne Room, for he was not able to walk, I took my place immediately, as well as the other women who enjoyed the same privilege, on the benches which were arranged around the Throne Room. There we found many gentlemen who had also the entrées, and, seated very comfortably, we talked until the moment when the King was announced, when we rose and took a more conventional and respectful attitude. Then we filed one by one before the Royal arm-chair. The King always had something droll or kind to say to me.

This same winter, the Duc de Berry gave two balls to which he invited all the principal members of the Bonaparte Party, the Duchesses de Rovigo, de Bassano and so on. None of them danced and all had a very disagreeable air, in spite of the advances and the attentions of the Prince and his aides de camp. Mme. de Duras and I took to one of these balls Albertine de Staël. After having obtained the consent of her mother, who, in spite of her fifty years, was always dressed herself like a tight-rope dancer, we had been permitted to dress her to our taste. Every one found her so changed and so improved that from that time on she abandoned her former custom of wearing English dresses. The Duc de Broglie fell in love with her, and, if I am not mistaken, it was at one of these balls that he decided to demand her hand in marriage.

Since I have named Mme. de Staël, this is the moment to say that shortly after my return to Paris, after the Restoration, I had renewed my former acquaintance with her. I had already seen her, nevertheless, in 1800, when I arrived from England, a little before the time when Napoleon obliged her to leave Paris, and had also met her at different periods since then. At the time of the 18 Fructidor, she had shown herself very Revolutionary, carried away by her intimate relations with Benjamin Constant. Her last transformation had been accomplished in England whence she returned a Royalist. She received at her house all the notable personages from all the countries of Europe who were present in Paris during the winter of 1814 and 1815.

I happened to be in her salon the evening of the day when the Duke of Wellington arrived at Paris. One hundred other persons, equally curious to see this personage, already well-known, were also there. My relations with the Duke went back to my childhood. Our ages were about the same, and Lady Mornington, his mother, had been closely associated with my grandmother, Madame de Rothe. Young Arthur Wellesley, his sister Lady Anne and I had passed many evenings together. Later I again met Lady Anne in England at Hampton Court, when I went to see the old Stadtholder, the Prince d'Orange. I was received by the Duke as an old friend. In this salon where all eyes were fixed upon him, but where he knew hardly any one, he was very glad to find some one to talk with him.

During the sojourn that the Duke made at Paris, before going to the Congress of Vienna, I met him almost every day. I presented my son Humbert to him, and he showed him much kindness. Humbert spoke English perfectly, as he had become familiar with this language, both in America and in England. He had also a good acquaintance with Italian. This winter when Paris was full of strangers, he was frequently taken for either an Englishman or an Italian. On leaving Paris, the Duke of Wellington set out for the Congress where Monsieur de La Tour du Pin was already present.

One evening during the first days of March, I was in the apartment of Mme. de Duras at the Tuileries. There were many people there, including General Dulauloy and his wife. Mme. Dulauloy appeared to fear something and showed a great desire to leave, especially when Monsieur de Duras passed through the salon after the King had retired. She rose and left the room taking her husband with her. I remained behind and waited for Mme. de Duras to return from the room of her husband where she had followed him. I saw that she was very much troubled and she said to me: "Something terrible has happened, but Amédée is not willing to explain." I then returned home accompanied by Humbert and we made all the conjectures possible except the right one. The following morning the news of the debarkation of Napoleon at the Golfe Juan spread through Paris. The news was brought by Lord Lucan. Having left the evening before for Italy, at several stages from Paris, he met the courier who was coming from Lyon with the news. He immediately turned around and came back to Paris where he spread the news.

The results of this event belong to the domain of history. I will therefore only recount those which concern me personally.

I was too well acquainted, on the one hand, with the Court, and on the other, with the strength of the

Napoleonic Party, to have for a moment any doubts regarding the efficacy of the measures which would be adopted.

Monsieur de La Tour du Pin, although one of the four Ambassadors of France at the Congress of Vienna and employed per interim in the diplomatic affairs of France, in Austria, had nevertheless retained his post of French Minister to Holland. I felt that I could not remain at Paris when Napoleon was about to arrive there and that I ought to go to Brussels or The Hague. My plans were submitted to the King by Monsieur de Jaucourt, Minister of Foreign Affairs per interim. He approved of my purpose and I therefore prepared to leave.

Humbert, as soon as the departure of the King was decided upon, was not able to leave the quarters of the Musketeers. Consequently, I was obliged to complete alone all the arrangements for my trip which I was about to undertake with my daughter Cécile, sixteen years of age, and my son Aymar who was eight.

In the evening, I went to the bureau of the Minister of Finance to obtain the amount of the salary due Monsieur de La Tour du Pin, which I wished to take with me. The same evening, 19 March, 1815, the King was to leave at midnight. On entering the cabinet of the Minister, Monsieur Louis, with whom I had been well acquainted for a long time, I found him in a state of terrible rage. Showing me a hundred little barrels, similar to those in which anchovies are sold, he said:

"Look, I have had these barrels prepared, each of

which contains 10,000 or 15,000 francs in gold. I wished to confide one to each of the Body Guard ordered to accompany the King, and these gentlemen refused to take charge of them, under the pretext that it was not part of their duty."

While saying these words, he signed my voucher for the sum which I was to receive at once. I next took the money to my man-of-affairs in order to have him change it into gold. I had strongly urged Monsieur Louis to let me have one of the barrels of gold in his cabinet, but he absolutely refused. When I left my man-of-affairs, which was after nine o'clock, he told me to come back at eleven o'clock and that he would then give me the gold which he had procured.

I then went to see my aunt, Madame d'Hénin, who had also decided to leave, to make my adieux. I found her in company with Monsieur de Lally in a state of great trouble, packing, gesticulating, urging her fat friend who was finishing nothing. On seeing me she cried:

"But are you not going to leave, that you have such a tranquil air?"

I left her in the midst of her packages to go and take leave of Monsieur de Jaucourt, my Minister, to have him visé my passport and obtain an order for the post horses, a very necessary thing, for it would probably have been impossible to find a single one at midnight. Finally, at exactly eleven o'clock, I returned to my man-of-affairs, Rue Sainte-Anne. He handed me 12,000 francs in rolls of napoleons. I had a cabriolet hired by the hour. Getting into the carriage, I said to the coachman: "Home." I was living at 6 Rue de Varenne. We wished to take the route by the Carrousel, but, on account of the departure of the King, no one was allowed to pass. My coachman then kept along the Rue de Rivoli. At the moment we arrived at the Pont Louis XVI (now Pont de la Concorde) he heard the clock strike twelve. Stopping short, he declared that for nothing in the world would he go another step. His home he said was at Chaillot, and the gates would be closed at midnight. He demanded to be paid and invited me to continue my route on foot.

I used in vain all of my eloquence and promised him a superb pourboire if he would take me only to the point where we met another hack. He refused. I was obliged to descend from the carriage, although seized with a mortal terror. Fortunately, at this moment I heard the noise of a carriage. It was a hack, and vacant, thank God! I entered and offered the coachman a generous gratification to take me home.

As soon as I arrived I sent in search of the post horses. In spite of my *service extraordinaire*, in spite of the signature of the Minister, I waited until six o'clock in the morning for two miserable horses which were to be attached to a little calèche in which I was to take my place with Aymar, Cécile and a little Belgian maid whom I had kept in my service.

Our journey was not marked by any incident. We arrived safe and sound at Brussels where I took a little lodging Rue de Namur, with a lawyer named Monsieur Huart. He has been since, I think, Minister of Leopold I, King of the Belgians. I was very impatient to receive news from Vienna. The dispatch of the couriers who were usually sent to the Foreign Affairs and by whom my husband and my daughter Charlotte wrote me, had undoubtedly been interrupted. Although I had advised them both of my departure for Brussels, I had good reason to feel that I would be a long time without news, which indeed was what happened. At Brussels I found all the persons of my acquaintance, both Belgian and French. Every one received me cordially, with the exception of the Bonapartists.

The King of Holland, William the First, was at Brussels. I went to see him and he received me cordially. We were seated upon a sofa in the former cabinet of Monsieur de La Tour du Pin. Turning to me he said:

"In this salon I try to find the inspiration to make myself loved like your husband."

Alas! the poor Prince did not succeed. I spoke to him urgently regarding the interests of my son-in-law who had now become his subject. Probably it was this conversation which opened to him the diplomatic career.

A little later my daughter Charlotte arrived alone from Vienna, accompanied by her maid and the valet of her father. She informed me that the Congress had dissolved at the news of the landing of Napoleon at Cannes. Every one had left in haste and the Powers who were all ready to become enemies had become reconciled before the imminent danger. They only thought now of making France pay dearly for the welcome given the hero who in making her so powerful and glorious had raised up for her so many enemies.

In the southern provinces, the Duc d'Angoulême had brought together a kind of party which might have become important under another chief. Some one was wanted to take to this Prince the assurance of the union of the Powers to overwhelm Napoleon. Monsieur de La Tour du Pin, with his usual zeal, accepted the mission of going to Marseille to join the Duc. He set out accompanied by his son-in-law, who went as far as Genoa, whence he brought me at Brussels news from my husband. Young Liedekerke rejoined his wife in that city, and I was able to inform him on his arrival that I had assured his position with the King, his master.

POSTSCRIPT

Life of Monsieur and Madame de La Tour du Pin After the First Restoration.— The Dillon Family.— Genealogical Table.— Biographical Notes.— History of the Dillon Regiment.

THE events of the life of Monsieur and Madame de La Tour du Pin, up to the epoch of the Hundred Days, have been told us in the foregoing Recollections.

At the moment of the debarkation of Napoleon at the Golfe Juan, Monsieur de La Tour du Pin was at the capital of Austria where he had been sent after the First Restoration, first as Minister per interim and then as one of the Plenipotentiaries of France to the Congress of Vienna.

After having signed the famous declaration of the thirteenth of March, 1815, which placed Napoleon outside the law, he went, accompanied by Monsieur de Talleyrand, to Toulon, to endeavor to hold Maréchal Masséna, Governor of that place, in the service of the King, and from there to Marseille to confer with the Duc de Rivière.

After this, his mission was to rejoin in the South the Duc d'Angoulême, who had received from the King the order to go to Nîmes. But having learned at Marseille the news of the surrender of this Prince at Pont-Saint-Esprit, after having taken, in concert with the Duc de Rivière, some indispensable measures, he chartered a vessel in order to go to Genoa, whence he expected to return to Vienna. The bad weather, or rather the ill-will of the captain of this vessel, forced him to go to Barcelona.

From there, by way of Madrid, he proceeded to Lisbon where he embarked for London. During the twenty-four hours that he remained in London, he had the honor of seeing the Duchesse d'Angoulême and put her in touch with the situation in France. The night following this interview, he left for Dover, passed over to Ostende and went to Ghent where he joined Louis XVIII.

After the battle of Waterloo, Monsieur de La Tour du Pin returned to Paris, at the same time with the King.

In the month of August following, he took part in the general elections as President of the Electoral College of the Department of the Somme. The seventeenth of the same month, he was named Peer of France by Louis XVIII.

As stated in the memoirs of his wife, Monsieur de La Tour du Pin, while acting as one of the Pleni-potentiaries of France at the Congress of Vienna, had kept the post to which he had been appointed a short time before of Minister to the Low Countries. In October, 1815, he went to Brussels to hand his credentials to the King, William I, and be present at his coronation.

Having returned to Paris, a short time later, to take his seat in the Chamber of Peers, Monsieur de La Tour du Pin took part during the first days of December in the debates over the trial of Maréchal

Ney. He voted in favor of his condemnation, but at the same time made a formal declaration in which he stated that he thought that the Maréchal was worthy of the clemency of the King.

As is well known, the clemency of the King was not accorded.

About the first of February, 1816, Monsieur de La Tour du Pin returned to The Hague to take up his duties as Minister Plenipotentiary to the Court of the Low Countries.

In the month of September, 1818, the Duc de Richelieu summoned Monsieur de La Tour du Pin to act as his assistant at the Congress at Aix-la-Chapelle, the object of which was to arrange the conditions for the evacuation of the French territory by the foreign troops. Immediately after the closing of this Congress, Monsieur de La Tour du Pin returned to his post at The Hague. At the end of the year 1819, he went again to Paris to take his seat in the Chamber of Peers, at the opening of the session, and was there at the time of the assassination of the Duc de Berry, the thirteenth of February, 1820.

A little later in 1820, he was appointed Ambassador at Turin and immediately joined his post, which he did not leave until the month of January, 1830, except for a sojourn of four months at Rome in 1824.

In the month of January, 1830, Monsieur de La Tour du Pin decided to retire from public life, as he was worn out and also dissatisfied at the turn taken by events. He accordingly took up his residence at Versailles, where he was living at the time of the Revolution of July, 1830.

POSTSCRIPT

The second of August at three o'clock in the morning, he left Versailles and directed his steps towards Orléans, thinking that the King, in leaving by way of Rambouillet, would take this route to go to Tours. The following day, learning of the abdication of the King and of his departure for Cherbourg, Monsieur de La Tour du Pin resolved to proceed to his estate at Le Bouilh, near Saint André-de-Cubzac. From there he addressed a letter to Monsieur Pasquier, President of the Chamber of Peers, in which he advised him that he was not willing to take the new oath of allegiance which was demanded of him, because it was directly contrary to that which he had already taken to Charles X. This letter was laid before the Chamber during the session of the twenty-first of August and appeared in the "Moniteur" the following day.

The events of the month of August had at the same time put an end to the mission with which Monsieur de La Tour du Pin was charged, in connection with the King of Sardinia. Free, therefore, from all engagements, he passed the end of the year 1830 quietly on his estate at Le Bouilh. During the course of the year 1831, his youngest son Aymar became involved in the movement in the Vendée and was arrested and put in prison. His father not wishing to be separated from him spent the four months of his detention with him. As soon as he was liberated in April, 1832, Aymar again went to the Vendée to rejoin the Duchesse de Berry. The failure of this attempt is well known.

After the arrest of Madame, Aymar was once more

pursued, but he succeeded in finding refuge in the Island of Jersey in the month of November, 1832. During his absence, he was condemned to death on account of his participation in the attempt of the Duchesse de Berry.

Several of the newspapers having attacked his son in terms which appeared outrageous to Monsieur de La Tour du Pin, the latter came vigorously to the defence of his son in a letter which was published by the "Guyenne." As a result, he was put on trial before the Cour d'Assises at Bordeaux, and the fifteenth of December, 1832, was condemned to pay a fine of 1,000 francs and to three months in prison. These three months, from the twentieth of December, 1832, to the twentieth of March, 1833, he was confined at the Fort du Hâ, in company with his wife who refused to be separated from him.

On leaving prison, Monsieur de La Tour du Pin settled at Nice, where his wife and son came to rejoin him. Having been compelled by political reasons to leave this city, he proceeded to Turin and from there to Pignerol, where he remained until the twenty-eighth of August, 1834.

At this time urgent business interests recalled Monsieur and Madame de La Tour du Pin to France. Here they remained exactly one year, and then again left France with the plan of settling at Lucerne, where they arrived towards the end of the month of November, 1835, after a sojourn of several weeks at Suze.

The twenty-sixth of February, 1837, Monsieur de La Tour du Pin died at Lucerne at the age of seventy-eight years.

POSTSCRIPT

The Marquise de La Tour du Pin has recounted to us in her Recollections all the notable events of the period of her life comprised between her childhood and the end of the month of March, 1815. Her history from that time on was closely connected with that of her husband, whom she followed to The Hague and later to Turin. She also accompanied him to Italy and then to Switzerland in the voluntary exile which he imposed upon himself, in order to share that of his son, Aymar, and she was at the bed-side of her husband at Lucerne at the moment of his death in February, 1837.

Some time afterwards, with her son, Aymar, she left for Italy and took up her final residence at Pisa in Tuscany, where she died the second of April, 1853, at the age of eighty-three years.

The Marquise de La Tour du Pin had six children — three sons, Humbert, Edward and Aymar, and three daughters, Séraphine, Charlotte and Cécile. Two of her children, Séraphine and Edward, died in infancy.

In the interval between March, 1815, the date at which the Recollections end, and the first of January, 1820, the date at which Madame de La Tour du Pin began to write her memoirs, she lost two other children, her eldest son, Humbert, and her youngest daughter, Cécile.

Humbert de La Tour du Pin was born at Paris the nineteenth of May, 1790. During the last years of the Empire he was Sous-Préfet at Florence and later at Sens. At the time of the First Restoration he was appointed officer in the corps of the Mousquetaires Noirs and became later aide de camp of Maréchal Victor, Duc de Bellune. He died under circumstances which were very sad and very dramatic.

At the time of his appointment to the Military Household of the Duc de Bellune, among the aides de camp of the Maréchal was the Commandant Malandin, an officer who had risen from the ranks. He was rough and uneducated, but audacious and courageous, with an open and loyal heart, but very susceptible upon the point of honor. He had won every one of his grades upon the different fields of battle of the Empire.

The very day that Humbert took up for the first time his service with the Maréchal, on entering the quarters of the aides de camp, he encountered the Commandant Malandin. The latter addressed him in a vein of pleasantry, regarding some unimportant detail of his uniform, but in terms which were coarse and unbecoming.

Before Humbert could make any reply, the Maréchal entered, upon a tour of inspection, and, while there, gave the Commandant a mission to the Minister of War.

As soon as Humbert was able to leave, he went immediately to the hôtel occupied by his family and entered the cabinet of his father. Here he recounted the incident, without omitting any of the details, except that he stated that the person involved was not himself, but one of his friends. He then asked his father what "his friend" ought to do. His father replied:

"Challenge the aggressor."

"And if apologies are offered?"

"Refuse them."

That evening Humbert sent a challenge to Malandin. The meeting was arranged for the following morning in the Bois de Boulogne. The weapons selected were pistols and the distance was twenty-five paces.

The duel took place the following morning in a clearing in the Bois de Boulogne.

When the distance had been measured off and the adversaries had been placed in position, before the signal had been given, the Commandant Malandin gave a sign that he wished to speak, and in a loud tone he pronounced these words:

"Monsieur de La Tour du Pin, in the presence of these gentlemen, I think that I ought once more to declare to you that I regret my wretched pleasantry. Two good fellows ought not to kill each other for that."

Humbert hesitated a moment and then walked slowly towards the Commandant. All the assistants had a feeling of secret relief at seeing the favorable turn which the affair had taken. But when the young man arrived close to his adversary, instead of offering him his hand, he raised his arm and with the butt of his pistol struck Malandin on the forehead.

"Monsieur," he said, "I think that now you will not refuse to fight!" and he returned to his place.

After such a scene, only one dénouement was possible. The signal was given; Monsieur de La Tour

THE DILLON FAMILY

GENEALOGICAL TABLE

I	II	III	IV	V	VI
1 THÉOBALD	2 Henry	4 Richard			
		5 Charles	11 Charles		
			12 Arthur		
		6 Henry	13 Henry		
			14 Frances		
			15 Charlotte		
	3 Arthur	7 James	16 Lucy m. Rothe	17 H.-Lucy m. La Tour du Pin	19 Humbert
		8 Edward			20 Charlotte
		9 Arthur R.			21 Cécile
		10 Laura m. Falkland		18 Th.-Lucy m. (12) Dillon	22 Aymar

POSTSCRIPT

BIOGRAPHICAL NOTES

1 THÉOBALD, VII Viscount Dillon, died 1691; married Mary, daughter Sir Henry Talbot.

2 HENRY, VIII Viscount Dillon, died 13 January, 1714; married 1687, Frances Hamilton.

3 ARTHUR, first Colonel-Proprietor of the Regiment of Dillon in the service of France, died 5 February, 1733; married Christina, daughter Ralph Sheldon. (From Ralph Sheldon were descended the cousins of the author, so frequently mentioned in her memoirs.) Children: five sons and five daughters.

4 RICHARD, IX Viscount Dillon, born 1688; died 1737; married Lady Bridget Burke, daughter Earl of Clanricarde. Daughter FRANCES who married her cousin (5) CHARLES.

5 CHARLES, X Viscount Dillon, second Colonel of the Regiment, died 1741; married his cousin FRANCES (above). No children.

6 HENRY, XI Viscount Dillon, third Colonel, born 1705; died 1787; married Lady Charlotte Lee, daughter second Earl of Lichfield, grandson of King Charles II by the Duchess of Cleveland.

7 JAMES, fourth Colonel, killed at Fontenoy, 1745. Never married.

8 EDWARD, fifth Colonel, died 1747 from wounds at battle of Lawfeld. Never married.

9 ARTHUR-RICHARD, born 1721; died 5 July, 1806; was Archbishop of Narbonne.

10 LAURA, married Lucius Cary, Viscount Falkland. She died 1741. One daughter (16) LUCY.

11 CHARLES, XII Viscount Dillon, born 1745; died 1813; married Henrietta Phipps, daughter Lord Mulgrave. Two

children: HENRY AUGUSTUS, and FRANCES CHARLOTTE, who married Sir Thomas Webb. He also had by Marie Rogier, whom he married after death of his wife, a natural daughter, CHARLOTTE, who married Lord Frederick Beauclerk, brother of the Duke of Saint Albans.

12 ARTHUR, sixth Colonel, born 3 September, 1750; executed 13 April, 1794; married, 1st, his cousin (18) THÉRÈSE-LUCY DE ROTHE. One daughter (17) HENRIETTE-LUCY, the author of "Le Journal d'une femme de cinquante ans." He married, 2d, Marie de Girardin, widow of Comte de La Touche, and first cousin of the Empress Josephine. One daughter FRANCES, who married General Bertrand, aide de camp of the Emperor Napoleon.

13 HENRY, Colonel of the Regiment in England, born 1759; married Frances Trant, and had two sons and two daughters.

14 FRANCES, born 1747; married 1767, Sir William Jerningham.

15 CHARLOTTE, married 1777, Earl of Kenmare. One daughter Charlotte, married Goold.

16 LUCY CARY, married General de Rothe. One daughter (18) THÉRÈSE-LUCY, who married her cousin (12) ARTHUR DILLON. One daughter (17)* HENRIETTE-LUCY.

17 HENRIETTE-LUCY DILLON, author of the "Recollections" was born at Paris, 25 February, 1770; died at Pisa, Italy, 2 April, 1853; married 21 May, 1787, FRÉDÉRIC–SÉRAPHIN, Comte de Gouvernet, later MARQUIS DE LA TOUR DU PIN. Two sons (19) HUMBERT and (22) AYMAR, and two daughters (20) CHARLOTTE and (21) CÉCILE, besides two children who died young.

18 THÉRÈSE-LUCY DE ROTHE, married 1768, her cousin (12) ARTHUR DILLON. She died 7 September, 1782. One daughter (17) HENRIETTE-LUCY.

19 HUMBERT DE LA TOUR DU PIN, born 19 May, 1790; died 28 January, 1816.

20 CHARLOTTE DE LA TOUR DU PIN, born 4 November, 1796; died 1 September, 1822; married 20 April, 1815, the Comte

de Liedekerke-Beaufort. Children: one son and one daughter: HADELIN, Comte de Liedekerke-Beaufort, born at Brussels 11 March, 1816; died at Brussels 3 January, 1890; CÉCILE, born at The Hague, 24 August, 1818, died at Paris 19 August, 1893; married Baron Ghislain, 28 December, 1841.

HADELIN DE LIEDEKERKE-BEAUFORT had a son AYMAR, born at Brussels, 19 May, 1846; died at Paris, March, 1909; married at Paris, 16 September, 1885, Louise Cécile Béranger. Children: three sons and one daughter: Hadelin, born at Paris, 8 October, 1887; Aymar, born at Paris 21 October, 1888; and Humbert, born at Paris 14 September, 1890.

21 CÉCILE DE LA TOUR DU PIN, born 13 February, 1800; died 20 March, 1817; never married.

22 AYMAR DE LA TOUR DU PIN, born at Le Bouilh 18 October, 1806; died at Fontainebleau 4 March, 1867; married; son: HUMBERT ADELIN MARIE, born 15 May, 1855; married 10 October, 1883, Gabrielle, daughter Comte Aynard de Clermont Tonnerre: three daughters.

HISTORY OF THE DILLON REGIMENT

Théobald (1), Lord Viscount Dillon, Peer of Ireland, chief at this epoch of the illustrious house of that name, raised at the end of the year 1688, upon his lands in Ireland, and equipped at his own expense, a Regiment for the service of King James II. In the course of the year 1690, this Regiment passed into the service of France, under the orders of Arthur Dillon (3), his second son. It formed a part of a corps of 5371 men of the Irish troops who debarked at Brest on 1 May, 1690, and who were given by King James II to Louis XIV in exchange for six French regiments.

After the capitulation of Limerick, in 1691, the number of Irish troops who entered the service of France was considerably augmented and reached a total of more than 20,000 men. From that time to the date of the French Revolution they served under the name of the "Irish Brigade" in all the wars of France and always with the most brilliant distinction.

Arthur Dillon (3), first Colonel of the Dillon Regiment, became Lieutenant General at the age of thirty-three years, having won this rank through his glorious deeds. He was for a long time Commandant in Dauphiné and Governor of Toulon. On 28 August, 1709, near Briançon, he defeated General Rehbinder, Commander of the troops of Savoy, who wished to invade France. He finished a glorious career in 1733, at the age of sixty-three years. He left five sons and five daughters.

In 1728, he had transferred his Regiment to Charles Dillon (5), the eldest of his sons. Charles Dillon, having become the head of the family in 1737, by the death of Richard (4), Lord Dillon, his cousin, kept the Regiment temporarily and then transferred it to his brother Henry Dillon (6).

Henry Dillon (6) on the death of Charles Lord Dillon in 1741, succeeded to the titles and property of his family, but nevertheless kept the command of the Regiment at the head of which he served until 1743. After the Battle of Dettingen the English, who up to that time had been auxiliaries, became the principal parties in the war. Lord Henry Dillon, in order to preserve his title of Peer of England and to avoid the confiscation of his estates, was, owing to this fact, obliged to leave the service of France, which he did with the consent and even by the advice of Louis XV.

James Dillon (7), Chevalier of Malta, the third brother, was then promoted to be Colonel of the Regiment, at the head of which he was killed at Fontenoy in 1745.

Edward Dillon (8), the fourth brother, was appointed Colonel of the Regiment by Louis XV on the field of battle, and like his brother found his death in action at the head of the Regiment at the Battle of Lawfeld in 1747.

Arthur Richard Dillon (9), the fifth brother, alone survived, but he had entered into orders and died in England in 1806 as Archbishop of Narbonne.

At the death of Edward Dillon (8), killed at Lawfeld, Louis XV was strongly urged to dispose of the Regiment under the pretext that there was no longer a Dillon to take command. But the King replied that Henry, Lord Dillon, had just been married and that he was not willing to consent to see go out of the family a property cemented with so much blood and of so remarkable services, so long as it was possible to hope for an heir. The Dillon Regiment consequently remained after 1747 under the successive command of a Lieutenant-Colonel and of two Colonel-Commandants until the Honorable Arthur Dillon (12), second son of Henry, Lord Dillon, was put in charge, on 25 August, 1767, at the age of seventeen years.

At the epoch of the French Revolution, the Irish Brigade was reduced to three infantry regiments, namely: Dillon, Berwick and Walsh. In 1794, what was left of the three regiments, including the greater part of the officers who had emigrated to England, passed into the service of the King of England. The Dillon Regiment, or the part still in existence, to which England was willing to attribute the name, was given to the Honorable Henry Dillon (13), third son of Henry, Lord Dillon, and brother

RECOLLECTIONS OF THE REVOLUTION

of Arthur Dillon, last Colonel of the Regiment in France, who had perished on the scaffold in 1794. This new Regiment was filled up by recruiting on the same lands which had furnished the first soldiers in 1688. A little later it embarked for Jamaica where its losses were so considerable that it was disbanded. The flags and ensigns of the Regiment were transported to Ireland and carefully deposited in the hands of Charles, Lord Dillon, chief of the family and eldest brother of the Colonel.